No Ghost in the Machine

Also by Rodney Cotterill

The Cambridge Guide to the Material World

No Ghost in the Machine

Modern science and the brain, the mind and the soul

RODNEY COTTERILL

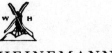

HEINEMANN : LONDON

To Marianne and Jennifer

William Heinemann Ltd
Michelin House, 81 Fulham Road, London sw3 6rb
LONDON   MELBOURNE   AUCKLAND

First published 1989
Copyright © Rodney Cotterill 1989

British Library Cataloguing in Publication Data

Cotterill, Rodney. *1933–*
    No ghost in the machine: modern science and the
    brain, the mind and the soul.
    1. Man. Mind, body and soul
    I. Title
    128

ISBN 0-434-14607-2

Typeset by Hewer Text Composition Services, Edinburgh
Printed and bound in Great Britain
by Butler & Tanner Ltd, Frome

'The sum of all the parts of Such –
Of each laboratory scene –
Is such.' While science means this much
And means no more, why, let it mean!
But were the science-men to find
Some animating principle
Which gave synthetic Such a mind
Vital, though metaphysical –
To Such, such an event, I think,
Would cause unscientific pain:
Science, appalled by thought, would shrink
To its component parts again.

ROBERT GRAVES
Synthetic Such

Contents

Acknowledgements

The author and publishers are grateful to the following for permission to quote from copyright works:
The Society of Authors on behalf of the Bernard Shaw Estate (extracts on p.29, p.76, and p.82); Cambridge University Press (extracts from Charles Scott Sherington's *Man on his Nature* on p.82 and p.105); The Executors of the Estate of Robert Graves ('Synthetic Such' on p.v); Longman Group UK (extract on p.181 from *The Blind Watchmaker* © Richard Dawkins 1986); *New Scientist* magazine (quotation from Stafford Beer on p.228); The Peters Fraser & Dunlop Group Ltd (extract on p.158 from John Mortimer's *A Voyage Round my Father* © 1971 by Advanpass Ltd); Routledge (extract from *Animal Thought* by Stephen Walker on p.228); Taylor & Francis Ltd (extract from Max Born's *My Life* on p.203).

Preface

It is frequently said that science tends to raise more problems than it solves. This is true in at least two senses. To begin with, the drawing aside of one of the veils of our collective ignorance invariably reveals further mysteries which clamour for explanation. Science would not want things to be otherwise. The fact that Nature continually throws up new challenges to our skill and resource is not usually seen as a difficulty; there is, on the contrary, general satisfaction that the scientific enterprise should be a story without an end. In the other sense, however, the problems that science generates cause difficulties that are both real and daunting. For when scientific advance is transmuted into society's tool, there is always scope for the unfortunate and unanticipated dimension. All too often, what at first appears to be a blessing later shows itself to possess a darker side; the boon has a penchant for becoming the bane. Of late, we have frequently seen this in the field of medicine. Mankind's newly acquired ability to manipulate the stuff of life, the gene, the embryo and the organ, for example, has caused much anguished introspection.

There has recently been a quickening in the pace of the scientific investigation of the brain. This has been caused by a number of technical advances which have permitted the monitoring of the brain's processes with a precision that would have been unthinkable even a decade ago. But, just as importantly, the advent of very powerful electronic computers has furthered the theoretical study of brain function and we appear to be on the threshold of understanding the mechanics of the mind, at the level of the brain's nerve cells and their mutual interactions. The upshot of these advances has been that things which formerly seemed mysterious now appear almost commonplace. It does not demand much from the imagination to see that this progress too will produce problems. It has long been assumed that there is an intimate relationship between the mind and what we call the soul, and it is difficult to see how our ideas about the one could be modified without a reappraisal being required of the other. Through its continuing encroachment on an area that many still regard as being out of bounds, science might seem to be on a collision course with some of society's most venerable establishments.

This book is intended to be a contribution to the debate on the mind–soul issue. Having reviewed what I believe to be a representative and responsible amount of the vast literature on the subject, I have come down rather strongly on the side of determinism, and this is reflected in the book's uncompromising title. I have presented the mechanistic view of the brain and its associated mind with all due vigour, but I have nevertheless tried to maintain the objectivity that never-ending science requires of its practitioners. This is conveyed in the latter part of the text, in which I have even attempted to guess at what types of new factor could radically change the picture that I have described. (One must nevertheless bear in mind, of course, that subsequent developments might give us an even more mechanical view than the one portrayed here.) It would be encouraging to know that this will assure the book a fair hearing, free of recourse to dogma of whatever stripe.

There is no denying, however, that some of the conclusions drawn in the final chapter will prove difficult to reconcile with those religious attitudes that advocate a dualist separation of body and soul. And it would be naive to think that the idea of the will as being individual rather than free can escape strong resistance, not to mention downright hostility. But the case for a revaluation of the concept of free will does seem to have become strong recently, and it is hard to see how this could avoid drawing the traditional view of the soul into question as well.

I would not have written this book if I did not feel that some good could come from an open discussion of these matters. For it is not obvious, to me at least, that the anticipated exchange between science and religion has to result in mutual detriment.

Given the proper type of dialogue, it might prove possible to salvage the best of what each side of the argument has to offer. To begin with, we do well to remind ourselves that science is the human enterprise which has enjoyed the best track record regarding cooperation between peoples. Not surprisingly so, indeed, because science is of us all and for us all. It is, to use John Ziman's excellent phrase, simply public knowledge, and knowledge cannot in itself be bad. To this, I would like to add my personal opinion that when organized religion does good, and its capacity for doing so is certainly large, it achieves this by operating in territory that is shared by all creeds. The discussion that is now in the offing could add something valuable to that common ground; there could be many beneficiaries.

The subject of the dispute is the nature of the soul, and my text goes against dualism and what I feel is too simplistic a view of the will. The traditional picture of the soul foists this facile attitude upon itself because it labours under a lack of nuance. It saddles itself with mutually exclusive extremes, and it has to invoke freedom of will to permit a choice between them. Its defence of that position rests heavily on the comfort and solace that the idea of the immortal soul has undeniably given countless individuals. But that same idea has also produced casualties, and I am not merely referring to those who have suffered religious persecution. Just as important are all the people whose organically dictated infirmities have been ascribed to a delinquent soul; less than a hundred years ago many mental illnesses were simply attributed to sin, and mental institutions were reasonable approximations to Hades. And even today it is often implied that the schizophrenic and the manic depressive, to cite just two examples, could be cured if only they would 'pull themselves together'. That is just one of the types of injustice that the idea of free will leads to.

The remarkable thing is that, by implication at least, the concept does not even enjoy our unqualified support. When mental impairment is too manifest, we consign the sufferer to an asylum without compunction. There are perfectly good practical grounds for doing so, and such confinement is not my bone of contention. The important issue is that the criterion for commitment to a protected environment figures as just one point on a scale that everyone acknowledges is a continuous spectrum of abilities; it is embodied in our universal acceptance of the idea of the intelligence quotient. And although the actual determination of a person's IQ can be a non-trivial challenge, there are not many who would question the basic validity of such a measure. In this book's final chapter, drawing on facts about the observed gradual decline towards dementia in certain patients, amongst other things, I argue that the will would have to be regarded as occupying a similarly continuous spectrum, and that as such it cannot be wholly free. This, in turn, diminishes the credibility of the individual soul, as normally envisaged, and leads to the suggestion that the soul of mankind has emerged as a collective phenomenon, related to the sophistication of our mental interactions with one another. The immortality of that collective soul is, I feel, at least as attractive an idea as the traditional one. Moreover, there seems to be no obvious reason why such a collective soul should not be able to survive our replacement, one of these millennia, by an evolutionarily more advanced species.

In a wider sense, the beneficiaries of the advocated change of attitude could be all of us. For although the currently standard view is comfort*ing*, as noted earlier, it is also too comfort*able*. It lets us off the hook too easily on at least two counts. For a start, it allows us to invoke the hereafter as a place where all manner of injustices will be compensated for; it permits us, consciences intact, to turn our backs on the miserable lots of so many of our fellow human beings who never really stood a chance in this world. Just as reprehensibly, it enables us to add insult to injury regarding all those who, through a combination of unfortunate genetic endowment and unhelpful environment, do not possess the competence required to succeed in our competitive civilization; the assumed freedom of will is altogether too convenient a device for letting us justify the belief that equality of opportunity is all that should be required of an equitable society. In so far as the recent discussion of ecumenism, in religious circles, is motivated by conviction rather than mere expediency, it might prove worthwhile to include consideration of the potentially unifying issues addressed in the following pages. They are, in any event, at least as worthy of debate as one of the current ecclesiastical favourites, namely the divisive question of whether to extend to the females of our species the equality that Nature conferred on them aeons ago.

A number of people rendered valuable aid in the production of this book. Numerous discussions with John Clark, before and during the writing, had a strong influence on the volume's general form. Christopher Cousins, Allan Mackintosh, Knud Særmark and Thomas Zeuthen generously offered to read the entire manuscript, and they made a number of important suggestions for improvement. Their collective advice made a vital impact on the shaping of the final work, as did that of three of my departmental colleagues, Steen Sloth Christensen, Claus Nielsen and Henrik Thovtrup. It is a pleasure also to thank Erol Basar, Søren Brunak, Christian Guld, Cameron Gundersen, Demetrious Haracopos, John Hertz, Gevene Hertz, Richard Hoffman, Henrik Jahnsen, Christof Koch, Teuvo Kohonen, Raymond Meddis, Margareta Mikkelsen, Graeme Mitchison, Harald Moe, Steven Rose, Morton Schatzman and Paul Wooley for stimulating discussions about specific topics. Carolyn Hallinger's help with the first draft was deeply appreciated, and I have also been much indebted to Ole Broo Sørensen, for his assistance with some of the figures, and Flemming Kragh, for photographic support. On the editorial side, Jane Carr and Karin Fancett removed a number of weeds and skilfully nurtured endangered areas. They managed to transform into an exciting enterprise what could easily have been just a chore.

Finally, I wish to thank the several colleagues who gave me permission to reproduce pictures taken in connection with their own researches; their names appear in the respective captions.

Rodney Cotterill

1

Beyond mere matter?
A natural history of the soul

When God is determined to win the soul of a person,
he calls upon his most faithful servant,
his most reliable messenger: sorrow.

SØREN KIERKEGAARD

There is no scientific evidence for the existence of an immortal soul, in either our own species or any other species. There is, on the other hand, a growing body of scientific data which indicates that all animals, including ourselves, can for most, and perhaps even all, purposes be regarded as organic machines, devoid of anything mystical.

The implications of those stark assertions are, I realize, as disturbing as they are profound. They are in obvious disharmony with certain religious beliefs and, in hinting that we might have to re-evaluate our attitude towards the mind and the issue of free will, they are in clear danger of falling into conflict with the ethical and legal foundations of human society.

The statements also seem to fly in the face of common sense; they are manifestly counter-intuitive. After all, one does not have to subscribe to the idea of an immortal soul in order to accept the concept of a human spirit, inseparably associated with an individual but somehow transcending the mere workings of his body. And most people would consider the existence of the spirit to be obvious. But what *on earth* is a human spirit, and how could it have an existence that is separate from that of its host? My main goal in this book will be to demonstrate that mind and spirit are simply natural attributes of the body, and that they enjoy no such autonomy. In addition to dismissing the concept of the immortal soul, therefore, I will also be endeavouring to demonstrate that the mortal soul might not be what we thought it was.

Of the many negative reactions which these propositions might elicit, one clearly demands immediate attention. I have indicated that the arguments are going to invoke scientific evidence, and this naturally raises the question of the scientific enterprise's limitations. Are there not, it could be asked, things which will forever lie beyond the reach of scientific investigation? It would be a bold scientist, indeed, who claimed that everything will ultimately fall within science's grasp, and this book will certainly not go that far. It seems more prudent to acknowledge that such points of dispute as the existence and nature of God, and perhaps also the creation of the universe, lie fundamentally outside our understanding.

But the inner workings of the human being might be quite another matter. Things which, at a given time, appear to be quite outside the scientific realm have a way of subsequently proving to be not only amenable to the scientific method but even open to scientific manipulation. Who, one hundred years ago, would have dared to predict that we would become so well acquainted with the workings of a cell's genetic machinery that we could actually modify it, for example? In view of the advances they have achieved during recent decades, there seems to be no reason why brain scientists should not expect to match the feats of their colleagues in genetics, regarding their understanding of, and dominion over, the object of their studies. Precisely what can be accomplished during the next hundred years cannot be predicted, of course, but my guess is that the concept of the immortal soul will have fewer adherents a century hence.

In this first chapter, my main purpose will be to explore the way in which the idea of the soul arose. But before we move on to that question, let us undertake a scientific expedition in our imaginations. It is going to help us to appreciate the issues involved in the idea of the soul. (The fact that one can make such a mental journey is interesting in its own right, of course, and one of the aims of this book is an explanation of this fascinating faculty.)

Every so often, one reads of the discovery of a group of human beings who apparently have never had contact with the outside world. The goal of our expedition is to observe these primitive people, under certain conditions, and let us assume that we do not have to bother with all the logistical details of travelling to their remote location and suitably bivouacking ourselves nearby. While the tribe is sleeping, we surreptitiously creep forward to place a radio receiver–transmitter in a prominent position, and retire to await their reaction to the device, the following morning. At the first signs of stirring from their night's slumber, and using a similar two-way radio, we covertly transmit a few bars of music. This would ideally be a fairly simple piece, such as a solo voice *a cappella*, the general idea being to give them something reasonably close to their own vocal capabilities. Their most likely reaction to the intruder would leave us mutely congratulating ourselves on our foresight in bringing several reserves; they would probably either smash it to pieces or throw it into the nearest river. The following night would thus see us placing our first reserve on the same spot we chose previously, and this would surely increase their wonderment upon discovering it the next morning; to its already mystical powers of vocalization would now have been added the capacity for reincarnation.

Let us consider how our experiment might continue, and what could be learned from it. Attracted by the piece of music, some of the tribe would gingerly approach the device, and before long we could be up to all manner of pranks. Transmission of taped animal sounds would have our primitive colleagues puzzled and intrigued, and it would be easy to record their own voices and play these back at them with just a few seconds' delay.

And, assuming the device survived their initial investigations, what would be the subsequent fate of the thing, in their hands? I believe that it would not for long be readily accessible to all the tribe's members. On the contrary, it would soon be numbered amongst the accoutrements of the tribe's witch doctor or holy man. It would be displayed and put through its paces only on special occasions, and it would no doubt soon become the hub of much folklore. The device's self-appointed custodian would use it as an instrument of power over his subordinates, who, in turn, would invoke its mystical powers in order to restrain their adventurous offspring. Some would say that we had wreaked damage on the tribe's social life; injury which could be made permanent by equipping the contraption with solar-powered batteries. Others might feel that we had increased the tribe's stability by giving it something supernatural to look up to.

Our experiment will have demonstrated that a person's attitude depends strongly upon his background knowledge. In this era of advanced space technology, when even telemetry across huge distances of open space leaves us somewhat blasé, we would look upon the gadget as something quite commonplace. To the primitive tribe, however, it would be a thing of great wonderment, and although an equivalent of the word 'paranormal' would probably not be found in their vocabulary, this would be the term that best described their evaluation of its properties.

Replace the radio, and its associated 'mind' and 'soul', by the human brain, and we become the primitive tribe. Down through the ages, we have generally been reluctant to demystify the things and phenomena which surround us. The change of attitude has usually required a period of controversy and upheaval, a particularly noteworthy example being that which embroiled the unfortunate Galileo Galilei in the latter part of his life. That great scientist's troubles began in 1611, not long after he had turned his telescope towards Jupiter, discovered the moons which revolve around that planet, and realized that his observations verified the views of Nicolaus Copernicus. The book *De Revolutionibus Orbium Coelestium* (The Revolution of the Heavenly Orbs) had been published by Copernicus in 1543, and it argued that the earth moves around the sun (as do the other planets), rather than vice versa. (The word 'revolution' now has another connotation, of course, and the second meaning actually stems from this event.) But the world was not ready for this revolution, and neither was it in a receptive mood ninety years later when Galileo published his *Dialogue on the Great World Systems*. Galileo was summoned to appear before the Holy Office of the Inquisition, forced to recant, and sentenced to spend the balance of his life under house arrest. The revolution was nevertheless underway, of course, and geocentrists are now about as common as flat-earthers.

The present book seeks to demystify the human mind, and explode the myth of the soul. Why should one produce such a volume? Isn't the entire exercise rather like deploying a battleship against a water-lily? Even if there is no such thing as the soul, why should one attempt to destroy the illusions of those who reap the benefit of blind faith? I have written this book because I believe that the concept of the hereafter also has negative dimensions. And in illustrating this point, I wish to suggest that it is no exaggeration to refer to the tyranny of the soul.

One of the most universal and durable of man's taboos is that which surrounds such speculation about the non-existence of life after death. René Descartes was acutely aware of this. His *Traité de l'Homme*, on which he was working when Galileo was running into such trouble, sought to expose the human body for the machine it is. Descartes sequestered it in a desk drawer, and it was not published until after the author's death.

Although an individual's soul would presumably be his own property, it has nevertheless always lain within the jurisdiction of the religious professional, who has had what could appropriately be called a vested interest in maintaining the myth of its existence. The concept of the hereafter is not the sole preserve of any one religion. Indeed, the idea is found in the majority of faiths, and it would be no exaggeration to call it the mainspring of virtually all of them. Anyone who doubts this should ask himself how many people will still go to church regularly if biologists ever find the secret of immortality. Although that might seem to be a very remote prospect, it is interesting to note that an article which appeared in the 8 January 1968 edition of the *New York Times* actually listed chemical control of aging amongst the possible scientific achievements by the middle of the 1990s.

Belief in life after death is a major facet of religion. It serves the obvious need of softening the blow of our realization of life's finiteness, of the inevitable snuffing out of each brief candle, of the fact that, as Mark Twain put it, no one gets out alive. One could say that it is the high price we have had to pay for the evolution of our minds. It is interesting to speculate on how long the notion of an afterlife has been with us. Perhaps it actually came with the development of consciousness. It is possible that it was already there in Neanderthal culture, because these pre-humans buried their dead festooned in garlands of flowers; they seem to have associated something spiritual with the departed state. But

although there has long been a case for hypothesizing continuity
of an individual's essence, through and beyond the grave, it
has been equally obvious that this must involve something
other than the body, putrid specimens of which are pungently
impermanent. In short, a non-carnal mediator of survival was
required, and hence the idea of the soul.

Compared with all eternity, the average life span of man
is a mere bagatelle, a drop in the ocean. But it was clear
at the outset that the soul could not fritter away its fleeting
stay on earth, marking time waiting for the death of its mortal
caretaker to release it into the infinite. On the contrary, the
biblical three score and ten years were accorded a disproportionately large significance. During this time, through divine but
devious beneficence, we were given freedom of will, to use or
abuse, and a sufficiently blotted copybook was to be rewarded
with everlasting damnation. However, the technical details of
the afterlife, pleasant or unpleasant, were at best nebulous.
How one was to experience eternal bliss or eternal anguish,
for example, without access to a central nervous system, has
never been made clear. That such questions arise is of course
a reflection of the fact that our intellects are unequal to this
cosmic challenge. Small wonder that we were forced to create
God in our own image.

But where, exactly, was the soul to be located during one's
period of stewardship? If we find amusement in the attempts
of ancient civilizations to grapple with this problem, we should
remind ourselves that anatomical investigations still lay in
the future. The only invasions of the body's interior officially
sanctioned in those remote days were made by the instruments
of battle, and the observations were consequently crude. The
Sumerians, Assyrians and early Israelites believed the soul to
reside in the liver. At the time, this was a reasonable guess;
the liver is a focal point of the circulatory system, and if a
sufficient amount of blood flowed out of the body, the soul also
seemed to depart. The Ancient Egyptians variously favoured the
bowels and the heart, regions still popularly associated with such
qualities and emotions as courage and affection, even though the
brain has long since become universally accepted as the seat of
the mind. One does not see the cerebral cortex used as a motif
on Valentine cards, for example.

Until the late sixteenth century, those who studied the brain's anatomy were preoccupied with its ventricles, rather than with the surrounding tissue. There are four of these chambers, but because the two at the front are symmetrically arranged, the brain theorists of that time believed that there were just three regions amongst which all the faculties were to be apportioned. The *sensus communis* was attributed to the front ventricles, which were perceived as a rendezvous point for messages arriving from the various senses, rather than as the seat of common sense. The central ventricle on typical anatomical drawings of that era was usually labelled with words such as *ratio* (reason), *cognatio* (thought) and *aestimato* (judgement).

Memory (*memoria*) was invariably attributed to the aftermost ventricle. The dualism of brain and mind, a concept later advocated by René Descartes, is depicted in this imaginative drawing by the Paracelsian alchemist and mystic, Robert Fludd. It attempts to display the links between the ventricles and the higher facets of the intellect, and it even includes a connection to the spinal cord.

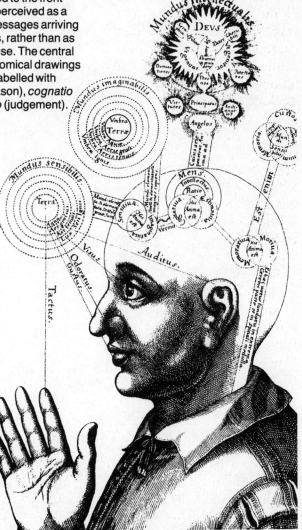

In the midst of this preoccupation with what could be called the geography of the issue, Descartes came up with a new angle which eventually won so much favour that it has survived until this day. The soul is not actually part of one's physical body at all, he told us. It is merely associated with the body. He even managed to pinpoint, to his satisfaction at least, the site where the body and soul make contact, namely the pineal gland, which is deeply embedded within the brain. The majority of people now willingly embrace Descartes' view, even though few would be able to correctly label it as 'dualism'. The idea has many illustrious adherents amongst the philosophical fraternity, some of whom probably feel that they are advocating an easily defended position. Isn't it rather obvious, after all? The various parts of the body are admittedly sophisticated; the Great Designer did a good job with them. But other animals have similarly impressive bits and pieces. You can see them at the butcher's shop. Even brains, in fact. You can make a jolly good brawn from a pig's head, including the brain, and warm monkey's brain on the half skull is as great a delicacy in the Orient as chilled oyster on the half shell is in Europe and America. We are clearly above what can be purchased across the counter; there must be something else. Some philosophers even have a crisp way of putting it for us: the whole must be greater than the sum of its parts. That is just the sort of catchy phrase we need, is it not, to express the idea of the soul, the immortal soul, temporarily saddled with its bodily associations.

But I have jumped ahead of my argument; the primacy of the brain has not yet been established. I am easily convinced that the focal point of my own consciousness, my 'me-ness', if you will, is located between my ears and a few centimetres behind my eyes, and this indeed puts it around the centre of my brain. But would I still feel this to be the obvious seat of my mind if I had been born deaf and blind? Probably not. And the early dissections of the brain can hardly have encouraged promotion of that organ to the hallowed position it now holds. They revealed little more than a series of channels through an otherwise featureless gelatinous mass, which led some to speculate that the brain might function like a piece of hydraulic plumbing. Many decades of painstaking anatomical investigation subsequently produced an exquisitely detailed picture, and revealed a complexity that seems more in keeping with the brain's lofty status. But it was not these commendable efforts which brought about the revolution, and the central figure in this upheaval was not even a scientist; he was a twenty-five-year-old railway engineer.

The thirteenth of September 1848 was a Wednesday, not a Friday, and there is, in any case, no record of whether the affable and popular young Phineas Gage of Vermont was superstitious. It was, nevertheless, to be his day of destiny. Although he would survive for another decade and a half, his life, as he prepared for work that fateful morning, was to all intents and purposes in its closing hours. The day's main task was the blasting of a boulder which lay blocking the route of a new branch line, and Gage, following standard procedure, had bored a hole and filled it with gunpowder. Rather imprudently, he then started to compact the charge by tapping its surface with a metal rod. But this time, alas, he inadvertently created a spark. The ensuing explosion shot the iron shaft upwards with tremendous force. It entered his head just above the left eye, passed through his forebrain, and emerged from the top of his skull, ultimately to land some fifty metres away. Miraculously, he did not succumb to this appalling injury, but the irreparable damage to his frontal lobe caused a profound change of character; gone forever was the mild and gentle manner and, for the rest of his days, Gage was obstinate, violent, mercurial and profane. It was in this macabre fashion that medical science was presented with irrefutable evidence of the mind's location in the brain.

Subsequent studies of patients with mercifully milder lesions have led to the pinpointing of the areas of the brain associated with the primary senses of sight, hearing, smell, taste, touch and balance, as well as those responsible for more complicated faculties such as the understanding of speech. The pinpointing has now reached two successively finer levels of detail: the cellular level and the molecular level. And as each curtain has been pulled aside, an increasingly mechanical picture has emerged. At no point on this journey to the brain's innermost recesses has one encountered what Gilbert Ryle facetiously referred to as Descartes' ghost in the machine, or what the earlier zealots called the 'homunculus', or little inner man. And our charting of the territory is now so complete that there is no hiding place left for that spectral entity. The brain stands revealed as an organic device. One of breathtaking complexity, admittedly, but nevertheless just a device.

In exposing the mechanical nature of the brain, science has, in effect, supplied the final chapter of another revolutionary story; one which began some twenty years before Phineas Gage's fateful explosion had served as a starting gun for modern neurobiology.

The experiment was a routine one, and Friedrich Wöhler had no reason to believe that the reaction proceeding in his test-tube would give anything more exciting than all the other products meticulously recorded in his laboratory notebook. Using the time-honoured strategy of thermally inducing parts of chemical compounds to exchange places, he heated a mixture of ammonium chloride and potassium cyanate and confidently awaited the precipitation of ammonium cyanate. To his astonishment, the concoction produced crystals of urea. This compound was well known at the time, but until then it had always been associated with the processes of life; it is present in the urine of vertebrates, for example, and each of us excretes about 30 grams of urea a day. Through his chance observation, Wöhler had shown the barriers between the organic and inorganic realms to be illusory. There is only one chemistry, and its rules apply to all materials. Nature makes no distinction between chemical combinations in living and dead substances; the matter contained in living organisms possesses no extra spiritual ingredient, no vital force. (An immediate beneficiary of this epoch-making discovery was, of course, medical science, which could now unhesitatingly add the entire inorganic domain to its inventory of potential cures.) For our purposes here, however, the decisive significance of Wöhler's deceptively innocent reaction lay beyond the confines of the bladder. He had exorcised the spirit from a single humble compound, but Descartes' ghost was now also on the run.

Why, then, have we not been able to run it right out of town? We have already seen how contemplation of death made us take to the idea of the soul as a duck takes to water, but there is more to the story than mere escapism. This book's adversary is tenacious because it comes in various guises, and it has been with us so long that it now pervades the entire fabric of human culture. Its place in mankind's intellectual baggage seems so justified, in fact, that many regard it as just another aspect of our biological makeup. The soul has, in short, acquired a natural history of its own, and it is to this that we now turn.

It seems strange, in retrospect, that the association of the mind and the brain had not already permanently established itself at the time of the Ancient Greeks. After all, the brain's claim to superiority did not lack support, even in those early times. But as Thomas Kuhn noted, in his book *The Structure of Scientific Revolutions*, published in 1962, new ideas establish themselves primarily through the demise of supporters of outmoded doctrines. We will see how this principle perversely backfired, and how Aristotle directed philosophy off into a blind alley, in which it proceeded to loiter for the next 2000 years.

We take up the story at the time of Democritus and Hippocrates, who both lived in the period from about 460 to 370 BC. We are indebted to Democritus for his introduction of the concept of the atom, of course, but he also anticipated modern neurophysiology by attributing even thoughts and sensations to the motions of elementary pieces of matter, which he called psychic atoms. That he was inclined to accord primacy to the brain is evident from his belief that this organ was the citadel of thoughts and intelligence, that it provided bonds to the soul, and that it stood guard over the upper limbs of the body. But he weakened his case through a penchant for hedging his bets; he assigned desire to the liver, and anger to the heart. There was no such vacillation on the part of Hippocrates. 'From the brain, and the brain only, arise our pleasure, joys, laughter and jests,' he wrote, 'as well as our sorrows, pains, griefs and tears.' And he went on to note that it is the brain which 'makes us mad or delirious, and inspires us with dread and fear.' He even ascribed 'inopportune mistakes, aimless anxieties and absent-mindedness' to the brain. His conclusions were based on observations of patients with brain injuries, and he was the first to appreciate that the left side of the brain controls the right side of the body, and vice versa.

Although Plato believed the brain to be the repository of the soul, which he referred to as 'the divinest part of us', we should not conclude that he was merely endorsing the clinical studies of his older colleagues. On the contrary, Plato was an advocate of pure thought, and would have no truck with experimental observation. The head, with its almost spherical shape, came closest to his ideal of mathematical perfection, and could thus be the only suitable habitat for the soul. And he backed up this contention with an even more bizarre train of reasoning. The colour and consistency of the brain bears a remarkable resemblance to semen, and this revealed, he believed, the route through which a man's offspring inherit the essence of their father's personality. (It was probably just as well for Plato that he did not survive long enough to experience the Women's Liberation Movement.) If anything, the case for the brain was already being diluted, and in his *Timaeus* Plato primarily concerned himself with the mechanism whereby the soul could survive the death of the body. He split the soul into three parts, placed in the head only that part which was destined for immortality, and chose the spinal cord to tie the immortal part to the two mortal segments.

The early foundations of neural science were beginning to totter, and it is ironic that Aristotle, by dint of having the final word in that era, should have been the one to complete the destruction; it was, after all, he who gave us the observational basis of the scientific method. Aristotle's efforts to get at the truth were commendably thorough, but the techniques of the day were inadequate to the challenge, and his observations woefully misled him. Nerves are too thin to have been discernible at that time, and Aristotle shared with his colleagues a preoccupation with blood vessels. Moreover, he had observed that the heart can be mechanically stimulated, whereas the brain, when it is exposed by injury or surgery, displays no such reaction. So although he pictured the sense organs as providing the soul with internal images, a concept we will have to return to and enlarge upon in a later chapter, his main conclusion was way off the mark: the soul resided in the heart, and the brain merely acted as a sort of refrigerator to keep the blood from overheating. We still loosely recommend that the head be allowed to rule the heart, of course, when seeking to evoke reason in our fellow men, but when today's young person tells others to 'cool it', he probably doesn't have Aristotle's ideas in mind.

Within a hundred years Greek scholars of medicine, following the principles of Aristotle's scientific method, actually made great strides forward. They discovered the distinction between nerves and capillary blood vessels, and showed that the former emanate from the brain and the spinal column, rather than from the heart. They also divined that some nerves are associated with movement whereas most merely convey sensation, and they were even on to the fact that the size of the brain in various species, relative to the body, correlates with mental ability.

But the damage had been done. The guardians of religious belief, who enjoyed a virtual monopoly of recorded knowledge, took those results of scientific investigation which they needed to bolster their dogmas, and ignored or even outlawed the rest. Their favoured science was creation science, which, of course, has continued to flourish ever since.

The prototypal misuse of the results of the scientific endeavour is exemplified by the work of one of the giants of Greek anatomy, Galen of Bergama. He focussed his attention on the ventricles, which are a system of cavities running through the brain, and on the *rete mirabile*, or 'marvellous net', a system of blood vessels at the base of the brain. Galen had actually made his observations on the brains of oxen and pigs, which have reti that are better developed than those found in human brains. In Galen's scenario, nutrients absorbed in the gut produced natural spirits in the liver, which were transformed to vital spirits in the heart, ultimately to become animal spirits in the rete mirabile. These animal spirits, or psychic pneuma, were finally envisaged as being stored in the ventricles. One can imagine how ready the early Christian Church was to embrace Galen's spirits; they could not have fitted more perfectly into the prevailing doctrine if they had been made to order.

The meanings of words like 'soul', 'spirit' and 'mind' can be hard to define. This is a good point at which to pause and take stock of what has become of the terms introduced by the ancient intellectuals. If one checks the dictionary for the meaning of the word 'psyche', which, as we have already seen, dates from the Ancient Greeks, one is referred onwards to the words 'soul' and 'mind', both of which are Anglo-Saxon. But the hunt then becomes something of a wild-goose chase, because the dictionary entry for 'soul' is likely to lead one on to the word 'mind', which in turn often has a cross-reference back to 'soul'. Similarly, an alternative route from 'soul' leads on to 'spirit', but this in turn branches both back to 'soul' or onwards to 'mind'. The term 'animal spirit' derives from the Latin words *anima* and *spirare*, the latter meaning to breathe. But although the etymology is unequivocal, the meanings of these different words are as nebulous as their religious concomitants. The situation is satisfactory only with respect to those definitions of the mind which call it the seat of consciousness, and the faculty by which we think. But then again, consciousness itself can be a rather difficult thing to pin down.

Nothing so attests to the power of the Church as the maintenance of the status quo for some thirteen hundred years, following the assimilation of Galen's findings. The ventricles had emerged in the second century, and they still held sway at the beginning of the sixteenth century. One sees them depicted schematically in the writings of Albertus Magnus, and the Carthusian monk Gregor Reisch apportioned the main faculties amongst these chambers. There are four ventricles, but the two frontally positioned chambers are arranged symmetrically, and they were thus collectively allotted to the *sensus communis*, or common sense. This term was not a reference to prudence; the frontal ventricles were merely seen as the confluence of the nerves which conveyed sensory information up from the ears, eyes, nose and tongue. Reisch's 'anatomical' diagram also identified the seats of fantasy, imagination, thought, judgement and memory.

But changes were afoot. The Church now had the Renaissance to contend with; its teachings on the anatomical ramifications of the soul were no longer being accepted without question. And although dissections carried out around the end of the fifteenth century were performed in surreptitious defiance of papal prohibition, the men of the faith could not gainsay the all too tangible results of these painstaking investigations.

The giants of that era were Leonardo da Vinci and Andreas Vesalius. Leonardo, working at the Santa Maria Nuova hospital in Florence, resourcefully developed a way of studying the form of the ventricles. This was no easy task. One can observe the shapes and arrangement of holes in a piece of Swiss cheese by cutting it into a series of thin parallel slices, but this is possible only because the cheese itself is reasonably rigid. The brain is too fragile to permit examination in a similar fashion, so

Leonardo hit upon the brilliant idea of injecting molten
into the ventricles and waiting for it to set. This produce
cast of the ventricles, not unlike the sculptor's bronze cast, with
which Leonardo was of course already familiar.

Leonardo's studies of such casts led him to re-evaluate his
earlier observations of both the ventricles and the surrounding
brain tissue. His previous conclusions had merely endorsed the
classic three-chamber model described earlier, but his new picture was radically different. He discovered that the sense organs
send their nerves not to the pair of ventricles at the front, but
rather to a region near the central ventricle. He consequently
relocated the sensus communis to the region previously reserved
for the twin faculties of cognition and estimation, that is to say
of judgement. It is not clear whether this was, in fact, the origin
of the term 'common sense'.

Although it was not immediately appreciated, Leonardo's
more important observation concerned the actual destination
of the nerves arriving from the sense organs. These did not
terminate at the central ventricle, but disappeared into a piece
of nearby tissue now known as the thalamus. The importance
of the ventricles had been undermined, and they were further
demoted when it was discovered that they contain cerebrospinal fluid; hardly the stuff of pneumatic animal spirits. One of
Leonardo's contemporaries, Berengario da Carpi, through his
own meticulous dissections, put paid to the mythical role of the
rete mirabile once and for all.

Leonardo had set new standards of anatomical observation,
and his mantle was taken up by Vesalius, whose book *De
corporis humani fabrica* (On the Fabric of the Human Body),
published in 1543, included an exquisitely detailed charting
of the nervous system. With Leonardo's virtual discovery of
the thalamus, the focus of attention was shifting from the
ventricles to the brain tissue, which until that time had been
regarded as little more than a sort of soft padding. Vesalius
produced drawings of the convolutions on the surface of the
cerebral cortex which remain remarkably accurate even by
today's exacting standards.

Was the message of these research advances getting through
to the men of religion and philosophy, however? If it was, it was
certainly being ignored. One could be charitable and say that

the philosophers, at least, must have found the prevailing intellectual climate oppressive. But the men of the Church were subject only to their own self-imposed and stultifying constraints. Science had long since given them all that their preconceived notions required, and the door which they slammed shut has, for many, remained closed until the present day. Within a few decades, Leonardo and Vesalius were dead and gone, and their beautifully illustrated writings, though not destroyed, were gathering dust on the bookshelves.

What, then, was claiming the attention of the intellectual advocates of the soul? It was primarily elaboration of the theme which the scientists had already demonstrated to be hopelessly outmoded. We have, as an example, a picture produced by the Paracelsian philosopher Robert Fludd. One sees the familiar pattern of ventricles, and their interconnecting corridors, but this has been embellished with the orbits of the mind, which are shown deployed around the surface of the head. And the heavy philosophical atmosphere was even getting to the anatomists. Their science was, if anything, running backwards. Franciscus de le Boë, also known as Sylvius, is looked upon as being one of the leading figures of the time, and yet he was back on the barren trail of the animal spirits, which he believed to issue from the cerebral lobes. And although officialdom had relaxed to the extent that universities could now put up theatres dedicated to the study of anatomy, these were equipped with small windows, to accommodate the prying eye of the Holy Inquisitor. Moreover, the brain and the sex organs were strictly off limits.

This brings us, once again, to Descartes, whose durable principle of dualism we encountered earlier. His speculations could not be called advanced, even for his time, because he thought in terms of pneumatic rather than nervous processes. But he correctly guessed that reflexes must be mediated by a system of conduits; he produced sketches of the paths taken by signals travelling from the limbs to the brain, and they show a marked resemblance to the nervous system. And it could have appeared that he had grasped the essential unity of the body and the mind, when he formulated his immortal phrase: *cogito ergo sum*, I think therefore I am. But, as we have already seen, he advocated complete separation of these attributes. That he should have so enthusiastically supported the idea of a mind,

L'HOMME
DE RENE
DESCARTES.
ET VN TRAITTÉ
DE LA FORMATION DV FOETVS
DV MESME AVTHEVR.

Auec les Remarques de LOVYS DE LA FORGE,
Docteur en Medecine, demeurant à la Fleche,
Sur le Traitté de l'Homme de RENE' DESCARTES;
& fur les Figures par luy inuentées.

A PARIS,
Chez CHARLES ANGOT, Libraire Iuré, ruë
S. Iacques, au Lion d'Or.
M. DC. LXIV.
AVEC PRIVILEGE DV ROY.

Although René Descartes is best remembered for his dualist view of body and mind, and for the phrase *cogito ergo sum* (I think, therefore I am), he was also responsible for introducing the idea of the reflex. Because the current wisdom saw all control as ultimately emanating from animal spirits, which resided in the brain's ventricles, it is not surprising that his conjectured reflex mechanism was based on the principles of hydraulics. The tubes in his system were dual structures that served to carry messages both to the brain from the skin and from the brain to the muscles. In this reproduction of one of his illustrations, the fire A displaces the skin of the foot, thereby tugging at the tube C and opening the pore D in the ventricle F. This releases animal spirits into the hollow core of the tube, and they flow down to the foot B, to inflate the muscles and cause the limb to be removed from the heat. The other figure shows Descartes' resourceful system of valves (such as the one marked H) which allows one muscle to relax as the other contracts when the spirits flow through tubes C and B.

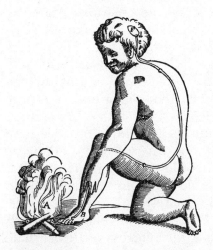

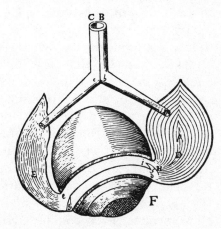

and by implication a soul, quite separate from the body, is hardly surprising in view of his devout Catholicism. And science really owed Descartes its gratitude, because he had unwittingly pulled off a diplomatic triumph; by separating the immortal soul from the mortal body, and cogently arguing that the latter is a mere machine, he was instrumental in bringing respectability to the anatomical investigation of the brain.

Because such investigation has certainly not diminished in respectability, during the intervening years, and since the dualist separation of body and mind is still with us, one might be inclined to conclude that this was the end of the story. But there was trouble brewing in the wings. Pierre Gassendi, an almost exact contemporary of Descartes, had put the cat amongst the pigeons by noting that since animals also have memories, and the ability, albeit limited, to rationalize, they too must therefore possess a soul. This was not exactly what the Church wanted to hear. And there was worse to come. Several experimenters had observed that the body of a decapitated frog retains the capacity for movement; its limbs can be made to twitch as a response to pinching and other forms of irritation. This was hardly consistent with the idea that such movements are provoked by the transmission of animal spirits from the ventricles down through Descartes' pneumatic tubes, since the latter would be cut through in the act of beheading the creature. An even more stringent rebuttal of Descartes' idea was supplied by an experiment carried out by Jan Swammerdam. He placed a frog's thigh muscle in a sealed flask that was equipped with a device for detecting changes in the volume of the air enclosed in the system, and showed that the stimulation and resulting contraction of the muscle was accompanied by neither an increase nor a decrease in volume. This refuted the idea that a muscle moves through the inflation caused by the inflow of animal spirits, just as a balloon swells up when air is blown into it. Some of Swammerdam's contemporaries, lacking his taste for careful experimentation, merely cut up frogs while they were submerged under water, and observing no tell-tale effervescence, they concluded that the pneumatic theory had also gone flat.

It would be naive to believe that these clever demonstrations made any impression on the Establishment, however. Descartes' dualism might have won a reprieve for experimental biology, but it had also emasculated it. Although anatomical work was now countenanced by those in power, presumably on the principle that all medical knowledge carried with it the potential for alleviating pain and suffering, any suggestion that the investigator's scalpel might also help to cut away the mystery surrounding the soul met with stern and peremptory opposition. The soul had, in effect, been declared to lie outside the domain of natural history. Contrary to popular opinion, this chapter of mankind's intellectual progress had not been closed, of course, but the climate was now such that works of great insight and wisdom made about as much impression on the public mind as does water on a duck's back. Thus when Etienne de Condillac produced his *Traité des Sensations*, in 1754, in which he argued that all properties of the soul derive from the information transmitted to the brain from the senses, his seminal and remarkably prescient message went largely unheard.

That the developments since de Condillac's time have proceeded beyond public awareness is attested to by the fact that dualism is still as much with us as it was when Descartes first introduced it. My task, in the remaining chapters of this book, will be to show that de Condillac's almost clairvoyant ideas have now been vindicated, to an extent which would surely have exceeded even his wildest dreams. I will chronicle the progress achieved during the last two centuries, and show how it reveals that what Plato regarded as the divinest part of us is not divine at all.

The great parting of the ways which dualism provoked provides our story with an obvious punctuation mark, so let me leave that scene with all its ambiguities and invective. I can do this by contrasting the fates of just two more figures of that time, and thereby epitomize the depth of the divisions which had arisen in the intellectual fraternity.

The first of these people is Julien Offray de la Mettrie. His view of the brain was supremely mechanical. He envisaged it as the origin of all the body's nerve threads, and through these it exercised total control over all bodily processes, however trivial or sophisticated. This, he claimed, explained everything, including the most abstract thoughts. The Establishment was scandalized, and when his book *Natural History* was published, the Parisian authorities decreed that it should be burned. De la Mettrie had to flee into exile, and he spent a period in what we now know as Holland. But when his pamphlet *L'Homme Machine* (Man Machine) appeared in 1748, he again found himself vilified and packing his bags, this time for the refuge of Frederick the Great's court in Prussia.

The other figure is Niels Steensen, also known as Nicolaus Steno, and in contrasting his fate with that of de la Mettrie there is a note of supreme irony. Steensen came from the same mould as the anatomist–architect–artist–engineer–mathematician Leonardo and the mathematician–philosopher Descartes, for although he belonged to the Baroque period, he embodied the protean ideal of the Renaissance polymath. Through his studies of the shapes of crystals, Steensen had founded the science of crystallography, while his discovery of various ducts and glands established him as one of the foremost anatomists of his time.

However, it is two of his other accomplishments which will concern us here. To appreciate the first, we must recall the famous systematic scrutiny of the Bible carried out by Archbishop Ussher and his colleague Dr Lightfoot in the middle of the seventeenth century. They had discovered that a consistent chronological sequence can be established, and they confidently announced that the creation of the world had commenced promptly at 9 a.m. on Sunday, 23 October, in the year 4004 BC. Steensen was also interesting himself in the origin of the earth, around this time. His authority was not the Bible, but the exposed strata of rock which he investigated during a visit to Italy. Chancing upon some suspiciously triangular-shaped objects, it soon dawned on him that they bore a striking resemblance to the teeth of the shark. He had, in fact, perceived the nature and origin of fossils. It did not take long before he had worked out a dynamical theory of the origin of the earth, and thus established yet another science, namely that of geology. And when reliable age determinations became available for fossilized material, it transpired that the Ussher–Lightfoot estimate of the earth's age was hopelessly short.

These were difficult acts to follow, but Steensen scored yet another success when he turned his attention to the brain.

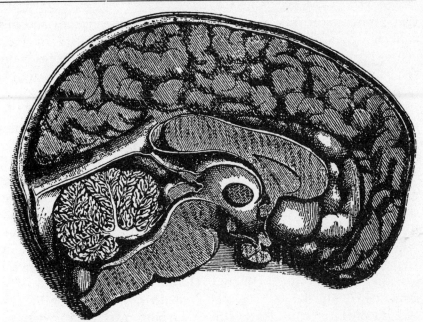

DISCOVRS

DE

MONSIEVR STENON,

SVR

L'ANATOMIE

DV CERVEAV.

A

MESSIEVRS DE
l'Assemblée, qui se fait chez
Monsieur Theuenot.

A PARIS,
Chez ROBERT DE NINVILLE, au bout du Pont
S. Michel, au coin de la ruë de la Huchette,
à l'Escu de France & de Nauarre.

M DC. LXIX.
AVEC PRIVILEGE DV ROY.

Niels Steensen, also known as Nicolaus Steno, must be one of the strangest figures in the entire history of brain study. Remarkably broad in his intellectual pursuits, he is credited with creating the sciences of geology and crystallography, and he was also one of anatomy's founding fathers. In 1667, still only 29 years of age, he turned his attention to the brain, and soon established himself as a leading expert in its anatomical exploration. At a time when most other people working in the field were barely getting to grips with the grey matter, Steensen quickly realized that the underlying white matter must be equally important in giving the brain the power of thought. The above picture shows one of the remarkably detailed illustrations from his most famous publication on the subject. Six years after it appeared in print, Steensen suddenly turned his back on all scientific investigation, and devoted the balance of his short life to religion. He had risen to the rank of bishop by the time he died, and he was recently elevated to sainthood.

Quickly realising that the pneumatic ideas of Descartes and his cohorts were untenable, Steensen started on a detailed charting of the paths taken by the nerves. He soon came to appreciate the central role played by a part of the brain which even today is unknown to the layman, to wit, the white matter (as opposed to the well-known grey matter). He rightly concluded that it is through the myriad connections made by this substructure that the brain controls the entire body, and that it is probably also responsible for all thought processes.

From these impressive accomplishments, we would be in no doubt as to which side Steensen should be placed in the controversy outlined above. He had delivered two body blows to the literal interpretation of the Holy Scriptures. But we have reached the ironic climax of this part of our story because, in 1675, Steensen converted to Catholicism and relinquished all his scientific pursuits. He took Holy Orders, indeed, rapidly rising through the clerical echelons to end his brief life as Bishop of Titiopolis. And while this book was being written, he was elevated to sainthood.

● Summary

Of all mankind's beliefs, the idea of a soul, associated with the body and yet distinct from it, has proved particularly tenacious. In ancient times, even the bodily connection was regarded as being tenuous, but successive civilizations identified a variety of organs as likely repositories of an individual's identity. For the Sumerians, Assyrians and early Israelites, it was the liver, while the Egyptians favoured the bowels and heart, regions still popularly associated with courage and affection. Early dissections of the brain revealed it to be disappointingly featureless, but personality changes in brain-damaged patients confirmed that this is indeed the seat of the mind. In spite of the steadily increasing precision with which the functions of the brain's various regions have been pinpointed, the dualist separation of mind and body, originally advocated by Descartes, remains virtually unopposed.

Mortal coils
The brain's anatomy

All man's reason has done for him
is to make him beastlier than the beast.
One splendid body is worth all the brains
of a hundred dyspeptic, flatulent philosophers.

GEORGE BERNARD SHAW
Man and Superman

Irrespective of whether one approaches London's Piccadilly Circus from Upper or Lower Regent Street, Piccadilly, the Haymarket, Coventry Street, or Shaftesbury Avenue – for this famous nodal point is the confluence of six great thoroughfares – one finds oneself staring at the beautiful bronze figure which everyone knows as Eros. Unveiled in 1893, it was actually intended by the sculptor, Sir Alfred Gilbert, to represent the Angel of Christian Charity. Perched atop the memorial fountain to the Seventh Earl of Shaftesbury, the Victorian philanthropist, the winged archer strikes a pose which is so familiar that we naturally regard it as commonplace: he is performing a one-legged balancing act.

Why should we be concerned with such an everyday feat in a book about the brain, the mind and the soul? Isn't it relatively easy to explain how the little fellow can poise himself thus? The muscles of the leg are obviously involved, of course, and we do appreciate that these are under the control of the nervous system, of which the brain is an important part, but surely the maintenance of balance is readily understood by anyone who has studied basic biology. One is taught that muscles come in pairs, and that it is the interplay between opposing members of each

pair which permits the type of equilibrium being displayed by
Gilbert's statue. But this is only the beginning of an explanation,
for what is it that enables each of the muscles in the opposing pair
to exert precisely the correct amount of tension? It is here that
we touch upon a central characteristic of the nervous system's
function, and the key word is automation.

However, before we consider this particular example of automation, let us contemplate the concept in the wider context of
engineering. Man might have been harnessing Nature's energy
since time immemorial, but his early machines were always
controlled by hand. The Industrial Revolution would not have
been possible had it not been for the ingenuity of engineers
in finding various ways in which machines can be made to
control themselves. Noteworthy amongst the regulatory devices
developed at that time was the governor, which keeps an engine
running at a constant speed. I recall owning a toy version of such
a gadget, in my younger days. It was equipped with two brass
spheres, which made the contraption look rather like two-thirds
of a pawnbroker's sign. Each sphere was linked by two rods to
a rotatable spindle, the connection between each of the upper
rods and the spindle being a simple hinge. Each lower rod, on
the other hand, was connected to a ring which could slide up
and down the spindle, and a further thin rod connected the
ring to a lever which controlled the amount of steam being
fed to the driving cylinder. Automatic control of my engine's
speed was achieved in the following way: any tendency for the
rotational speed of the spindle to increase would raise the level
of the twirling brass spheres, and this decreased the amount of
steam being fed to the engine; the spindle's rotational speed
was thereby decreased and the brass spheres fell back to their
original most stable positions. A momentary drop in the engine's
speed was compensated for in like manner. This self-correcting
mechanism in my simple governor embodied the same principle
as that used in more sophisticated machines, and the principle
is known as negative feedback.

Returning to the nervous system, we find that negative feedback is as important as it is ubiquitous. Each muscle is equipped
with sensors which send information about the state of the muscle's tension up to the brain, and the brain returns corrective
instructions to the muscles, thereby permitting just the right

amount of tension to be maintained. If Gilbert's winged archer had been flesh and blood, this is the piece of neuromuscular circuitry that would have allowed him to hold his tiptoe balance. Our understanding of these processes dates from the pioneering work of Charles Sherrington, who studied the interruption of the reflexes in experimental animals by removing parts of their cerebral cortices and making observations on the resulting muscular rigidity.

The negative feedback principle is a central theme in the story of the brain, mind and soul, and we will encounter it on various scales of size. But in order to appreciate how it conspires to make us the automatic machines we are, we need to prepare the ground with a thorough account of the anatomical background. The best way of getting down to that job is to return to the historical events which were being chronicled in Chapter 1.

We left the story at the great parting of the ways. Anatomy and physiology had been given free rein to probe what we could call the body's hardware, namely the structures which human beings and the higher animals have in common. The ways in which we form internal images of the external world, however, were not only left unexplained but assumed by many to be unexplorable. It was generally believed that perception and the formation of concepts were the preserve of human beings and that, because such faculties were really attributes of the soul, anatomical dissection was not likely to shed any light on them.

The word 'generally' is important here, however, because the opposing view, that man and beast differ only in degree and not in type, was again beginning to make itself heard. I wrote in Chapter 1 of Aristotle's dispatching philosophy into a 2000-year sojourn up a blind alley. If one takes that figure literally, the middle of the seventeenth century would seem to provide philosophy with a cue for its reawakening, and the first person to champion the animal cause was John Locke. He could be called a charter member of the empiricist school, which maintained that knowledge is the sum of accumulated experience rather than the expression of preordained mental rules and intuitions. The mind, according to Locke, started life as a blank tablet, a *tabula rasa*, on which an individual's experiences were subsequently written. He believed that animals

can perceive and remember, and even reason, but that they fall
short of man in not being able to abstract. This flew in the face
of the majority view, which drew the animal–man dividing line
on the other side of reason; Locke was attempting to move the
mental Rubicon to a different place on the philosophical map.
In this, he enjoyed the support of Gottfried Leibniz, who cited
the case of a dog cowering in fear of an anticipated beating when
its master reaches for a stick previously used for that purpose.

Thomas Willis, another contemporary of Locke and Leibniz,
and also of Steensen, whose work was mentioned in Chapter
1, was particularly influential amongst the anatomists of the
time. More adroit with the scalpel than with pen and brush,
he enlisted the artistic talents of Sir Christopher Wren, better
known as the architect of St Paul's Cathedral in London. The
combination of painstaking anatomical investigation and superb
illustrations gave this collaboration well-deserved influence, and
Willis began to undermine the view that sensation is a spiritual
rather than a bodily function. He produced a remarkably mechanistic theory of hearing, showing it to involve the transformation
of sound by activation of a receptor mechanism in the cochlea of
the inner ear. (The cochlea is the part that resembles the coiled
spring of a pre-electronic clock or watch.)

Hearing was not the first sense to be given a mechanistic
'explanation', in fact, because Johannes Kepler had done the
same thing for vision several decades earlier. As an astronomer,
he was familiar with optical instruments, and he proposed a
mechanism of seeing which involves the formation, by the eye's
lens, of an image on the nerves contained in the retina. Kepler's
ideas have remained valid to this day, but like those of Willis they
explain only the initial stage in the production of a sensation.

Willis was especially concerned with the way in which anatomical features peculiar to the various parts of the brain make
them suitable for specific functions. He attributed the role of
memory to the cerebral cortex, the convoluted surface of which
had already been studied by Vesalius. The *corpus callosum*, a thick
bundle of fibres which connects the brain's two hemispheres,
was conjectured to imbue the mind with imagination, while the
cerebellum, a large clump of nerve tissue that lies to the rear of
the brain, below the cerebral cortex, was seen as providing the
basis for involuntary movements. Finally, Willis believed the

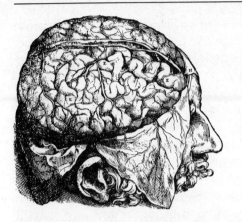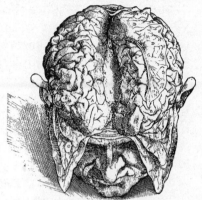

Medieval biological investigations were subject to the taboos that naturally accompanied vitalism; the interior of the human body was the vessel of the soul, and was thus out of bounds. Anatomical dissections of that era were therefore carried out in surreptitious defiance of papal prohibition. The relaxation of restrictions in the Renaissance period permitted brain studies to flourish and the greatest anatomist of the time was Andreas Vesalius. But although these illustrations from his *De humani corporis fabrica*, published in 1543, showed the cortical convolutions in admirable detail, Vesalius attached little importance to these structures; he likened them to the random clouds drawn by schoolboys. His primary concern was with the underlying features, such as the ventricles, and the corpus callosum, which is indicated by the letter L in the right-hand figure.

corpus striatum, which lies centrally located beneath the cerebral hemispheres, to be the focal point for all sensory inputs, and therefore the most likely site for the origin of reason. There was a grain of truth in each of these speculations, even though his ideas have long since been superseded.

Although Willis had made major contributions to the demystification of the senses, he personally believed in the existence of the soul. Or should we rather say that he publicly acknowledged it? Perhaps he merely saw wisdom in not crossing swords with the politically powerful Archbishop of Canterbury. In any event, he too felt obliged to pinpoint the location at which the body makes contact with the soul, and he chose not the pineal body favoured by Descartes, but rather the corpus striatum, no doubt because its presumed association with reason made it an obvious candidate.

There is not room in this book to record all the advances which led to the detailed picture we now have of the brain.

Neither can I find place for a roll call of the names of all those whose work gradually pushed back the frontiers of ignorance. Their collective efforts improved anatomical techniques, and the written reports of their investigations often included philosophical conclusions that were remarkably perceptive. In this respect, mention must be made of two giants. Johann Reil was the first researcher to use organic preservatives and hardening agents, thus making the brain firm and permanent enough to permit reliable and reproducible dissection at leisure. He thereby did for the soft brain tissue what Leonardo had achieved for the ventricles. Reil exploited the new possibilities that this opened up, and he must be credited, either directly or indirectly, with charting the connections between the brain's various substructures. Reil was not in opposition to Descartes' dualism, but he emphatically brooked no diminution of the brain's role in the scheme of things. On the contrary, he saw it as 'the mysterious nuptial bed where the body and the soul celebrate their orgies'.

Pierre Cabanis went one bold step further: he stated that there is no independent soul, and that consciousness, the uppermost manifestation of mental activity, is inextricably related to the natural functioning of the brain. In the previous chapter, we saw how the lack of tell-tale bubbles from frogs decapitated under water led some to deride the idea of animal spirits. Cabanis became preoccupied with similar, but even more macabre, notions. The guillotine had recently dispatched many of his compatriots, and in some cases spectators swore that they saw the eyes of the executed victims turn in their sockets. Could a guillotined head briefly retain consciousness, Cabanis speculated. He tried to resolve the issue by experiments in which exposed animal brains were locally stimulated. This produced muscle convulsions, but it supplied no conclusive answer to his grisly question. On the subject of the mind, however, Cabanis was in no doubt. In *Histoire physiologique des sensations*, which was the second volume of his *Rapports du physique et du morale de l'homme*, published in 1802, he calls the brain a 'particular organ, specially designed to produce thought, just as the stomach and the intestines contribute to digestion'. And he goes on to note that 'impressions, arriving at the brain, make it spring into action, just as food, falling into the stomach, excites the latter into producing gastric juice.' So the brain was seen as secreting thought, just as the liver secretes bile. These seminal ideas of Cabanis were indeed food for thought.

Our narrative has reached an episode which was intriguing, bizarre, and yet undoubtedly important. It was touched off by the emergence of an attempt to identify various mental faculties with specific locations in the cerebral cortex, to a much greater degree of precision than had previously been accomplished. Its originator, Franz Gall, had, since his early days, been fascinated by observations of the shapes of his friends' heads. There appeared to be correlations between certain cranial features and the mental make-up of their possessors. The clever members of his circle, for example, all boasted high foreheads, while those with good memories had protruding eyes. (The former of these observations was perhaps responsible for the term highbrow.) Gall became a qualified anatomist, in fact, and deservedly achieved respect as a dissector of the brain. He hit upon the clever idea of carrying out post-mortem dissections on the brains of individuals whose intellectual capacities and character traits he had previously made a note of, but his attempts to match mental propensity with internal structure produced nothing conclusive. His earlier preoccupation with the external shape of the skull thus gradually gained the upper hand, and he began to extend his investigations well beyond the ranks of his immediate acquaintances. He became particularly interested in institutions which, by their very nature, suggested associations with particular mental characteristics: learned societies, lunatic asylums, prisons, and so on. We must leave to the imagination the question of how he came to link sexiness in the female with bumps behind the ears.

When Gall had compiled a sufficiently large inventory of his correlations, often based on flimsy evidence, he felt justified in launching his new 'science' of cranioscopy, now more commonly referred to as phrenology. The general idea was that an excess or deficiency of a particular faculty, in an individual, would be respectively reflected in a surfeit or deficit of brain tissue in the area from which the faculty arises. This, in turn, would produce a bump or a depression on the surface of the skull. Because brain tissue is very soft, while the skull is quite hard, it might be felt that the idea was a non-starter, but we should bear in mind that the skull is quite soft and pliable during

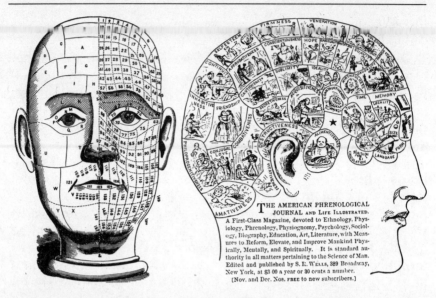

THE AMERICAN PHRENOLOGICAL
JOURNAL AND LIFE ILLUSTRATED.
A First-Class Magazine, devoted to Ethnology, Physiology, Phrenology, Physiognomy, Psychology, Sociology, Biography, Education, Art, Literature, with Measures to Reform, Elevate, and Improve Mankind Physically, Mentally, and Spiritually. It is standard authority in all matters pertaining to the Science of Man. Edited and published by S. R. WELLS, 389 Broadway, New York, at $3 00 a year or 30 cents a number.
[Nov. and Dec. Nos. FREE to new subscribers.]

The most bizarre chapter in the history of brain science started in 1790, when Franz Gall put forward the idea that mental propensities are reflected in the contours of the scalp. A bump in a given area was taken as an indication of strength in the corresponding aspect of personality. Several different systems subsequently appeared, all claiming to most accurately chart the various phrenological regions. The most elaborate of these was due to J.W. Redfield, M.D., of New York City (left figure); it listed 160 numbered faculties. The fact that Republicanism (region 149) is adjacent to Faithful Love (148) and Responsibility (149A), in his system, probably reveals more about Redfield's political sympathies than about his medical qualifications. But the most advanced scientific knowledge of any period takes time to filter through to the public awareness; the *American Phrenological Journal* (right figure) was still thriving in the 1930s, and the British Phrenological Society was not disbanded until 1967.

infancy. If mental make-up is either congenital or determined in one's youngest years, Gall's ideas perhaps ought not to be dismissed out of hand.

In scientific circles at least, phrenology soon fell into disrepute, however. Its decline amongst men of medicine was no doubt accelerated by the unjustified fervour of Gall's disciples, prominent amongst whom were Gall's pupil Johann Spurzheim, and George Combe, a lawyer turned philosopher, phrenologist and liberal reformer. Gall's original phrenological map charted the locations of twenty-seven mental faculties, but his zealous followers continually augmented the terrain with increasingly more detailed sites, the pinpointing of which was the product of pure fantasy rather than of reliable observation. Gall's acolytes seem to have been particularly proud of their towering foreheads, which, according to their own charts, reflected the very brand of intellectual superiority that would be natural amongst their science's leaders. The truth was, of course, that their energies were being squandered on a pseudo-science, the popularity of which was attributable to its tempting scope for quackery. It reached its grotesque zenith at the end of the nineteenth century, when one practitioner, a certain Dr J.W. Redfield of New York, published the most elaborate system of phrenological localizations ever conceived. It comprised no fewer than 160 regions, including one at the rear of the jaw identified with Republicanism. This province, according to Redfield, lay immediately adjacent to areas having dominion over faithful love and responsibility, a mapping which probably reveals more about Redfield's political sympathies than his medical qualifications.

There are several lessons to be learned from the phenomenon of phrenology. One is that theories, irrespective of their soundness, tend to be well received if they tell the layman what he wants to hear. Phrenology survived for over 150 years; the Ohio State Phrenological Society was still publishing its journal in 1938, and the British Phrenological Society was not disbanded until 1967. (Amongst the paraphernalia produced for adherents of phrenology were porcelain busts on which were indicated the locations of the various character traits and faculties. These have now become collectors' items, and one would pay far more for just one of them than for an entire anatomist's demonstration skeleton. The bizarre and the fanciful have always held a peculiar fascination for the souvenir hunter.) A particularly sinister and nefarious dimension was added to this story during the Second World War, when the leaders of the Nazi movement condoned 'anatomical studies' aimed at correlating skull shape with genetic proximity to the politically desirable Aryan race.

Gall and his crackpot followers inevitably fell victim to their own exaggerated claims, what nowadays would be called their own hype. By the 1820s, their case had become ripe for demolition. The *coup de grâce* was delivered by Marie-Jean-Pierre Flourens, who specialized in the technique known as surgical ablation, or the cutting away of portions of tissue. He showed that removal of the cerebellum, for example, deprived a subject of the ability to coordinate movement, while breathing became impaired if the *medulla*, which lies near the posterior ventricle, was excised. He established that the cerebral cortex is the seat of the functions usually associated with the mind. Animals robbed of their cerebral lobes lost their ability to perceive, judge and remember. They sat immobilized, as if in a trance, but they were nevertheless capable of movement when suitably prodded. This led Flourens to the most far-reaching of his conclusions, namely that the cerebral lobes are the origin of volition, that they are the true seat of the will.

But if Flourens was able to wreak such havoc on Gall's theory, and lay derelict the cult of its motley compilation of cranial bumps, why have I stated that phrenology played an important role in the development of our knowledge of the brain? For it must not be overlooked that Flourens, on the basis of his observations, believed each mental faculty to be spread throughout the entire cerebral cortex. The ideas of the two men were thus diametrically opposed: strict localization against wide distribution; only one of them could be correct.

In contemplating Gall *vis-à-vis* Flourens, we see science in its most typical state: seemingly presented with a crisp decision between black and white, it was actually required to make a calculated yet tentative step forward in a fog of thick grey. To begin with, the work of Flourens was not really all it was cracked up to be. His scalpel was not always wielded with the precision demanded of his far-reaching claims; it sometimes unwittingly cut into the tissue of underlying brain components, producing physiological malfunctions that Flourens incorrectly ascribed to the cerebral cortex. Just as importantly, his investigations were largely confined to birds and lower vertebrates, which have subsequently been shown to have cortices that are much less specialized than those of humans and the higher mammals. Finally, he must be defaulted in respect of his behavioural analyses; the tests to which he submitted his tissue-ablated subjects were far too crude to justify comparison with the pinpointing of faculties being attempted by the phrenologists. What must be credited to Flourens, on the other hand, is the fact that he shifted the focus of scientific attention away from the barren landscape of the skull and scalp, and placed the cerebral lobes firmly in the centre of the stage. They have been there ever since.

What, then, salvages Gall's position in the history of the subject? It is primarily the fact that he helped to divert the public preoccupation from the nebulous and immaterial world of the soul towards the tangible and material world of anatomical structure. Phrenology is a good example of a theory which, while being essentially wrong, was interesting enough to promote scientific thought. And on the question of localization versus delocalization, Gall emerges as the clear winner. Although mesmerized by the head's outer surface, he retained his interest in the cortex's *gyri* (the folds originally charted by Vesalius) and *sulci* (the fissures which lie between the gyri), and he believed until his dying day that the various faculties were specifically located in different cortical regions. In this, as subsequent explorations have amply demonstrated, Gall was right. He had divined the truth, but he had missed supplying the evidence because of his incorrect approach and his indefensible data.

As had been seen before, and as has occurred many times since, a thesis and an antithesis were mutually at bay, and the result was synthesis. After the above couple of hiccups, brain science was ready to get down to the serious task of being cartographer for the cortex's hills and valleys, and to the job of matching these to faculties and functions. And within a hundred years or so, it succeeded in producing the sort of detailed map that would surely have warmed the cockles of Gall's heart. Let us take a closer look at some of the chief milestones.

A specific date can be put to one of these: the fourth day of April, 1861. The scene is a meeting of the Société d'Anthropologie in Paris, and the four leading characters are Louis Gratiolet, who had provided many of the cortex's gyri and sulci with identifying names, Pierre-Paul Broca, the meeting's secretary, who had already gained renown as an anthropologist and anatomist, Jean-Baptiste Bouillaud, whose scientific reputation had survived his brief flirtation with phrenology, and Bouillaud's son-in-law, Simon Auburtin. Despite the odium which was now associated with phrenology, in scientific circles at least, Bouillaud was an enthusiastic supporter of Gall's belief that the faculty of language is localized in the brain's frontal lobes.

At the society's meeting on 21 February, in the same year, both Gratiolet and Broca had presented papers which attempted to establish a link between brain size and intelligence. (Gall's brain, incidentally, his high forehead notwithstanding, was about 25 per cent smaller than the average for an adult male.) Now, during the postponed discussion of these learned contributions, the two scientists came under fire from Auburtin, who expressed the opinion that faculties must be linked to parts of the brain rather than the whole. In support of his father-in-law's proposition, he cited his own clinical studies of a patient who had attempted suicide but who had merely managed to shoot away a part of his skull, thus laying bare part of his still-intact brain. 'During the interrogation of the patient,' Auburtin reported, 'the blade of a large spatula was placed on the anterior lobes; by means of light pressure speech was suddenly stopped; a word that had been commenced was cut in two. The faculty of speech reappeared as soon as the compression ceased.' To preclude possible criticism on the grounds that the pressure could have been transmitted to other parts of the brain, Auburtin added that the pressure had been directed so that only the anterior (frontal) lobes were affected, and that neither paralysis nor unconsciousness had been provoked by the spatula. (The society's meetings were obviously no place for those with delicate constitutions.)

During the ensuing exchange, Broca was prudent enough not to take umbrage. On the contrary, Auburtin's narrative reminded Broca of an inmate he had encountered at the Bicêtre asylum. The man had been incarcerated two decades earlier after losing almost all of the power of speech. His real name was Leborgne, but he was known as Tan because that monosyllable was all the unfortunate fellow could utter. Broca referred to the affliction as aphemia, but it is now called aphasia. As fate would have it, Tan died on 17 April, and Broca himself joined in the post-mortem the following day. The autopsy's result vindicated Broca's learned colleagues: the anterior lobes of Tan's brain were singularly atrophied, and there was a lesion around the middle of the left hemisphere. This region, which lies near to those areas subsequently demonstrated to control the tongue and the larynx, now bears Broca's name, in recognition of his follow-up studies of numerous other patients who displayed the same deficiency. We should particularly note that Broca's area lies on only the left side of the head.

As we are going to see shortly, other researchers continued this developing tradition of locating the cortical regions responsible for the various faculties. But it would be well to inject a note of caution, at this point. Is it obvious, after all, that we should expect to be able to match region with type of mental function, right down to the merest nuance of intellectual activity? Herbert Spencer, who to a certain extent anticipated Darwin's idea of evolution, suggested that a more hierarchical arrangement of faculties within the lobes might be closer to the truth. In such a scheme, basic functions would be easier to pinpoint than the more complex attributes, while such nebulous capacities as the emotions might be distributed rather widely throughout the brain. John Hughlings Jackson, a friend and disciple of Spencer, and, several decades later, the aptly named Henry Head found evidence of such subtlety. Head in particular showed that injury to the cortex, even if it were localized to a quite specific region, never led to the complete loss of a mental function. A case in point concerned one of his patients who seemed to understand most questions, and could supply the answer 'yes', where appropriate. Although a 'no' was beyond his impaired abilities, he could substitute it with 'damn!' There is more to relate about the quest for localization, but we will anticipate things by noting that the more complex a mental faculty is, and the more it is related to volition, the greater is the tendency for it to involve simultaneous activity in a number of cortical regions.

In the meantime, however, let me go back to Hughlings Jackson and to his work in the 1860s. His specialty was epilepsy, an affliction which subjects its victims to incapacitating fits. A brilliant observer, Hughlings Jackson was able to formulate far-reaching neurological concepts even without performing experiments. One common feature of the infirmity intrigued him: for a given patient, the epileptic fit would invariably start at the same part of the body, and then gradually spread outward to engulf adjacent areas, ultimately producing massive convulsions. For one patient, the seizure initiation point was one of the thumbs, while for another the spasms would always start at the corner of the mouth. Hughlings Jackson concluded that the trouble was caused by a particularly vulnerable spot on the cortex, and of course a different one for each patient.

Many of his contemporaries considered the hypotheses of Hughlings Jackson, based as they were on clinical observation and deduction rather than surgical dissection, to be ingenious but fanciful. His conjectures did not have to wait long for experimental verification, however. In 1870, two young pioneers opened up a new era of cortical localization which has lasted until the present time. They were Eduard Hitzig and Gustav Fritsch, and their technique was electrical stimulation. Their first experiments were carried out in Hitzig's bedroom, of all places, and their subjects were dogs. Some weeks earlier, Hitzig had actually carried out a cruder test on a man, and had found that the passage of a mild electrical current through the back of the head caused the eyes to move involuntarily. 'The question arose,' he wrote, 'whether this method caused the eye movements by circuits or currents penetrating to the base, or, whether the cerebrum, contrary to the generally accepted view, is endowed with electric excitability.' To resolve this issue, Hitzig and Fritsch realized that direct stimulation of the cortex would be necessary. They accordingly removed part of a dog's skull and started to gently prod the creature's exposed brain with their electrified wires. This might sound like cold-blooded cruelty, but in fact the brain's surface possesses no pain receptors, and there was the added advantage that the tests could be performed without the possibly distorting presence of an anaesthetic.

What the young experimenters observed must have filled them with awe. Most areas produced no response at all, but they discovered a well-defined strip in which stimulation caused movement of part of the body. At one point, the electrical irritation caused a foot to twitch, while another was obviously related to a shoulder, and so on. In later experiments they combined electrical stimulation with ablation, the surgical removal of tissue discussed earlier, and this enabled them to map out the region that is now known as the motor cortex. They were also able to confirm something we have already touched upon, namely that the left side of the body is controlled by the right hemisphere of the cortex and vice versa.

The direct stimulation technique was applied a couple of

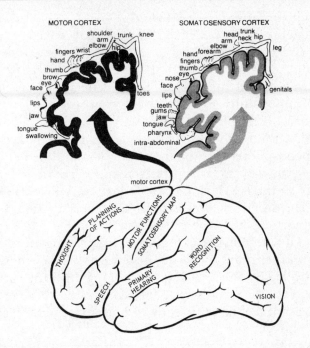

Around the beginning of the present century, practitioners of the new technique known as cyto-architectonics produced the most detailed charts of the cortex ever seen. Microscopical investigations of the appearances of cells and fibres provided a new way of classifying the various regions, and they also revealed that brain tissue becomes increasingly differentiated during evolution. The leading figures in this exciting field were Walter Campbell, Cecile Vogt and her husband Oskar, and Korbinian Brodmann. The lower figures show the latter's drawings of the cortex's outer surface (left) and a cross-section (right). Many of the cortical areas have also been linked to the corresponding faculties through observations on patients with brain damage, and also by direct stimulation of the surface of the grey matter (above).

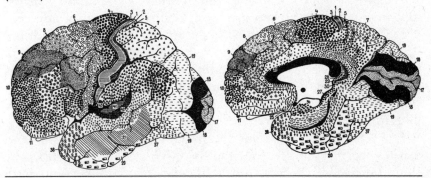

years later to primates, by David Ferrier, who produced a far more detailed map which showed that adjacent parts of the body are governed by adjacent parts of the motor cortex. Ferrier inferred, moreover, that humans too must possess a motor cortex. As in the case of Broca's decisive investigation, a clinical opportunity to test a bold idea was soon to present itself. Roberts Bartholow, a Cincinnati physician, had a patient named Mary Rafferty whose cranial defect exposed parts of each cerebral hemisphere. He was thus able to stimulate her brain in much the same way as Hitzig, Fritsch and Ferrier had employed with their animals. Bartholow's report makes for harrowing reading. He describes how stimulation of a certain point on the right cortical hemisphere caused the girl's left arm to be thrown out, with fingers extended. His probing needles must have been rather blunt, because the left leg, which is now known to be controlled by a nearby but distinct region of the cortex, was caused to jolt at the same time. Mary complained of a very strong and unpleasant feeling of tingling in both extremities, especially the arm, and yet she smiled as if amused. An increase in the strength of the current caused her great distress, however, and she began to cry. When Mary later died of meningitis, Bartholow was able to find the marks made by his needles. It was in this morbid fashion that the existence of the human motor cortex was established.

Thanks particularly to the work of Albert Grunbaum, who changed his surname to Leyton in 1915, and Charles Sherrington, it was later demonstrated that a second band runs close to and parallel with the motor cortex, and it is from here that skin sensation emanates. This is the sensory, or somatic, cortex, and in this area too there is a continuous mapping of adjacent areas of the body. But, as with the motor cortex, the mapping involves considerable distortion. Edgar Adrian found that a disproportionately large amount of a pig's sensory cortex is devoted to the snout; in a mouse it is the whiskers that are most generously represented. The best represented areas clearly give the greatest sensitivity.

One can easily trace out the paths of one's own motor and sensory cortices. Place your hands on your head in such a way that the tips of the two index fingers are touching, and with the tips of the two middle fingers also in contact. Adjust the hands if necessary so that these paired fingertips are positioned at the top of the head. Now draw the hands downwards, at each side, so that the fingers in question move towards a spot just in front of the ears. The left middle finger will have traced the path of the motor cortex of the left hemisphere, while the index finger will have passed over the sensory cortex of the same hemisphere. But remember, from what has already been described, that these two cortical ridges (or gyri, to give them the correct name mentioned earlier) are related to the right side of the body! The moving fingers of one's right hand will similarly have run the lengths of the motor and sensory cortices which govern the body's left side. Incidentally, the motor and sensory ridges are separated by one of the deepest valleys in the entire cortex, namely the central sulcus, which is also called the sulcus of Rolando after its most prominent explorer, Luigi Rolando. Another deep valley, the lateral sulcus, runs forward and downward from the above-mentioned point just in front of the ear. Its alternative name honours Sylvius, whose work was mentioned in Chapter 1.

The appearance on the surface of the cortex of two continuous maps of the body's outer form naturally intrigued the world of medicine. And the collective name they were given by the anatomists is no less thought-provoking. These learned men used a word we encountered in the previous chapter: the homunculus, or little inner man. It is as if there were suddenly a rearguard action in defence of Descartes' dualism. But we must not underestimate science's capacity for mordant humour and self-irony.

Place your hands once again on your head, with the opposing fingertips touching, but this time with the fingers splayed out as far as they can be stretched. Your thumbs will then lie above the occipital region at the rear of the brain. The collective efforts of Bartolomeo Panizza, who studied ravens, chicks, ducklings and later mammals, Hermann Munk, whose favoured subjects were dogs, and Gordon Holmes, who reluctantly took advantage of the numerous cases of human brain injury provided by the First World War, established that this is the area of the cortex which receives visual signals from the retina. Panizza, moreover, made the important discovery that the thalamus, a structure centrally situated beneath the cortical lobes, also plays a vital role as a sort of relay station in the visual pathway. Munk's investigations of mild damage to the cortex revealed that dogs, and evolutionary equivalent animals, are able to rally from visual (and also auditory) impairment, but the human casualties examined by Holmes showed no similar capacity for recovery. The potential for repair unfortunately seems to diminish with increasing sophistication.

The regions where your thumbs join the palms of your hands are covering (if you have kept your hands positioned on your head while reading) the temporal areas of the cortical hemispheres. These are responsible for hearing, as was established jointly by Edward Schafer and Sanger Brown, their preliminary work being carried out on monkeys. There is an area just below the temporal region which appears to provide the sense of time.

Because your fingers are splayed out this time, your index fingers will not cover the somatosensory regions as they did earlier. Now, instead, they lie over the parietal lobes, which appear to be related to a sense of actual existence. A patient injured in this region of one lobe ignores the opposite side of the body; half the beard goes unshaved, and half the hair goes uncombed. Around the middle of the triangle formed by the parietal, temporal and occipital regions lies a second language area. It was discovered in 1874 by Carl Wernicke, and in distinction to Broca's area, which governs speech, this second area controls understanding of both the spoken and the written word.

Let us turn, finally, to the frontal lobes which lie under our outstretched little fingers when we encompass our head within our hands. We have already seen, in connection with the appalling injury to Phineas Gage described in the previous chapter, that this region of the cerebral cortex plays a major role in the formation of the personality. But that is not an easy thing to pin down. Some aspects, such as sociability, seem well defined, but just how one is to quantify the mixture of personality's more tenuous facets is not so obvious. Amongst those who have attempted to elucidate the problem experimentally, Leonardo Bianchi deserves particular mention. His early subjects were monkeys, and he favoured the popular technique of surgical removal of tissue. His ablated monkeys appeared to lose their 'psychical tone', by which he meant their capacity for 'serializing and synthesizing groups of actions'. He also found his operated subjects singularly lacking in initiative, friendship, gratitude, jealousy, maternal and protective impulses, dominance and authority, and above all a sense of personal dignity. By any standards, Bianchi noted, such frontally ablated animals would be judged to be imbecile.

Ablation of the frontal lobes took on a grim new dimension in the late 1930s. Following up a report on work that was clearly inspired by Bianchi's pioneering efforts, and which indicated relief of anxiety in an experimental chimpanzee, Egas Moniz decided to extend the approach to humans. Working with surgeon colleagues, he developed the technique known as lobotomy. The desire to alleviate mental frustration and distress was laudable enough, but the justification for such an extreme surgical measure was very weak. By the time it lost its popularity, lobotomy had turned many thousands of human beings into vegetables. Perhaps the one positive thing to emerge from this regrettable episode was the finding, in some of the few patients who emerged relatively unscathed from this practice, that there is a marked impairment in the planning and sequencing of motor functions. Some researchers have generalized this, and concluded that the frontal lobes govern the planning of actions.

We have now constructed for ourselves a fairly detailed picture of the cortical hemispheres, and have placed on the map the most prominent features. The points at which three of the senses feed information into the cortex have also been identified, those senses being touch, hearing and sight. The remaining senses of taste and smell enter at the olfactory bulb, which lies just below the frontal lobe. It thus lies not far above the uppermost regions of the nostrils.

This description of the cortex would be glaringly incomplete, however, if I did not mention the thick bundle of nerve fibres that provides the main connection between the two hemispheres. This is the corpus callosum. In the 1860s, Jules Déjerine and Hugo Liepmann made independent investigations of stroke-related damage to this important bridging structure, and found evidence that the various mental faculties are associated with particular hemispheres. The surgical severance of cortical connections has already been mentioned in connection with lobotomy.

The corpus callosum has also been cut in an attempt to alleviate a variety of ills, most notably epilepsy. In the 1950s and early 1960s, many patients were successfully treated in this way, but Roger Sperry discovered bizarre qualities in such split brain individuals. I will postpone until the final chapter a discussion of the significance his observations have had regarding the issue of consciousness. It may be noted here, however, that Sperry's work strengthened the case for specializations of the two hemispheres. The right side appears to be primarily concerned with emotion, intuition, creation, spatial relationships, and the appreciation of art and music. The left hemisphere, apart from looking after speech and the understanding of language, is dominant for analysis and logic, abstraction, coordination, and the sense of time.

Let us now stand back, as it were, and take a more global view of the body's nervous system. And let us do so in a series of steps. To begin with, we see the overall picture of the cerebral hemispheres, with their familiar convoluted walnut-like appearance, and we note that the specific areas that were identified and discussed in the preceding paragraphs do not, collectively, make up the entire structure. There are spaces in between which have not, to date, been linked with any easily defined function. There are strong indications that these are the regions which provide the brain with the ability to handle the incoming sensory information at a higher level of complexity; they are very likely the seat of the higher mental functions. And a simple series of surgical slicings reveals the reason for the cortex's hills and valleys, which, since the time of Vesalius, had so fascinated the anatomists; the cortex is actually a sheet of tissue varying in thickness between 3 and 5 millimetres, with each hemisphere covering a total of about 1000 square centimetres, and the corrugations are the inevitable consequence of these sheets being packed into the confined space available in the skull.

Backing off another step, we see that the brain comprises more than just the two cerebral halves. We have already encountered some of these associated bits and pieces, and the point has arrived at which the most prominent of these should be put in the proper context. The hemispheres, which are collectively called the cortex, are the main feature of what is known as the forebrain. The latter also contains the amygdaloid complex, the hippocampus, the septum and the basal ganglia. The amygdala takes its name from the Latin word *amygdale*, meaning the almond, which it resembles in shape. It has been physiologically linked to the control of emotions, defence reactions, and feeding and reproductive behaviours. The hippocampus, too, takes its name from Latin, the allusion this time being to the form of a seahorse. Since the late 1950s, there has been growing evidence that this part of the brain plays a major role in memory. The word septum always indicates a dividing wall; the septum in the nose separates the two nostrils, for example. In the forebrain, the septum provides the wall between two of the ventricles. The basal ganglia help to control movement and posture, and impaired function of these structures has been implicated in the tremor, involuntary movements and muscular rigidity observed in patients with Parkinson's and Huntington's diseases.

The midbrain lies at the next level of depth within the head, and it is thus broadly surrounded by the forebrain. It comprises the thalamus, the hypothalamus and the cerebral peduncles. The latter connect the midbrain to the cerebral hemispheres. The thalamus, as we have already noted, is one of the brain's main relay stations. It plays an absolutely major part in the functioning of the senses. The hypothalamus has a key role in several of those bodily functions which fall outside our conscious control.

The innermost part of the brain is referred to as the hindbrain, and it is actually continuous with the top of the spinal cord. Its major components are the pons (which reminds one of the French word for bridge, of course), the medulla oblongata, the cerebellum and the brain stem. The pons is known to be involved in the generation of emotions and the experience of pain, while the medulla oblongata has a decisive influence on spontaneous respiration, blood pressure and heart rhythm. (In passing, and to touch on a grim subject, we may note that brain death is judged to have occurred when all electrical activity in the medulla and the hypothalamus has been lost.) In terms of size, the cerebellum (or little cerebrum) far outstrips any of the other brain structures except for the cortex itself. Its function is now very well understood: it orchestrates and coordinates the movements of our limbs and all our other movable parts.

There are other ways of apportioning the brain's more salient members, a particularly significant one being the identification of functional groups. Paul MacLean was responsible, in 1952, for an especially noteworthy example of such a classification. Stressing that the evolutionary development of extra brain tissue led to acquisition of new faculties, and arguing that the various regions retained their original associations, he proposed a model of what he called the triune brain. The innermost region, in MacLean's scheme, is the reptilian complex. Located around the top of the spinal column, it is the brain's oldest part, a remnant of those remote days when our ancestors inhabited the primordial swamps. The reptilian complex is enveloped by the limbic system, which, in the higher species, is surrounded by the cerebral cortex. The name limbic derives from the Latin word *limbus*, which means border. It is thus called because it lies deployed around the inner edges of the cortex. The limbic system comprises the anterior part of the thalamus, the hypothalamus, the amygdala, the hippocampus, the septum and the basal ganglia, all of which we have already encountered, as well as the cingulate gyrus. The word 'cingulate' means girdling or encircling, and the latter structure does indeed wrap itself around the hippocampus. In MacLean's model, the reptilian complex governs the most fundamental functions, those that determine, in the final analysis, the sheer survival of their possessor. The limbic system was seen as being responsible for the more overt aspects of behaviour, those which are usually associated with emotion. The subtle facets commonly linked with intellect are, according to the model, the province of the cerebral cortex.

The pituitary gland, which controls other glands, and through them the body's endocrine system, is also part of the limbic system. Endocrine imbalance is a recognized source of behavioural aberration, while surgical destruction of the amygdala has been used to quell extreme aggression. MacLean, in collaboration with a number of colleagues, has presented weighty evidence for his own theory. Working with hamsters, he surgically removed the cerebral cortices immediately after birth and observed no impairment of their innate behavioural traits. The decerebrated animals romped, foraged, copulated, and generally displayed either affable or aggressive reactions where appropriate. But when those parts of their limbic systems

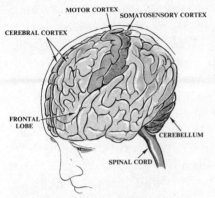

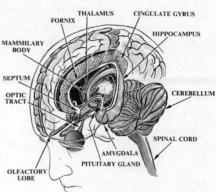

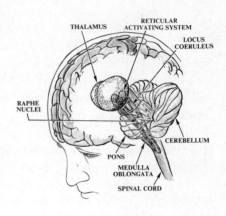

The brain consists of many different structures, of which the familiar cerebral cortex (above left) is merely the largest and the outermost. It is the main part of what is known as the forebrain, from which we derive our intellectual faculties. The midbrain (above right) lies below and inside the forebrain, and it governs the more overt aspects of behaviour and the emotions. The innermost part of the brain, which is actually continuous with the top of the spinal cord, is referred to as the hindbrain (below right). It controls the most fundamental functions: those connected with survival. To the rear of this lies the cerebellum, or little cerebrum, which coordinates limb movements.

not essential to survival were also removed, the creatures became morose and apathetic, and the females appeared to be robbed of their maternal instincts.

Arthur Koestler has given his own interpretation of the triune brain. We have already seen that MacLean compared the most primitive part of the human brain with all the brain that a reptile possesses. Many of the less developed mammals, such as the horse, have brains that encompass both the reptilian complex and the limbic system, while only man and his closer cousins enjoy the additional benefits of a well-developed cerebral cortex. If the psychiatrist's couch is usually a sturdy affair, it is probably because it has to simultaneously bear the weight of an alligator, a horse and a human, as Koestler has facetiously observed.

We have been taking mental steps backwards to provide ourselves with increasingly more global views of the body's nervous system. When we do this just one more time, our bird's-eye view encompasses as much as we could require; we see things in their entirety. The system consists of just three components: the central nervous system, which itself comprises the brain and the spinal cord; the peripheral nervous system, whose members stretch out to all the body's surfaces and to the extremities of every limb; and the autonomic nervous system, the main function of which is to regulate all those bodily processes over which we have no conscious control. It is at this point that we should come to grips with a couple of terms that are not in colloquial usage but which will prove useful because of the crisp distinction they provide. An 'afferent' nerve conducts information towards the central region of one of the above three nervous systems. An 'efferent' nerve, on the other hand, carries information away from the central region towards the farther reaches of the body. We see immediately that the senses employ afferent nerves, while the motor cortex must use efferent nerves to dispatch its commands to our voluntarily movable parts.

This begins to smack of machine-like control, does it not? But it is control of a type that ought to make us decidedly grateful. Let us look at an example of the way in which the autonomic nervous system stands sentinel over our well-being. The underlying principles were first appreciated by Claude Bernard, the idea being that the workings of the body will be optimal only if the internal environment, as it were, is maintained at a constant state with respect to temperature, blood pressure, blood sugar, and a number of other things. The situation is not unlike that which prevails when a good car driver casts an occasional glance at the dials on the dashboard, and reacts accordingly. In the context of the body the regulatory process is called homeostasis. This composite term comes from the words *homeo*, which means the same, and *stasis*, which means stability or balance. The balance is achieved by the interplay between two watchdog subdivisions of the autonomic nervous system, namely the sympathetic nervous system and the parasympathetic nervous system. Working in a complementary fashion, they influence, in one way or another, all our organs.

Let us observe them at work. Your plane has just taken off, and the 'Fasten Seatbelts' sign has already been extinguished. The stewardess delivers an appetizing lunch, and it is not long before your parasympathetic nerves have slowed down your heart beat and stepped up your digestive activity. The meal over, you start to doze off. Then the Captain's voice shatters your siesta. The outer starboard engine is on fire, and he is returning immediately to the point of departure. Fasten Seatbelts! Fasten Seatbelts! Your sympathetic nerves take over, diverting blood from your digestive system to increase the flow through the muscles and brain; expanding your lungs to provide more oxygen; activating your sweat glands to promote cooling should you need to exert yourself; dilating your pupils to give you more light. This is an extreme example, of course, but it illustrates the way in which these two counteracting systems seek balance automatically, without the intervention of one's consciousness.

We started this chapter in the centre of London's Piccadilly Circus, gazing at Eros frozen in his balancing act. Let us take our leave of him by assuring ourselves that we now possess the wherewithal to appreciate his not-so-common accomplishment. It stems from another of these pairs of nervous systems, the stand-off in this case resulting from the pitting of the motor nerves against those of what is known as the proprioceptive system. The former send signals down from the brain to the muscles, and these latter are equipped with sensors. Such sensors are called muscle spindles, and they are the muscular equivalent of my toy engine's brass spheres, which we encountered at the beginning of this chapter. Another set of nerves convey information on the state of the spindles back up to the brain. Collectively, the opposing nerve systems produce what is known as the stretch reflex, a well-known example of which is the involuntary knee jerk provoked by the doctor's little rubber hammer. If the flesh-and-blood counterpart of Eros had started to topple forwards, the resultant stretching of the various muscles down the back of his supporting leg would have triggered the spindles to send signals up the proprioceptive nerves. This, in turn, would have automatically caused the motor cortex to instruct those same muscles to contract, and thus restore the balance. Any tendency towards toppling in another direction would have been similarly compensated.

We have now identified our machine's major parts, and we have begun to sense the automatic regulation which keeps it running on schedule, day in, day out. The heart of the person writing these words has now beat a total of some two thousand million times, since the hour of his birth, all without any conscious effort on his part. Irrespective of whether he is awake or asleep, his hypothalamus and medulla oblongata are always on duty. A machine which embodies a high degree of automation is not the worst thing one could be.

● Summary

Anatomical and physiological investigations, undertaken during recent decades, have elucidated the roles of almost all of the brain's components. Some are associated with specific senses, whereas others function as more general control or relay centres. Information is transmitted to and from the brain, and within the brain itself, by nerve fibres. The dominating principle is that of balance between opposing tendencies, and the body thereby seeks equilibrium. This is achieved by a variety of compensatory mechanisms, not unlike those provided by the mechanical governors and electrical feedbacks encountered in engineering. The brain does indeed resemble a sophisticated machine.

3

From molecule to man
The brain's physiology

> Had I been present at the birth of this planet
> I would probably not have believed on the
> word of the Archangel that the blazing mass,
> the incandescent whirlpool there before our eyes
> at a temperature of fifty million degrees would
> presently set about the establishment of empires
> and civilizations, that it was on its way
> to produce Greek art and Italian painting.
>
> W. MACNEILE DIXON
> *Gifford Lectures, Glasgow (1935–37)*

The venue was as unlikely as it was depressing. It lay, oddly enough, just a few miles east of Piccadilly Circus, the point at which we started the previous chapter. And one of the two central figures of the day's event played nothing more than a minor role in the history of brain science. But he was at least less obscure than the other character, whose name appears to have escaped the record entirely. The scene was the dreaded Newgate Prison, near London's St Paul's Cathedral, and the man who took the most minor part was a criminal, freshly executed that very morning. The issue from which the scene drew its motivation was, on the other hand, one of the most famous in the history of science, and the fervour of Giovanni Aldini was understandable enough; he was desperately trying to defend the reputation of his more illustrious uncle, Luigi Galvani.

But before we consider what took place on that sombre occasion at the beginning of the nineteenth century, let us turn the clock back still further. To 20 September, 1786, in fact. This was the momentous day when Galvani and his wife Lucia made their first observation of the spontaneous twitching

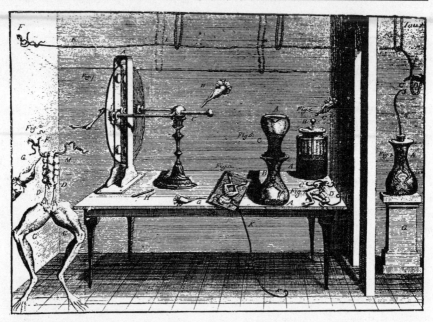

The emergence of controllable electrical phenomena in the early eighteenth century caught the imagination of biologists, and Luigi Galvani showed that a frog's leg could be made to twitch by connecting it to an electrical generator. He and his wife Lucia, in 1786, noticed spontaneous convulsions in a leg that was not in contact with such a device. They concluded that limb movement is driven by animal electricity rather than by animal spirits. But the leg had been suspended from a hook arrangement involving two different metals, and Allesandro Volta soon established that this produces electrical effects having an inorganic origin. Galvani's subsequent demonstration of spasms in a frog's leg muscle that was brought into contact with the frog's bared spinal cord, proved that there really are sources of electricity inside the creature. This illustration appeared in his report published in 1791. A generator is positioned on the left side of the work bench, and two legs are seen hanging from a hook on the left-hand wall.

of a frog's leg. They had actually been trying to demonstrate the influence of atmospheric electricity on the creature, which hung from the copper hook upon which it had been impaled, the point of the hook actually being embedded in the spinal cord. Their excitement stemmed as much as anything from the fact that the weather was crisp and bright, with no sign whatsoever of electricity in the air. Here, surely, was the ultimate proof of the existence of animal electricity, for all external agencies could be ruled out as the source of the frog's convulsions.

That animal electricity should have preempted animal spirits, by the time of Galvani, is not surprising. The science of electricity was establishing itself around this time, and it was providing experimental enthusiasts with the primitive pieces of apparatus we can now see in museums. And it was natural that one should investigate the influence of this new-found force on nerves, which, after all, bear a certain resemblance to wire conduits. Stephen Hales had made the suggestion, as early as 1732, that nerve conduction might involve electricity. Galvani was not the discoverer of animal electricity, in fact. The electrical properties of certain aquatic creatures had been known since antiquity, and John Walsh, a member of the British parliament, had demonstrated the generation of an electric voltage in the torpedo fish, in 1772. But the frog in Galvani's experiment was apparently isolated from any external source of electricity. This is what made his observations so thrilling, and news of the experiment soon spread well beyond his native Bologna. In Pavia, it reached the ears of Count Alessandro Volta, and it aroused his scepticism. That copper hook from which Galvani's frog was suspended had itself been attached to an iron bar. It was not long before Volta came to realize that an electrical voltage is automatically generated at every junction between dissimilar metals. The term 'voltage' honours his discovery, and he must be credited for giving birth to the science of metallic electricity.

Galvani's name also became a household word, however. We have the term 'galvanization', which has even acquired a colloquial dimension. I have been galvanized into writing this book, for example. So let us return to that grisly day in Newgate Prison, and to Aldini's attempt to vindicate his uncle Luigi, in the Galvani–Volta dispute. He had served as apprentice to his senior relation, and was present when Galvani had induced spasms in a frog's muscle during an experiment from which all metallic objects had been banned. The creature's spinal cord and also the muscle of one of its legs had been exposed by dissection. Galvani bent the latter upwards so as to bring it into contact with the bared spinal cord. The muscle obliged by contracting, and Galvani's belief in animal electricity had been shown to be fully justified. In 1838, when both Aldini and his uncle were dead, their compatriot Carlo Matteucci actually managed to measure the electrical current generated by a muscle, but at the time of Aldini's demonstration at Newgate Prison the general air was one of disbelief. So, to convince his onlookers, he laid bare the spinal cord and brought a severed leg muscle into contact with it – essentially a repetition of the experiment on the frog; he won many converts. They had witnessed the first demonstration of animal electricity in a human being.

But the demonstration of the existence of a phenomenon is not the same thing as supplying an explanation of its occurrence. Galvani had no more given an explanation of animal electricity than Volta had of metallic electricity. And for both phenomena, the causes were revealed only when one had gained access to the atomic level of the associated structure. This has, indeed, been one of the great messages of twentieth-century science: knowledge of the atomic structure of an object frequently sheds a decisive light on that object's mode of functioning. My quest in this book is to expose the brain for the machine it is, and to show that there is nothing particularly mystical about the working of the mind. I will now proceed to dig downwards through several scales of size, until the atomic heart of the issue has been reached.

The first stop on this journey, and it will be a rather long one, is provided by what must be called one of science's major mileposts. In 1608, Zacharias Jansen placed crude lenses at either end of a tube and thereby fashioned history's first microscope. It had only a modest magnifying power, no more than a factor of about a hundred, but this did not prevent Robert Hooke from using a facsimile of the device to make the first microscopic observations of living organisms. He was rewarded, in 1665, with the discovery of the cell, the elementary unit of which all animals and plants are composed. The body of an adult human being, for example, comprises about one million million cells.

The users of the early microscopes were plagued by the aberrations produced by their crude lenses, and they were often fooled by mere haloes and other optical artefacts. Particularly misleading were the 'globules', which were interpreted as being the elementary building blocks of nervous tissue, but which were actually just figments caused by the microscope's chromatic deficiencies. The introduction of the achromatic compound instrument, in the 1820s, thus raised the field of microscopy to a new level of acceptability. Before this development, Marcello Malpighi had turned his attention to the cerebral cortex and reported observing what he referred to as 'minute glands'. But these translucent white structures were apparently easier to see when the brain was given a prior treatment in boiling water, a fact which hardly makes one confident that Malpighi was really looking at the brain's individual cells.

Similarly, the reports of studies of nerve fibres made by Antoni van Leeuwenhoek cannot be taken at face value. Influenced by the still-common idea that nerve conduction was mediated by spirituous substances that flowed through tube-like passages, his investigations were biased in favour of a hunt for such structures. One of his reports, written in 1717, tells that 'single nerves, as far as they extend lengthwise, were hollow or pervious like a kind of channel'. He also mentions seeing 'a large number of small particles swimming and floating in the water . . . that had issued from the vessels.' Leeuwenhoek's microscope did not have the power and precision of a modern instrument, of course; it could only magnify about 300 times, and resolve objects down to a diameter of about 0.002 millimetre. If he had had access to one of today's optical microscopes, which permit magnification by several thousand times, he would have been able to discern the inner structure of a nerve fibre. Thus, although his description is in striking agreement with the actual state of affairs in a fibre, it is not likely that he was really resolving such detail.

We have, until this point, been using the two terms nerve cell and nerve fibre without revealing how they are related. One could be forgiven for guessing, for example, that the fibres are composed of cells. The lack of clarification has been deliberate because it reflects the situation that prevailed before the advent of the achromatic compound microscope. Once this instrument was placed in the anatomist's hands, the situation changed dramatically. Robert Remak had soon made definitive observations of the thinnest fibres and had even suggested that these are connected to nerve cells in some way. He also demonstrated that the fibres are frequently sheathed by a sort of insulating material. The latter is now known as myelin. Jan Purkyne arrived at similar results, independently and at about the same time, and he made the important extension of showing that nerve cells elsewhere in the nervous system are not essentially different from those found in the cerebral cortex.

The so-called cell theory, which established that the fibres are definitely extensions of nerve cells, and that the brain's white matter is composed of fibres while the grey matter consists of both fibres and cell bodies, was put forward in 1839 by Theodor Schwann. He also showed that the myelin sheathing is produced by other cells which surround the actual nerve cells. These cells now bear Schwann's name. A major development around this time was the discovery of certain chemical substances which can be used to stain cells and thus render them more visible under the microscope. The early list of such substances included chromic acid, carmine and indigo. Their availability was a key factor in the advances made by Otto Deiters, advances cut short by his tragically early death from typhus. His posthumously published reports showed a wealth of detail hitherto unsuspected; they told that 'the body of the cell is continuous uninterruptedly with a more or less large number of processes which branch frequently but have long [unbranched] stretches between them.' Most importantly, Deiters was able to differentiate between two types of process: protoplasmic processes, which are now known as dendrites; and nervous processes, which have come to be called axons. (A comment is obviously necessary regarding the word 'process'. As used here, it refers to an extension or prolongation of the nerve cell, not unlike a tentacle protruding from the body of an octopus. The *Oxford Dictionary* lists this meaning – i.e. outgrowth or protuberance – of the word, which is of course more commonly encountered as 'method of operation' or 'course of action'.)

One of the greatest mileposts in the study of nerve cells was reached in 1873, when Camillo Golgi first described a chemical method of rendering entire cells visible in an optical microscope. This advance opened a new era, not only in the tracing of individual nerve fibres, but even more importantly in the revelation of the spatial relationships between different cells. The technique was based on a silver stain and cells selectively coloured in this way were seen silhouetted against a white or yellow background. By carefully controlling the staining conditions, Golgi was able to obtain situations in which only a small fraction of the cells in a piece of tissue became coloured at one time.

Oddly enough, Golgi himself soon veered off course in one important respect. He became an ardent advocate of the view that the processes of different nerve cells are in actual physical contact with one another, and that this produces a vast continuous net, like an irregular version of a fishing net, but one which spreads out in three dimensions rather than just two. The other school of thought saw the individual cells as independent entities, and in chronicling the manner in which this view's proponents gradually gained the ascendancy, we will bring our story into its present, twentieth-century, form.

The net theory first began to wobble when Wilhelm His made a systematic study of brain tissue specimens taken from subjects at different stages of development, actually starting with embryonic samples. He was able to report, in 1887, that the young nerve cell is not only independent but that it is also devoid of processes. These subsequently sprout out from the cell body, the axon appearing first and the dendrites considerably later. Within a couple of months, August-Henri Forel had provided a strong endorsement of the His result, by essentially reversing the latter's approach. Forel's forte was retrograde degeneration of nerve cells, and he showed that the atrophy provoked by injury to an axon never extends beyond the nerve cell in question.

These beautifully complementary efforts were soon to be reinforced at the hands of the greatest nerve cell anatomist who has ever lived: Santiago Ramon y Cajal. And as if to add insult to injury, Ramon y Cajal mounted a withering attack on Golgi's belief in the nerve cell net by employing Golgi's own staining technique. Reporting on his exquisite observations of the cellular arrangement in the cerebellum, he showed that individual cells are often contiguous but never continuous with one another; they might make close contacts, but they are not physically joined. Ramon y Cajal also discovered something that was later appreciated as being highly suggestive of the way in which nerve cells interact: he noticed that the axon of one cell would often make near contact with a dendrite of one of its neighbours.

The sheer amount of Ramon y Cajal's published data is impressive by any standards, and it attests to a life devoted to quiet and painstaking observation. It is thus surprising to catch him in an uncharacteristically bellicose mood. The person who elicited his ire rejoiced in the name Heinrich Wilhelm Gottfried von Waldeyer-Hartz. The nerve net theory had proved to be remarkably stubborn, and Waldeyer took upon himself the onerous task of adjudicating its merits *vis-à-vis* the independent cell view. He must at least be given credit for carefully sifting through a large amount of data, which led him to come down in favour of the independent nerve cell, for which he coined the name neuron. This infuriated Ramon y Cajal. 'All Waldeyer-Hartz did,' he bitterly remarked, 'was to publish in a weekly newspaper a resumé of my research and to invent the term "neuron".' There is no denying that Waldeyer-Hartz did have a flair for neologisms: he also created the terms 'chromosome' and 'plasma cell'. And in any event Ramon y Cajal received adequate compensation in the form of a Nobel Prize, in 1906, which he ironically shared with Golgi.

Let us pause and take stock of what all this research had revealed about the cells in the brain and their spatial relationships. From the readily measured distance between adjacent neurons, one can easily calculate that there must be about one hundred thousand million of these cells in the brain. Each cell has up to ten thousand or so tentacle-like protuberances, or processes, these being of two types: the dendrites and the axon. The numerous dendrites tend to lie on one side of the cell body, spreading out like the limbs, branches and twigs of a tree. Indeed, one refers to the dendritic arborization. Dendrites typically spread out over distances of up to 0.5 millimetre from the cell body. A single axon emerges from the opposite side of the cell body, and it can extend over distances of several millimetres, and in some cases even centimetres, from the cell body. The axon invariably displays considerable branching near its extremity, the appearance being something like an arm branching out into multiple fingers. An earlier, more major, branching also occurs in some cases, the secondary processes thereby produced being referred to as axon collaterals. It turns out that the dendrites carry information towards the cell body, while the axon provides the route for information transmitted from that central region of the neuron. The terminology we encountered in the previous chapter, in connection with the grosser aspects of signal transfer in the nervous system, is equally applicable at the level of the individual neuron, so the dendrites are said to be afferent processes while the axon is an efferent process.

The grey matter of the cerebral cortex derives its appearance from the presence of both cell bodies and the thousands of associated dendrites. The axons frequently emerge from the grey matter, run along its inner surface for distances of up to a few centimetres, and then re-enter the grey matter at another site. The vast network of axons thus produced forms the white matter. Under a powerful microscope, it looks not unlike a huge telephone exchange. In the spinal cord, the arrangement is reversed; the white matter lies on the outside, surrounding a rather smaller core of grey matter.

But what has all this to do with the electrical phenomena studied by Galvani and his contemporaries? We are, in fact, approaching the answer to that central question, but let us first look back at what Isaac Newton believed of the nature of nerve transmission. He saw it as a disturbance passing through an ethereal medium, in a manner which we now know does apply to electromagnetic waves such as those of light and radio. These waves travel at stupendous velocities, however: about 300,000 kilometres per second. The belief that messages were transmitted along the nerves at immeasurable velocities persisted until Hermann von Helmholtz actually measured the velocity in 1849. His method was borrowed from that which he himself had applied to the determination of the muzzle velocity of a bullet fired from a gun, and in the case of nerve transmission the result was surprisingly modest: a mere 24 to 39 metres a second.

This speed is nevertheless adequate to account for the observed rates of limb movement in the adult human. It is instructive to consider a simple example. In 1988, Canada's Ben Johnson set the new (but later disqualified) world record of 9.79 seconds for the 100 metres run. If we assume that his stride spanned approximately 2 metres, we find that this record run consisted of about fifty paces, each of which occupied about 0.2 second. Now the distance from Johnson's brain to his leg muscles is about a metre and a half, and from von Helmholtz's measurement we see that the nerve messages could travel from brain to leg in about 0.05 second. So the speed of the nerve signals is not the limiting factor in such limb movement.

Remarkable advances were already well under way before von Helmholtz had made his historic measurement. The work of Emil Du Bois-Reymond was particularly noteworthy, and he has been called the father of electrophysiology. Considering that he was active at a time when the atomic nature of matter was still an issue of dispute, his concept of the origins of animal electricity were impressively prescient. He saw the nerve fibre as being perpetually in a ready-to-fire state by dint of a 'resting potential difference' (i.e. a voltage) between the fibre's inner and outer surfaces, and he postulated that this arose because of the polarizing effect of nearby molecules. This was the first appearance of the idea of the excitable axon, and his electrical measurements on the thigh of the frog led him to the conclusion that nervous conduction involves the passage along the fibres of trends of 'negative variation'. Du Bois-Reymond's work set a new high-water mark for the materialistic and mechanical pictures of the brain and the nervous system, and this new thrust soon began to enjoy the support of other researchers. In the hands of his student, Ludimor Hermann, Du Bois-Reymond's trend of negative variation became an experimentally detected 'current of action' having the form of a well-defined wave; it was, in other words, not simply a continuous electric current.

The quest to provide these electrical phenomena with an atomic-level explanation took a giant step towards fruition when Julius Bernstein suggested that Du Bois-Reymond's nerve resting voltage is produced by the ions in the salt solutions that are demonstrably present in all living animal tissues. (It should be noted, here, that atoms are normally electrically neutral because they contain equal numbers of positive and negative electrical charges. When an atom loses one of its negatively charged electrons, it is left with a net positive charge and thereby becomes what is known as a positive ion.)

Bernstein's beautiful membrane theory, as he propounded it in 1902, was so close to the modern view that it deserves a fuller description here. Augmented in detail by Ernest Overton, it suggested that the tube-shaped nerve fibre consists of selectively permeable membrane which, in the fibre's resting (and polarized) state, separates internal potassium ions from external sodium ions. Excitation at one point of this membrane locally increases its permeability and the negative ions inside the fibre pass through it, thereby producing a state of depolarization. The small electric currents thus generated stimulate adjacent parts of the membrane, and the process is repeated, producing a self-propagating wave of negativity (as described by Du Bois-Reymond) which passes along the fibre. The Bernstein–Overton picture, or model as it would be called nowadays, was wrong in just one important respect. Both potassium and sodium ions are positively charged. (When table salt, which is the compound sodium chloride, is dissolved in water, the molecules break up into positive sodium ions and negative chlorine ions.) In invoking the passage of negative ions, the theory puts the onus of nerve conduction on chlorine ions. Although chlorine ions are indeed present in nerve fibres, we now know that they do not carry the sole responsibility for animal electricity.

Fifty more years were destined to pass before that particular question was satisfactorily resolved. Meanwhile, the discovery of pulses of electrical activity in nerves raised other interesting and important issues. Was the magnitude of a sensory impression reflected in the amplitude of the nerve pulse it produced? Were there indeed several impulses, and if so, did they form some sort of pattern as with the dots and dashes of the Morse Code? In short, what sort of signalling does the nervous system employ?

Although there were some prior suggestions from other scientists working with these problems, the chief credit for answering the questions posed above must be given to Keith Lucas, who enlisted in the Royal Flying Corps at the outbreak of World War I and was killed in a flying accident, and his student, Edgar Adrian (whose work on the cortex was described in the previous chapter). It transpired that a nerve functions in an all-or-nothing fashion; if the stimulus applied to it is not sufficiently intense, nothing is transmitted at all, but if the intensity (or, to be more precise, the degree of depolarization of the voltage across the nerve membrane) exceeds a certain threshold value, an impulse is generated and it passes along the nerve fibre at the velocity first measured by von Helmholtz. Impulses, moreover, always have a standard amplitude. If the stimulus continues to be applied for more than about a hundredth of a second, which would normally be the case, of course, more than one impulse is generated and transmitted. But although the impulses are generated more frequently the greater the stimulating intensity, the time lapse between two successive impulses cannot be less than what is termed the refractory period, which is about one hundredth of a second.

It is a simple matter to measure the threshold value that determines whether or not an impulse is to be dispatched out along the axon. There is some variation between different cell types, but the thresholds generally lie just under 0.1 volt. Even when compared with the modest voltages of the batteries in such things as transistor radios and hearing aids, this value might seem low. But one should remember that the fatty membrane which must withstand this voltage is a mere 0.000005 millimetre thick. The resulting electric field across the membrane is, in fact, only about a factor of ten below what would cause electrical breakdown. This gives the lie to the quiescent picture that one might otherwise have had of the typical neuron; it exists on the verge of a shower of sparks.

What happens in the typical neuron is therefore as follows: information in the form of electrical waves moves along the dendrites towards the body of the cell and, depending upon whether the total effect of all the incoming waves is greater or less than the above-cited threshold, a nerve impulse will or will not be transmitted out along the axon. It is, then, at the body of the neuron that the 'decision' is made whether an onwardly travelling signal, now known as an action potential, is to be dispatched, and this function can be explained without invoking any external intelligence.

We can, in fact, put the capstone on this purely mechanical process without further to-do. In 1936, John (J.Z.) Young had discovered that the nervous system of the squid *Loligo forbesi* includes some axons which can be as large as 1 millimetre in diameter. These are large enough to be pierced by a carefully manipulated hypodermic needle, and Alan Hodgkin and Andrew Huxley were soon exploiting this fact in an attempt to lay bare those final elusive details regarding the ionic movements which provide the basis of the nerve impulse. Using a modified hypodermic needle which could measure electrical effects, they were able to show that the impulse is initiated by the inward flow of sodium ions, and that its termination is caused, about a millisecond later, by the outward flow of potassium ions. At present, the structures of the molecules which serve as the voltage-sensitive 'gates' for these ions are close to being elucidated right down to the atomic level, and it is already clear that they possess narrow passages through which the ions can just manage to squeeze, when the depolarization of the trans-membrane voltage exceeds its threshold value.

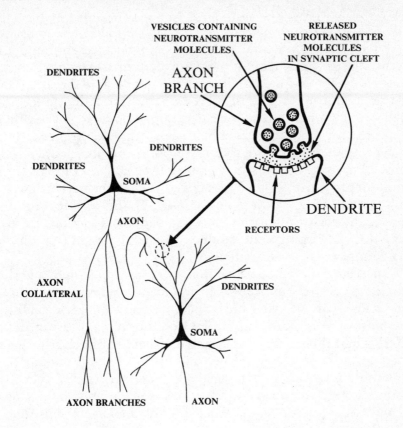

VESICLES CONTAINING NEUROTRANSMITTER MOLECULES

RELEASED NEUROTRANSMITTER MOLECULES IN SYNAPTIC CLEFT

DENDRITES

AXON BRANCH

DENDRITES

DENDRITES

SOMA

AXON

DENDRITE

RECEPTORS

AXON COLLATERAL

DENDRITES

SOMA

AXON BRANCHES

AXON

In the late nineteenth century, it became clear that signalling in the nervous system is mediated by special cells known as neurons. Their outer surfaces have long extensions called processes, and these act as electrical (actually, electrochemical) conduits. The processes are of two types: the dendrites, which conduct signals towards the centrally located soma, and the axon, out along which the neuron sends an impulse if the sum of the incoming signals exceeds a certain threshold value. Axons can be many centimetres long, and the nerve fibres that carry signals from the brain to the various parts of the body are composed of bundles of these processes. Within the brain, the axon divides into several parts, the subsidiary members being known as collaterals, and both the main axon and the collaterals show considerable branching at their extremities. The latter closely approach other cells, particularly at the dendrites, the small remaining gaps, known as synapses, being traversed by the signalling substances called neurotransmitters. Molecules of these compounds are released when small membrane-bounded units known as vesicles fuse with the terminal membrane of the axon branch, this occurring only when that region receives a signal from the soma. This synaptic transmission of signals between neurons is of major importance to the functioning of the brain.

Striking corroborative evidence that the millions of protein molecules that dot the surface of an axon's bounding membrane do indeed have tunnel-like passages running through them has recently been provided by work on certain toxic substances. These are the components in snake venoms, and the stings of scorpions and certain spiders. X-ray studies of the molecules of these components have revealed that they have shapes that would permit them to fit snugly into the tunnel entrances, thus precluding the entrance of sodium or potassium ions, depending upon which protein was being put out of action. This in turn would deprive the axon of its ability to conduct nerve signals, and the upshot is either paralysis or, if the affected nerves were sufficiently important to a life-support function, death. For snakes, scorpions and spiders, this is of course a question of a square meal or starvation.

The passage of a nerve impulse along an axon could be compared with the progress of the burning zone along a fuse. But a fuse can be used only once, whereas an axon's life is indefinite. For a start, only a few sodium and potassium ions slip through their nearest respective protein channels, during a single impulse, so the aqueous solutions inside and outside the axon remain virtually unchanged after such an event. Cyclically moving a leg, an arm or a finger, as quickly as possible, has an only imperceptible influence on the ionic concentrations in and around the nerves that activate them. But prolonged movement would gradually lead to depletion of the water-borne ions if it were not for the counteracting efforts of other protein molecules. These return to the outside those sodium ions that have passed through the sodium gates, and the same molecules simultaneously transfer potassium ions in the other direction. So important are these particular protein work-horses to the nervous system's continued functioning that they use up about a quarter of all the energy that a person consumes.

We noted earlier that the beauty of the Golgi staining technique lies in its ability to single out a cell and reveal it under microscopical examination, isolated from the obscuring presence of all the surrounding cells, which, lacking the stain, remain invisible. The description of the individual neuron given in the preceding pages may have conjured up, in the reader's mind, a similarly insular structure, hovering in space. The actual situation could hardly be more different. If one inspects even a minute fragment of brain tissue under a different type of microscope, namely a scanning electron microscope, in which one can examine unstained specimens, one sees what at first appears to be a tangled pile of worms. These are the neuronal processes, the axons and the dendrites, and the observations permit verification of the presence of structures whose existence was postulated long before such high-powered instruments were invented. Let us now consider these important additional details.

As we have already seen, an axon branches into numerous extensions near its extremity. It transpires that these reach out towards those inwardly signalling processes of the surrounding neurons which we have identified by the term dendrites. There is no actual physical contact, however, the overall effect being more reminiscent of those almost-touching fingers as God creates Adam in Michelangelo's painting on the ceiling of the Sistine Chapel. Yet another type of microscope, the transmission electron microscope, which can actually resolve distances down to the diameter of a single small molecule (i.e. about half a millionth of a millimetre), can be used to reveal the presence and structure of such regions of near-contact. The extremity of the axon branch and the surface of its target dendrite approach to within about twenty millionths of a millimetre, which is roughly forty diameters of a typical small organic molecule.

This type of junction has proved to be a structure of great significance. Indeed, as explained below, it provides the nervous system with its most sophisticated capacities. In 1897, Charles Sherrington named such junctions synapses, and noted that they link the individual cells of the brain into a vast neural network, which he likened to an 'enchanted loom'. Before describing how subsequent investigations have painted a progressively less romantic picture, let us see how the existence of the synapse had been anticipated a couple of decades earlier. In 1877, Du Bois-Reymond had conjectured that 'there must be either a stimulating secretion in the form perhaps of a thin layer of ammonia or lactic acid or of some other substance on the outside of the contractile tissue so that violent excitation of the muscle takes place, or the influence must be electric.' The latter alternative was subsequently ruled out because, as we have seen, there is no direct contact between an axon and the dendrite to which it feeds its signals. Du Bois-Reymond was actually referring to the axon–muscle junction rather than the axon–dendrite junction, but this does not alter the fact that he was suggesting chemical transmission of the nerve message.

The first evidence, albeit rather indirect, for such chemical transfer across the synapse was provided by studies of the effect of another toxic substance, but this time one used by man. It was curare, the poison with which South American Indians tipped their arrows, and it had become an object of curiosity for Claude Bernard. One of his experiments closely paralleled that which Galvani had employed in his ultimate demonstration of animal electricity; it too involved laying bare the hind limbs of a dissected frog and stimulating them either directly or via the lumbar nerve. But in Bernard's experiment, reported in his book *Leçons sur les effects des substances toxiques et medicamenteuses* in 1857, the frog was first paralysed by placing curare under the skin of its back. Bernard found that attempts to influence the muscles indirectly by stimulating the nerve caused no movement, whereas the muscles went into violent convulsions when stimulated directly. His conclusion that curare was destroying the motor nerves turned out to be fallacious, and the real reason for the paralysis was not discovered until almost fifty years later. It came, interestingly enough, from that most basic of bodily functions, urination, and the observations were made on cats by Thomas Elliott. Elliott discovered that injection of adrenalin, which is secreted by the adrenal glands and which had been isolated and purified some years before his experiments, causes the bladder to relax. It was already known that this is what the hypogastric nerves also do, so Elliott concluded that adrenalin must resemble the chemical which is responsible for the transfer of the nerve's message, and might even be the very substance which carries out this function. And he stated the opinion that such a chemical mediator must be released from the nerve endings.

The capstone for these developments was provided by Otto Loewi, and his inspiration came through a dream in 1921. He reported having fallen asleep while reading a light novel, and awakening suddenly with the idea that the (vagus) nerves which slow down the heartbeat do so by liberating a substance related to the chemical compound muscarine. His dream showed him how to prove this: extract some of the substance from one frog heart and demonstrate that it inhibits a second frog heart. He scribbled the plan on a scrap of paper, but when he woke the next morning he could not decipher his own writing! Fortunately the dream recurred the following night, and this time the plan was properly remembered, soon put into action, and carried through to a successful conclusion. The upshot of Loewi's efforts was the unequivocal demonstration that messages are passed across the synaptic cleft by the transfer of a chemical compound, and he subsequently identified it to be a substance called acetylcholine.

Much later, after the Second World War in fact, Bernard Katz and Ricardo Miledi showed just how this substance, which is now referred to as a neurotransmitter, is actually liberated from the nerve terminus. The molecules are of course produced inside the neuron, and they are packaged into little round bags, each of which contains a few thousand of them. The envelope of each bag consists of the same type of fatty membrane which provides the neuron with its outer skin, and the bags are now called vesicles (pronounced '*vee*-sicles'). When the nerve impulse reaches the nerve terminus, a few vesicles fuse with the terminal membrane, close to which they were located, and they thereby liberate their cargo of neurotransmitters into the synaptic cleft. The process resembles the laying of eggs, but with the eggs breaking as they are laid. The neurotransmitter molecules drift across the gap and reach the bounding membrane of the receiving dendrite, a journey which takes them a mere ten thousandth of a second. They then dock with other (protein) molecules called receptors, on the surface of the dendrite, and this induces an onwardly travelling signal in the latter, and so on.

These elementary processes of the nervous system, now ame-nable to the most exacting chemical and physical analyses, are well understood. Using a minimum of detail and technical jargon, we have formed a reliable picture of a typical area of the cerebral cortex: a vast network of cells, the decision-making bodies of which receive and (can) send signals, with the intercellular communication being the responsibility of the neurotransmitters and their targets, the receptors. Without implying a belief that it functions like a traditional electronic computer, because that can easily be shown to be too simple a comparison, we could say that this is the hardware, the brain's circuitry. The software is the manner in which the circuits perform, and it is at this point that we must decide whether Descartes' ghost, despite our scepticism, could still be lurking amongst the wiring.

Imagine that we describe for a Martian (assuming that we can overcome the language barrier) the physical structure and attributes of a typical human being. Even if the visitor was given a detailed account of the means by which two people can communicate, he would be unlikely to guess at the complexity of society. Indeed, he might not even anticipate the existence of society at all, let alone its structure and its institutions. In considering the brain, we are confronted with a similar problem. We might feel that we have grasped the gist of the synapse, but perceiving how the myriad brain cells perform collectively is a much taller order; one cannot see the network for the neurons. It is hardly surprising that so many still believe the loom to be enchanted.

On the basis of what has been described thus far it must be admitted that the neural network, despite its hundred thousand million units, each with its several thousand connections to other units, does not seem to be the sort of thing that would be capable of human emotions and faculties. After all, a grain of salt contains about a million times as many atoms as the brain contains neurons, and the atoms interact with each other, but there is no life in one of these little crystals. There are several complications which we must now add to the above picture, however, complications which really do hold the promise of enriching the situation, and giving it the complexity of mental processes. The first of these broke upon the scene just after Loewi's introduction of acetylcholine into the story. Henry Dale confirmed the earlier suggestions that some neurons have an inhibiting rather than an exciting influence, and he went on to show that there are other neurotransmitters than acetylcholine and adrenalin. To date, several scores of these chemical signals have been discovered, and it seems unlikely that the inventory is complete.

In describing Dale's contributions to neuroscience, I have introduced something of major importance, namely a microscopic explanation of the self-regulatory mechanisms which were discussed in the previous chapter. The existence of both inhibitory and excitatory synapses makes possible, at the neuronal level, counteracting controls of the type that underlie the functioning of the engineer's governor. We are

MONOAMINE NEUROTRANSMITTERS

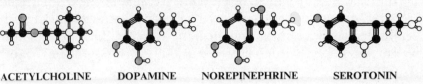

ACETYLCHOLINE   DOPAMINE   NOREPINEPHRINE   SEROTONIN

HALLUCINOGENIC DRUGS

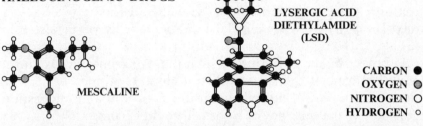

LYSERGIC ACID
DIETHYLAMIDE
(LSD)

MESCALINE

CARBON ●
OXYGEN ◉
NITROGEN ○
HYDROGEN ○

Neurotransmitters are synthesized in the neuron, near the terminals of the axon branches, and packaged into the membrane-bounded vesicles. The arrival of a nerve impulse releases approximately 10,000-molecule bursts of these chemical messengers, which thereupon diffuse across the roughly 0.00005-millimetre synaptic cleft. They then dock with receptor molecules in the dendritic membranes of the adjacent cell, thus provoking an ongoing electrochemical signal. Many neurotransmitters are small molecules, like the ones shown here, and some, such as norepinephrine, also serve elsewhere in the body as hormones. Several hallucinogenic drugs owe their potency to a structural similarity with certain neurotransmitters. Examples are mescaline, which can mimic dopamine and norepinephrine, and lysergic acid diethylamide, otherwise known as the infamous LSD, which can masquerade as serotonin.

starting to glimpse the mechanisms which imbue the brain with its powers of automation. And the additional capabilities provided by the existence of two opposing types of synapse are far more numerous than one might suspect. It is not just a question of producing the ability to balance, which we discussed in the context of the statue of Eros in the previous chapter. These mechanisms provide the basis of such things as attention and curiosity, through the action of neurons which seem to exploit the suppressing habituation of their neighbours as already described. Indeed, it would be no exaggeration to say that it is the presence of conflicting synapses which, in the final analysis, makes it possible for all living creatures to participate in the eternal competitive struggle that Nature has foisted upon us through Darwin's inescapable principle.

One of the most influential books ever written in the field of neuroscience was published in 1949. Its title was *The Organization of Behavior*, and the author was Donald Hebb. Amongst many seminal ideas which first saw the light of day in this monumental work, two deserve particular attention: synaptic plasticity and the neuronal assembly.

The first of these Hebbian ideas has proved to be of such profound significance that it would be wrong not to quote the relevant passage in full. It reads: 'When an axon of cell A is near enough to excite a cell B and repeatedly or persistently takes part in firing it, some growth process or metabolic change takes place in one or both cells such that A's efficiency, as one of the cells firing B, is increased.' And Hebb continues with: 'The most obvious and I believe much the most probable suggestion concerning the way in which one cell could become more capable of firing another is that synaptic knobs develop and increase the area of contact between the afferent axon and efferent soma.'

Hebb was essentially suggesting that the synaptic connection between two cells would be strengthened if the one were persistently helping the other to fire off an impulse. Synapses were thus being seen, for the first time, as modifiable, and in proposing this radically different view Hebb was thrusting into the hands of neuroscience a beautifully simple explanation of memory. Just as water running down the side of a mountain will gradually cut a channel, which will subsequently serve as the preferred route, so will experience tend to increase the transfer efficiency at certain synapses and thus create favoured pathways for later nerve impulses. This type of mechanism has, not surprisingly, come to be known as Hebbian learning.

Hebb's other idea was just as exciting because it enables us to tackle the daunting prospect of a structure comprising one hundred thousand million neurons and upwards of a hundred million million inter-neural connections. He simply suggested that under a given set of sensory stimuli, only very few of these cells would be active and that, moreover, the active cells would tend to lie close to one another by dint of their mutual electro-chemical influences. Such a group of simultaneously, or almost-simultaneously, firing neurons is known as a neuronal assembly.

The analogy drawn earlier to human society is particularly useful. Analogies are seldom exact, and one could cite the obvious difference that people move around whereas neurons (except in their early stages of existence, at least) remain in one place. The parallels are nevertheless close enough to be instructive. The impressive sophistication of modern society derives from the diversity of skills possessed by its individual members, while in the brain we find many different types of neurons, several of which have special names. Then again, there are many diverse modes of communication between people, and in the brain we have already noted the multiplicity of neurotransmitters. And society is divided up into smaller groups of individuals who pool their efforts and achieve collective goals. But there are numerous interwoven and yet independent sets of divisions; during the week one works with one set of colleagues while at the weekend one might be part of a sports team or an orchestra composed of quite different individuals. This is similar to Hebb's neuronal assemblies with their changing constellations of cells firing in, or close to, unison. Finally, we note that the interactions in human society are not always harmonious, and in accepting that there is both friendliness and enmity we are reminded of the fact that some synapses are excitatory while others are inhibitory. All in all, then, the view of the brain as a vast society of neurons is a quite useful one.

As attractive as these ideas are, however, one would naturally want to be shown evidence that they provide the most appropriate picture of an assembly of neurons. And the evidence should preferably be clear cut, with none of the obscuring factors that could easily arise because of the brain's sheer complexity; we would like to learn of examples in which the relationship between sensory stimulus and behavioural response is relatively simple and straightforward, and we would hope that the associated changes in the neuronal circuitry, and especially in the synapses, could be easily measured. This is why the present period of physiological research is so exciting; there really are such clear cut examples. We will examine a particularly famous one shortly, but to appreciate the significance of some of its detail we will need a brief preamble.

The name of Ivan Pavlov will always be linked to the concept of the conditioned reflex. Pavlov's unimpeachable scientific credentials were actually established through his efforts with the more pedestrian issue of gastrointestinal secretions, and he did not turn to the question of reflexes until he was fifty-five. His

initial discoveries in this latter area were in fact serendipitous.
The first observations concerned what we would now call
unconditioned reflexes. Using salivation as his main observed
response, he defined an unconditioned reflex as one in which
those properties of the object to which the saliva is physiologically
related (e.g. texture, chemical composition, dryness) are effective
as a stimulus. In the conditioned reflex, on the other hand, a
response is observed for stimuli which have no such physiological
role. A good example of the latter class is colour.

I invariably think of Pavlov when I order my favourite dish
for lunch at the canteen in which I take my midday meal. The
call for that particular recipe is not so great that the cook has
it on hand, so I order it and am told that a signal will be given
when it has been prepared. The signal is the tinkling of a small
bell, and I display a typical conditioned reflex as I respond to its
call, my mouth watering at the prospect of the appetizing food.
And I display this reflex even on days when I have not ordered
my favourite meal; my mouth still waters when I hear the little
bell calling others to come and collect their own choices.

Pavlov studied dogs and made the interesting observation that
the sight of dry bread actually provokes stronger salivation than
that of fresh meat, even though the latter causes far more antici-
patory movement and general excitement. Pavlov went on to
show that salivation becomes inhibited if a dog is repeatedly
shown food but is denied access to it. We have already encountered, in previous chapters, experiments involving the removal
of all or part of the cerebral cortex. Pavlov showed that such
decerebration deprives a dog of the ability to develop conditioned
reflexes, and his conclusion was that such reflexes require
appropriate adjustments in the highest centres of thought.

Pavlov's pronouncements did not meet with universal app-
roval. Amongst those who even went so far as to ridicule him
was George Bernard Shaw, who vouchsafed the opinion that
'Pavlov is the biggest fool I know; any policeman could tell you
that much about a dog.' This was GBS at his cantankerous best,
and we should not take his remarks too seriously. After all, there
must have been a good reason why Pavlov was awarded the
Nobel Prize for physiology (albeit for his work on digestion)
while Shaw received it for literature.

We are now better primed to appreciate the beautiful work

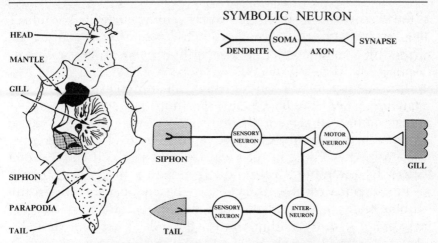

SYMBOLIC NEURON

HEAD

MANTLE

GILL

SIPHON

PARAPODIA

TAIL

DENDRITE   SOMA   AXON   SYNAPSE

SIPHON   SENSORY NEURON   MOTOR NEURON   GILL

TAIL   SENSORY NEURON   INTER-NEURON

The first demonstration that synapses are modifiable, as Donald Hebb had surmised, was made by Eric Kandel and his colleagues. They studied the simple nervous system of the sea hare *Aplysia*, which displays some of the types of conditioning seen in more sophisticated creatures. If the syphon (or the mantle) is touched, the gill withdraws immediately, but prolonged gentle stimulation of that same area, with a jet of water for example, causes habituation, and touching the siphon (or the mantle) then has no effect. In the highly simplified circuit diagram, in which groups of parallel neurons are represented by a single neuron, this habituation occurs because the synapses between the siphon's sensory neurons and the gill's (withdrawal reflex) motor neurons gradually lose their efficiency. (Similar circuits connecting the mantle to the gill function in much the same way.) The siphon's influence on the gill can be returned to normal by a pinch on the tail. This activates the facilitating interneurons, which have synapses that are capable of modifying the siphon—gill synapses, by sensitizing them. Kandel and his colleagues were able to detect the biochemical changes, in the synapses, that underlie these various behaviours.

of Eric Kandel and his colleagues on *Aplysia californica*. This rather large aquatic snail gets its nickname, sea hare, not from its speed across the seabed, but rather from the large ear-like protuberances on its head. For our purposes here, we need to pay particular attention to four of its other physical attributes: the tail, the siphon, the gill, and a centrally located structure known as the mantle shelf, which lies adjacent to the gill and is indeed bordered by the latter. Under normal circumstances, the gill contracts almost instantaneously if the mantle shelf is touched. Kandel and his colleagues have studied the structural changes in certain synapses of the creature under a variety of situations. The first of these, and the simplest, is habituation. If the siphon is repeatedly stimulated by a small jet of sea water, the gill withdrawal response is gradually diminished; the sea hare's nervous system apparently accommodates to the fact that the gentle disturbance in the region of its siphon poses no threat, although, as we shall see, this involves no intervening 'thought'.

The 'wiring' of the relevant part of the creature's nervous system is quite simple, but not the simplest one that could be imagined; if a single neuron had its dendrites embedded in the mantle shelf while its axon activated the muscles that control the position of the gill, it is feasible that this cell could alone cause the gill-withdrawal reflex. In practice, things are slightly more complicated. A sensory neuron having its dendrites in the siphon makes a synaptic contact with a motor neuron, which activates the muscles that control the gill. (There are actually several copies of this circuit, and they function in parallel.) It is the presence of a synapse in the route which makes the habituation possible, and subsequent physiological examination shows that changes have occurred in the presynaptic membrane's ability to allow the inward passage of calcium ions (which should not be confused with the sodium and potassium ions that are involved with the transmission of the nerve impulse). Earlier work had shown that when a nerve impulse arrives at the nerve terminal (i.e. the presynaptic membrane), there is a sudden influx of calcium ions, and these permit the simultaneous laying and breaking of the neurotransmitter-laden vesicles, as described earlier. Any decrease in the amount of calcium-ion influx during the process would, in turn, decrease the amount of neurotransmitter being passed on to the motor neuron that drives the gill-withdrawal reflex. This is apparently what happens during habituation.

Kandel and his colleagues went on to study sensitization in the same aquatic species. When the tail is given a stimulus that it does not like, and a sharp pinch is sufficient for that purpose, the gill-withdrawal reflex becomes more pronounced than earlier; it thus causes the direct opposite of habituation. Physiological monitoring this time revealed an enhanced ability of the presynaptic membrane to allow the passage of calcium ions. An additional piece of nerve circuitry makes this possible. The dendrites of another sensory neuron are present in the tail, and the axon of this cell synapses onto what is called a facilitator interneuron. This interneuron's axon makes a synaptic contact to that region of the siphon sensory neuron's axon that lies close to the latter's synapse to the gill-withdrawal motor neuron. When the tail is provoked, the message is passed from the tail's sensory neuron on to the facilitator interneuron, which releases the neurotransmitter serotonin, and this ultimately leads to the increased ability of the siphon sensory neuron's synapse to take in calcium ions.

It even proved possible to elicit, study and analyse a conditioned reflex in *Aplysia*. If the tail and the syphon were irritated at approximately the same time, subsequent stimulation of the syphon alone caused a more vigorous gill-withdrawal reflex in contrast to what is observed in habituation. This too has proved amenable to physiological analysis, and although things are obviously more complicated, a tentative scenario has been proposed for the enhanced calcium-ion intake.

These brilliant studies, as well as similar work on insects, leeches and a few other species, have revealed a strikingly unromantic picture of the nervous system. At the level of the axon, the dendrite, and the synapse, all appears utterly mechanical. Descartes' ghost in the machine would sit in the presynaptic membrane only with acute discomfort.

The fact remains, however, that creatures like *Aplysia* occupy a very humble rung on evolution's ladder. (In 1986, Stephen Kelso, Alan Ganong and Thomas Brown managed to demonstrate Hebbian modification of the synapses in the hippocampus of an experimental rat, and a year later, Alain Artola and Wolf Singer observed a related effect, known as long-term potentiation, in the visual cortices of members of the same species.) We need to consider what extra advantages are enjoyed by those species which, like us, possess a cerebral cortex, and why having a larger number of neurons in one's nervous system should make such a profound difference. Parallels to the phenomena just described for the sea hare are certainly much in evidence of course. One fascinating exploitation of the possibility of habituation appears to lie behind the mesmerizing wave of the cobra's head; it lulls its victims into a false sense of security. And one sometimes wishes that certain public speakers were more alive to the perils of too monotonous a delivery. But these are examples of mere projection of simple synaptic effects up to the level of many neurons; this produces only differences in degree,

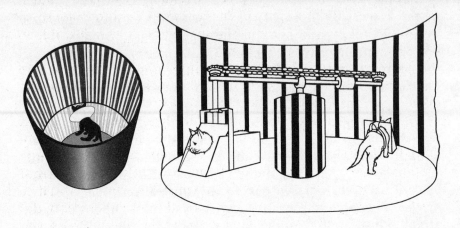

The coarser consequences of the synaptic modification demonstrated by the pioneering studies of *Aplysia* (see previous illustration) have also been detected in evolutionary higher creatures. The two classic experiments depicted here established different manifestations of these effects, in the brains of cats. In the work of Richard Held and Alan Hein (right), newborn kittens, their head movements restricted by neck-yokes, were confined to a cylindrical room decorated with exclusively vertical stripes, the active subject being free to walk about whereas the passive member rode in a gondola. The active kitten's grosser movements were imposed upon its partner by a rod and chain mechanism; both therefore had the same visual experiences. The goal was to show that the acquisition of appropriate motor responses depends upon conditioning during early development, and the post-training tests included blink reflex to an approaching object, visually guided paw placement, and visual cliff trials. In the latter, the kitten was confronted with a choice between shallow and deep drops when descending from a platform, the entire environment again being covered with vertical stripes. (An invisible glass floor prevented injury during descents on the deep side.) The actively trained kitten always chose the shallow drop, whereas its motor experience deprived sibling could not appreciate the danger on the deep side; the latter's brain presumably lacked neurons that had recorded the visual-motor associations. In Colin Blakemore and Grahame Cooper's experiment (left), a newborn kitten was similarly confined to a vertically decorated environment, and a fitted collar even prevented it from seeing its own body. Within a few months, it had become quite clumsy, bumping into objects as it moved about. Direct electrical recording from neurons in its primary visual cortex revealed the reason: neurons sensitive to horizontal lines were sparse, whereas their vertically tuned counterparts were over-represented. This demonstrated, in addition, that nerve cells are able to change their preferred direction.

not of kind. In the next chapter, therefore, I will take a much closer look at the interplay of some of the structures described in Chapter 2, but this time with the advantage of being able to take a neuronal view of things.

Let us close by paying another brief visit to that macabre scene with which the chapter opened. I wonder if Aldini really appreciated what he was starting that day when he first demonstrated animal electricity in man. Did he realize that he was lifting the corner of a veil which until then had been hiding a breathtakingly exquisite piece of machinery, a structure whose complex behaviour derives not from any ghost-like input but merely from the sheer numbers of its constituent units? And if he did begin to travel down that mechanical road, in his mind, did he see where it might be leading him and the physiologists who came after him? Did he, in particular, see what it might imply regarding the judgement that had, that very day, so conveniently provided him with a human experimental subject? For if one accepts the mechanical picture which is gradually unfolding in this book, what must be one's attitude towards culpability, since guilt is unavoidably contingent on the concept of free will? These are, in more than one sense, heady issues.

● Summary

The brain comprises approximately a hundred thousand million cells, known as neurons, the signalling capabilities of which derive from the structure of their membranous surfaces. These fatty films are dotted with numerous protein molecules that allow the armlike cell extensions to act as electrical conduits. Those extensions are the nerve fibres. The passage of information from one neuron to another is mediated by the chemical neurotransmitter molecules, which diffuse across the narrow intercellular gaps known as synapses. The efficiency of this transmission is modifiable by experience, and this imbues the network of neurons with the possibility of memory. Certain chemicals can mimic the action of neurotransmitters and thus provoke the altered brain states experienced by users of hallucinogenic drugs. The mind can thus be subjected to external control, just like any other machine.

4

Exorcising the Homunculus
Senses and actions

> What made this brain of mine, do you think? Not
> the need to move my limbs; for a rat with half my
> brain moves as well as I.
>
> GEORGE BERNARD SHAW
> *Man and Superman*

> To move things is all mankind can do, and for such
> the sole executant is muscle, whether whispering or
> felling a tree.
>
> CHARLES SCOTT SHERRINGTON
> *Man on his Nature*

Before the scientific endeavour started to collect information
about the internal workings of the human body, it was natural
that what we call the mind should have been taken for granted.
And because the results of some recent research are not yet
widely known, the assumption of dualism is rarely brought into
question. It seems obvious, indeed, that the mind should travel
around with the body, riding like a passenger somewhere up
in the head, and yet be definitely separate from it. One never
hears a sports commentator describe how a boxer has given
his opponent a left-uppercut to the mind, for example (though
this is precisely what he has done, if the opponent was struck
anywhere on the head). Our eyes seem to act as windows, and
our ears as funnels, both conveniently placed to provide a means
of observing the world from our cosy nook within. Let us take a
closer look at the senses, therefore, and pay particular attention

to the one that has been studied most intensely, namely vision, and see how we are fooled.

In the early days of photography, it was the recording medium rather than the apparatus which occupied the ingenuity of Louis-Jacques Daguerre, William Fox Talbot, and their contemporaries. The wooden cameras of that time now appear to possess an antique beauty, but they were simple structures: essentially a box with a single lens and a means of adjusting the latter's position relative to the sensitized plate. All control was in the hands of the user, and although the device for choosing the correct level of illumination did bear a superficial resemblance to the iris of the eye, its setting was manual. The pioneers would not have found this hardware impressive. After all, you can get an excellent image with a pin-hole camera (also known as a camera obscura), which has no lens at all.

Confronted with a modern camera, however, those same enthusiasts might have felt quite disturbed. For today's state-of-the-art camera seems to have what the early photographers must have assumed would always lie with the operator: the final word. The modern apparatus, in an almost eerie manner, usurps the function of the mind. You can stand it on a tripod, and listen to it quietly adjusting itself to a change in the lighting conditions or to a change in the distance to the object on which it is automatically focussing. But biology is aeons ahead of even modern photographic technology. Many of the nervous system's circuits are linked up in a manner which permits a high degree of feedback, and the visual system is no exception to that rule. This, together with the fact that both excitatory and inhibitory synapses are much in evidence, allows the eye and its associated part of the brain to achieve self-regulation, just as the incorporation of a governor in an engine produces self-control of the engine's speed. The result is automation of both focus and light controls.

The automation of the light control function in the eye is easily demonstrated. Using a mirror, look at your pupils in a dimly lit room, and notice how they quickly shrink down to a smaller diameter if the level of light suddenly increases. The reaction is quite involuntary. So automatic are all the components of the visual system, in fact, that it takes a conscious effort to defocus one's eyes or to go cross-eyed, and many people cannot achieve either situation. The eye does not serve as a window *for* the mind; it supplies us with a window *on* the mind.

One often speaks of seeing something in the mind's eye, and there is an understandable temptation to give this a literal interpretation in terms of an inner screen located somewhere in the head. Indeed, this assumption seems not at all far-fetched in view of the fact that the sense of touch is linked up to a region of the cortex (i.e. the somatosensory cortex) where there is even a continuous mapping (albeit distorted) of the body's surface. We noted that this tactile map had been facetiously referred to as the 'homunculus'. If that diminutive fellow is also to exploit the fact that we have visual systems, he will need something to look at. And it is natural to think in terms of an internal screen, with the eyes serving as twin television cameras. The dualist point of view actually seems to demand the existence of a homunculus, not one with arms and legs of course, but nevertheless some sort of presence in 'mission control', up there in the head, to monitor the dials and gauges fed by our senses and make decisions accordingly. An obvious shortcoming of this idea is that the inner being would itself need a similar apparatus, and in contemplating how that worked we would in effect be back where we started. The homunculus could, in other words, never be solitary; there would have to be an infinite hierarchy of them. Our poor heads would be crowded. Far better to exorcise the entire bunch. This is what we will now proceed to do, and we will replace the little inner man with something remarkably mechanical, something almost menacing in its simplicity.

We noted earlier that the eye provides us with a window on the mind. That window is never so transparent as when it reveals the visual system being wrong-footed. This is a quite common occurrence, in fact, and we know it as the optical, or visual, illusion. The brain's machinery can be fooled for the simple reason that, like any other well-organized device, its bits and pieces function according to the logic of their arrangement and their mutual interactions. Any marked departure from the conditions under which the system functions optimally will inevitably show up the machine's flaws, and although the human visual system is remarkably adaptable, it nevertheless does have its limitations. Just as the chameleon cannot sit with comfort on a piece of tartan, so does the sense of sight sometimes have to admit that too much is being asked of it. In some cases, indeed, its performance is only mediocre in situations that do not appear to be at all demanding. These give rise to some of the better known illusions, which are often useful in revealing some basic facts about the way in which the visual machinery is constructed.

However, before we go into these pieces of optical sleight of hand, it will be necessary to look a bit deeper into the visual system's circuitry. We start with the eye itself, and immediately run into something fascinating. As noted earlier, the left side of the brain controls the right side of the body, and vice versa. But each eye's single lens inverts the field of view it focusses on, so that up becomes down and left becomes right when an image of the external world is formed on the retina. This means that what lies to the left of the body is focussed on the right side of the retina, and this is true for both eyes. Conversely, what lies to the right of the body is focussed on the left side of the retina in both cases. Coordination of hand and eye would be a complicated affair if both visual and tactile components did not follow the same rules. This means that the nerves running from one eye to the brain must become subdivided at a certain point so that those emanating from the right side of the retina are routed to the right cerebral hemisphere, while left is linked to left. This is precisely what happens, and the point of division (and rearrangement, since two eyes have to be catered for) is called the optic chiasm.

In order to appreciate what is achieved by the connections between eye and brain, we should take a closer look at the eye itself. Let us follow the light beams as they travel inward from the environment. They are partially focussed by the outer protective layer, the cornea, while that job is completed by the lens, which has the advantage of being adjustable by the associated muscles. The rays also pass the iris, which controls the amount of light entering the eye by the automatic adjustment of its inner diameter, this being one of the responsibilities of the autonomic nervous system that was described in Chapter 2. Finally, the rays are brought to a focus on the retina, which covers the rear of the inside of the eyeball. It is here that we encounter, for the first time in this book, the special type of neuron known as a receptor cell. The ones in the retina are photoreceptors. They are sensitive to light, but there are analogous receptors which serve the other senses. It turns out, in fact, that there are two types of photoreceptor: the rod cells, which detect brightness, and the cones, which monitor contrast, motion, size and colour. The rods are about five hundred times more sensitive to light than are the cones.

These receptor neurons are quite small; a thousand of them placed side by side would span a mere millimetre. There are about 120 million rods in each eye, and they are distributed over the entire retina except for the blind spot, and the region which handles the centre of our gaze, namely the fovea. The fovea consists exclusively of the other type of receptors, the cones, and it contains about 6 million of them. The grand total of about 126 million cells in each retina should be considered in comparison with the approximately half a million spots that go to make up a television picture. There is a more tightly packed area at the centre of the fovea itself which contains only about 2,000 cones, and it serves a small fraction of the total field of view, corresponding to an angle of about one-third of a degree. A yet smaller patch can be identified within the latter, on the basis of microscopical examination, and this contains a mere few dozen cells. We use this small team of receptors every time we examine things at the limit of our powers of resolution. A convenient measure of this is the observed difference between a full stop (period) and a comma on the printed page the reader is now scanning; at the distance of most comfortable reading, the full stops and commas can be reliably discriminated.

The question now arises as to how these receptor cells are connected up to the brain. We have already referred to the links, when discussing the optic chiasm, but are we to assume that they are simply the axons of the receptors? The answer is an emphatic no. It turns out that a number of other cell types intervene, so that a minimum number of three synapses must be crossed on the route from the receptor to the cerebral cortex. Things are thus complex, if one judges against the convenient yardstick provided by the sea hare we encountered in the previous chapter. And the reason for the complexity lies in the fact that the retina is best regarded as part of the brain itself. This is apparent if one studies the brain's development; the embryonic retina is clearly an extension of the immature

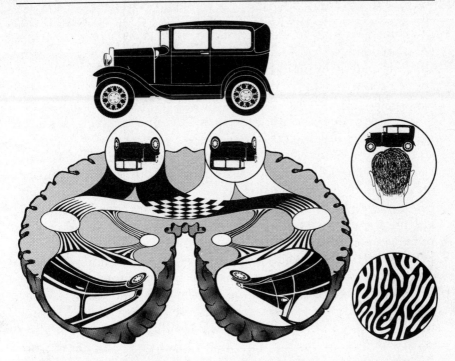

The brain's left side controls the body's right, and vice versa. The visual system thus has a problem, because each eye lens produces an inverted image on the retina, as indicated in this highly schematic rear view (see upper inset) of a horizontal section through the brain. The solution lies in a division of each optic nerve, half the fibres passing to the primary visual cortex at the rear of the same hemisphere while the remainder go to the corresponding area in the other hemisphere. They are not joined directly to those visual regions, however; the connections are via the lateral geniculate nuclei (the larger ovals in the figure). These also receive counter-running fibres from the primary visual areas, and this permits the feed-back control vital to the visual system's correct functioning. The smaller ovals represent the superior colliculi, which give the system its gaze-holding ability when the head or an observed object are in motion. They also produce 'blind sight' when the main path is damaged. The marked distortion of the image when it reaches the primary visual area is noteworthy, as is the fact that it is split down the middle. A conjectured internal observer would have an even harder job interpreting what goes on in the higher visual areas, where the representation is still more abstract. Depth perception is produced by the left–right alternation of fibres feeding the primary visual area; the existence of this arrangement was established by David Hubel and Torsten Wiesel, who injected a radioactive substance into one eye, let it diffuse to the visual area, cut a slice from that region, and located the radioactivity-bearing cells by placing the slice against a photographic film (see lower inset).

brain. This enables the retina to perform a sort of pre-processing of visual information, and it might come as a surprise to learn that the animal world boasts more complicated retinas than those found in humans, monkeys and cats. The possessors of these retinal masterpieces do not enjoy the advantages of our highly developed cortices, and they are thus dependent upon being able to employ their retinas for quite exacting tasks of prey capture and predator avoidance.

The silt-seeking fish known as the mudpuppy (*Necturus maculosus*) has proved to be an invaluable source of information on retinal physiology because its large neurons permit relatively easy piercing by the electrical measuring probes called electrodes. During the last two decades, John Dowling and Frank Werblin, in particular, have exploited this advantage, while Steven Kuffler has carried out the trickier analogous work on cats and monkeys. The five main cell types involved are the receptors, the bipolar cells, the ganglion cells, the horizontal cells and the amacrine cells. The main route taken by the nerve signals is from receptor to bipolar to ganglion, and it is the long axons of the ganglion cells which make up the optic nerve. But the optic nerve from each eye comprises only about 800,000 axons. With the efforts of 126 million receptor cells being fed out through this relatively small number of fibres in the optic nerve, it is clear that a good deal of pre-processing must indeed have occurred, and this is mediated by the horizontal cells, which lie in the plane of the retina, around the level of the receptor–bipolar synapses, and the similarly oriented amacrine cells, which occupy a level near the bipolar–ganglion synapses.

One of the peculiarities of our eyes is that the retinas are back to front; the incoming light has to pass the cells of the four other types before it reaches the receptors. An important consequence of this arrangement is that the axons of the ganglion cells lie on the inner part of the retina, and they thus have to pass through the latter in order to emerge from the eyeball and form the optic nerve. In so doing, they leave a receptor-depleted zone at their point of escape. This creates the well-known blind spot. It is interesting to note that although this region of the retina is devoid of rods and cones, we are unconscious of it. This is true even when we see with one eye closed and therefore lack the benefit of overlapping visual fields. There must be some mechanism whereby the brain compensates for the missing information. It is also interesting to note that some creatures, including the squid and the octopus, have retinas with the 'correct' orientation, and they therefore lack the blind spot.

What purpose does all this complicated retinal circuitry serve? Or rather, since Darwin's random and competitive principle of survival of the fittest forbids us to imply an underlying design or goal-oriented strategy, what evolutionary advantage does such intricate wiring bestow on its owner? The answer is surely that it makes the retina more efficient, more flexible, and more discerning. And it is the laterally deployed neurons, that is to say the horizontal cells and the amacrine cells, which play the key roles. Because their function is primarily inhibitory, and because they typically form links with a number of the cells of one or more of the other three types, one could say that they mediate the competition between the latter. Thus each horizontal cell receives excitation from a number of receptors, and passes on inhibition to a number of bipolars. Similarly, each bipolar receives excitation from several receptors. The upshot of this arrangement is a retina which can adjust itself to a really impressive range of lighting conditions (think about how well one sees in the almost dark, after a brief period of accommodation), and one which can perform the commendable feats of fine-scale discrimination that were mentioned earlier. This latter function follows directly from the manner in which the horizontal cells (and later the amacrine cells) restrict the lateral spread of the visual signals over the retina.

Kuffler, and also Dowling and Werblin, each working with his preferred animal, discovered interesting details about the optimal responses of the different types of retinal neurons in the main route from receptor to cortex. Performing experiments in which the positions and patterns of light stimuli in front of the animal's open eye could be varied, while the electrical response of a given neuron was monitored, they found that peak output in a ganglion is elicited either by a dark circular spot surrounded by an illuminated ring or an illuminated circular spot surrounded by a dark ring. Some ganglions thus respond best to a light stimulus in the shape of a doughnut while others prefer a doughnut hole. These two patterns are of course mutually exclusive, so a ganglion which is excited by an off-centre/on-surround pattern will be strongly inhibited by an on-centre/off-surround pattern, and vice versa. It follows that there will be little or no response from either cell to uniform illumination (which is equivalent to an on-centre/on-surround situation) because the inhibiting tendency from one region (hole or surround) will be balanced out by the excitatory tendency from the other (surround or hole).

It is this unevenness of optimal response within the plane of the retina, with some ganglions reacting to one type of pattern while others are activated by the opposite pattern, that ultimately provides the visual system with its powers of discrimination. It is also this structure, however, that gives a system which can be fooled remarkably easily. One of the first visual illusions to be discovered, and certainly one of the most famous, was stumbled across by Ernst Mach around 1860. It is also one of the most remarkable of the illusions because it catches the visual system performing below par in a situation which seems quite undemanding. A series of stripes with systematically varying shades of grey are placed side by side, with no gaps between them. The illumination level of each of the steps in this echelon arrangement is quite uniform, but an illusion appears at each inter-step junction: a ghost-like lighter line is seen in the darker strip, just to one side of the junction (and lying parallel to it), while an analogous phantom dark line appears in the lighter strip. Mach's speculations about this surprising phenomenon led him to the conclusion that lateral inhibition must play a part in visual processing, and this was in fact the first appearance of that concept. The modern explanation of Mach bands, as they are now called, involves a second concept, namely that of the spontaneously active cell. It turns out that some cells in the visual system emit nerve impulses even when the illumination level is zero. Their job appears to lie in reporting that 'It's dark, it's dark'. An obvious advantage follows from a situation in which the quiescent state corresponds to a certain level of activity rather than a total absence of activity: this level can be either increased or diminished; in contrast to the zero level state, it can respond in either direction. These two concepts, invoked together, provide an explanation of Mach's observation. Near the boundary between two different levels of grey tone, the discontinuity of illumination causes an imbalance in the degree of lateral inhibition and this extends across the boundary to give a locally enhanced (on the dark side) or diminished (on the light side) activity level.

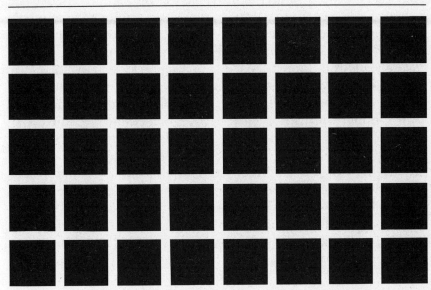

The optical illusions of greatest interest to the neurophysiologist are those related to fundamental processes early in the visual pathways. This is true of the Hermann grid phenomenon shown here. Nebulous shadows are seen at the intersections of the white strips, but they seem to evaporate if one stares directly at them. The retina's ganglion cells respond maximally either to a light central circle surrounded by a dark ring or vice versa. The intersections in the grid's image on the retina come closest to the former of these optimal stimuli, and the slight departure from the ideal gives rise to the shadows. But it is still not known why they disappear when one looks directly at them.

Another illusion, which also appears to stem from the way in which signals are handled in the retina, was discovered in 1869. The pattern, now known as a Hermann grid, that gives rise to this effect is a simple array of black squares separated by a series of white lines. Its overall form thus resembles a bird's eye view of the blocks and streets of a city. The illusion in this case is the appearance of dark nebulous patches at the corner intersections, and the mystery is heightened by the fact that the spots seem to evaporate if one stares directly at them; they are most clearly discerned in the peripheral regions of one's field of view. The explanation of this effect is to be found in the existence of the centre-surround responses of the ganglion cells, which were described earlier. An on-centre/off-surround ganglion reacts maximally when the excitatory response arising from a centrally located bright region is fully augmented by a second dose of excitation from a dark surrounding 'doughnut'. But at the intersections in the Hermann pattern, the four local side-streets are white and they therefore contribute four portions of inhibition. This is apparently sufficient to cause the evanescent dark patches. In the regions of the white lines lying between two intersections, there will be only two portions of inhibition, and this appears to be inadequate to cause the observed effect. The illusion is quite symmetrical: with a pattern of white blocks separated by black streets, one sees white ghosts, and the illusion then derives from disturbances to the normal environment of off-centre/on-surround ganglions. An interesting extension of this illusion involves the use of a lay-out in which the blocks maintain their standard size while the widths of the still-parallel streets gradually increase across the pattern. The spots appear most clearly for a given street width, and this enables one to measure the actual diameter of a centre-surround visual field.

Let us leave the retina, and follow the 800,000 or so fibres of the optic nerve as they travel on towards the brain proper. Now that we have put all the complexity of the retinal circuitry behind us, can we look forward to an uneventful trip, with the ganglial axons synapsing directly onto neurons in the cortex? Again the answer is no. There is another station en route, and it will prove to be a veritable Clapham Junction! This is the thalamus, which acts as a sort of combination interchange and relay device for not only the visual system but also several of the other senses. The parts of the thalamus concerned with vision are known as the lateral geniculate nuclei, while the medial geniculate nuclei serve the sense of hearing in an analogous manner. There are two lateral geniculate nuclei, one serving each eye, and the dendrites of their neurons make synaptic contacts with the ganglial axons arriving from the retina via the optic chiasm. Sight is dependent on a mapping (of the retinal image) onto an area of the cortex, and this could hardly be possible if there were not also an intermediate mapping at the half-way house collectively provided by the lateral geniculate nuclei. That is what is observed, but we must bear in mind that there is a great degree of compaction, with the information from the 126 million receptors being channelled through just 800,000 fibres. Just as with the sense of touch, some regions are far more generously represented than others, and in the case of sight it is those few dozen cells at the centre of the fovea which get the most favoured treatment. In fact, there is about one fibre for each of these cells, but we must bear in mind that there is nevertheless some redistribution of the overall optical signal between them because of the action of the horizontal and amacrine cells.

What makes these thalamic structures so special is that they both send signals to the cortex and receive signals from the cortex. The former, onwardly travelling, transmission is mediated by the optic radiations, while the return route is via what are known as the corticofugal fibres. This arrangement allows the cortex to have a considerable degree of control over what is being sent to it! So it is at this point that we find the principle of negative feedback creeping into the picture again, just as it did with the sense of balance in Chapter 2. It is through this mechanism that the visual system becomes self-regulating, and it accomplishes that feat with a precision that would put even the most sophisticated camera to shame.

Two other related brain structures should be mentioned here. One is the reticular activating system, which lies at the top of the brain stem but which sends connecting fibres up to the lateral geniculate nuclei. It controls the degree of awareness, and it is in fact the responsible agency when we are aroused into consciousness. The other system, which has one of its two component parts in each cerebral hemisphere, is the superior colliculus. Many of the ganglial axons have collateral branches which are diverted off to the superior colliculus shortly before the lateral geniculate nuclei are reached. The connections between the retina and the superior colliculus are also such as to retain the (distorted) mapping, just as is observed in the 'main' route. The neurons of this second centre send their axons to a region of the thalamus known as the pulvinar, the size of which seems to provide a particularly good indication of a species' position on the evolutionary ladder. The role of the superior colliculus is to guide visual attention, and it does this not only by detecting sudden changes in the visual scene but also through the sense of hearing, because it also receives input from the audio system.

It turns out that there is a hierarchy of visual areas in the cortex, and the optic radiations connect the lateral geniculate nuclei to what is known as the primary visual area, which is also known as the striate cortex, a name deriving from the stratified appearance of its cross-section when examined by a microscope. (The Latin word *strea* means a fine streak.) The most important question is obviously: which part of the retina is connected (via the corresponding lateral geniculate nucleus) to which part of the striate cortex? And to be even more specific: does one again find a direct mapping? The answer is yes, but it is a qualified yes; the map is rather heavily distorted, with the fovea being far better represented than the peripheral areas of the eyes' fields of view. If the intention of Nature's grand design had been to furnish a homunculus with an internal screen, the plan has been a miserable fiasco. The pictures on the screen would make for very difficult viewing.

I should pause here, and describe how the existence of this map on the primary visual cortex has been verified. The experiments have been carried out not on humans but on our near relatives, monkeys, as well as on such other mammals as cats and various rodents. The subject is temporarily anaesthetized with its eyes open, and with the gaze thus fixed on a point straight ahead. The skin at the rear of the head is cut and drawn aside, and a small piece of the cranium is removed. The subject's vital functions are continuously monitored, and the breathing is assisted by a hydraulic device. (The brain itself has no pain centres, and the experimental animal is in no form of discomfort. I have been present at such experiments, and have seen the animal romping about in its cage the following day, quite unaffected by the measurements that have been made on it.) Finally, an electrical probe (i.e. an electrode) in the form of a very sharp metallic needle is inserted with great precision into the part of the striate cortex that is under investigation. When the electrode impales a neuron, the nerve impulses are detected as blips on a display screen, if the cell is active. To relieve the experimenters from the tedious job of keeping one eye on the screen while they are carrying out their adjustments, it is standard practice also to link the electrode's output to a loudspeaker, and the impulses are then heard as sharp clicks. Indeed, if the cell being monitored is maximally active, that is to say giving off impulses at a rate of a hundred per second or more, the loudspeaker emits sounds reminiscent of the firing of a machine-gun. But, in general, a cell will be 'silent' unless a light stimulus appears in just the correct region of the experimental animal's visual field. It is in this way that one can establish which point in the latter corresponds to which point in the striate cortex, and one finds that the visual field is represented in the cortex by a highly distorted map.

If this distorted map is not a screen provided for an internal presence, and it certainly is not, any more than the sensory somatic cortex is a relief map intended for braille-like reading, what precisely is it? To answer that question, we need to look somewhat more closely at the physical structure of the cortex, and at the spatial arrangement of the approximately one hundred thousand million cells it contains. We have already noted that the human cortex is a mere 3 millimetres thick, and that its numerous convolutions are simply a consequence of the fact that a sheet of cortical tissue almost 2,000 square centimetres in area has to be fitted into the relatively confined space within the cranium. When we think of a cross-section through the cortex, therefore, we are imagining a cut made at right angles to the surface of the cortex rather than to the skull. Such a cross-sectional cut reveals that the cortex is stratified, the layers lying parallel to the cortical surface. There are six of these, and they are traditionally numbered from the outside. Layer 4 is clearly seen to be further subdivided, the accepted nomenclature for the sub-divisions being 4A, 4B, 4C-alpha and 4C-beta. It is found that the axons from the lateral geniculate nuclei, which as we have seen collectively form the optic striations, do not enter the striate cortex at layer 6. This might seem to be the logical entry point since it is the first layer that an axon would encounter. Instead, the afferent axons penetrate past the bodies of the cells in layers 6 and 5, ultimately making synaptic contacts with the dendrites of cells in sub-layers 4A, 4C-alpha and 4C-beta.

The fibres of the optic striations are not the only afferent axons to enter a given area of the striate cortex. We have already noted that the white matter consists of axons belonging to cells in the cortex, and that these run along the inside of the latter and then re-enter it, to form synaptic contacts with other cells. The broad characteristics of these other connections can be summarized as follows: white-matter axons that carry information to cells in the same cerebral hemisphere tend to stem from layers 2 and 3; white-matter axons bound for the other hemisphere (via the previously mentioned corpus callosum) arise from cells in layers 2, 3, 4, 5 and 6; white-matter axons taking either of the latter two routes re-enter the cortex and make synaptic contacts with cells in layers 1, 2, 3, 5 and 6; axons passing from the cortex to the superior colliculus come from layer 5; and finally, axons which the cortex uses to dispatch information back to the lateral geniculate nuclei come from cells in layer 6. (If this recitation of a bunch of numbers sounds like a dull exercise, and I admit that it does, one ought to ponder the fact that I have just described the blue-print of our minds!)

This variety of routes, and the way in which things are organized according to a strict code of rules, indicates some underlying strategy. But what is it? A large hint at the answer to these questions was stumbled across by David Hubel and Torsten Wiesel in 1959 during studies of the monkey striate cortex. They were searching for the visual field corresponding to a particular cortical neuron they were monitoring, and they were doing this by shining patterns of light on a screen, using an ordinary slide projector. To their surprise the loudspeaker suddenly gave out the tell-tale machine-gun sound as a slide was being inserted into the projector. They soon realized that the cell in question was responding to a moving stimulus, the edge of the slide in fact, and they went on to demonstrate that a given cell of this type is maximally sensitive to a line lying at a particular angle and moving in a particular direction. Moreover, cells lying in areas adjacent to each other tend to respond best to line orientations that are almost parallel. There is, in other words, a systematic variation in the preferred angle as one moves about in the plane of the cortex. Hubel and Wiesel went on to show that there are other cells that respond best to more complicated patterns, which nevertheless still have a well-defined directionality. Thus some cells in a given area seem to prefer bars of light rather than edges between light and dark, while still others respond best to bars of dark on a light background. All of these directionally sensitive cells, for a given preferred orientation, lie in a column that runs at right angles to the cortical surface. But they do not lie in layer

4; it seems that the mechanism which underlies the directional sensitivity does not get under way in this input layer.

The answers are thus beginning to emerge. The incoming visual signals are subjected to an analysis in the striate cortex, and this breaks up the incoming picture into its component edges and corners, and also into its motions, if the observed scene is not static. No mention has been made of colour, but this too is analysed for. We saw earlier that information from a particular side of the fields of view of both eyes is fed to the same hemispherical lobe, this being made possible by the rearrangement of the optical fibres at the chiasm. Hubel and Wiesel found that there are slabs of neurons about half a millimetre in width in which signals from a given eye are processed. Passing from one of these slabs to the next, one finds that the dominance has shifted from one eye to the other. This arrangement provides the basis for depth perception.

This is a good point at which to take a look at another intriguing optical illusion. The first time I experienced this one, I thought that something was going seriously wrong with my sight. It happened on a railway journey, and I had been staring absent-mindedly out of the window for several minutes. The train stopped, and then it seemed to begin travelling slowly in the reverse direction, as if the train were on a slight incline and the driver had inadvertently released the brakes. But there were none of the other signs of motion, such as the usual clickety-click of the wheels moving over the joins between the rails. And, just as importantly, those objects on the station platform that lay at the periphery of my field of view were not passing out of sight. Yet, at the centre of my gaze there seemed to be a steady and inexorable drift. The overall effect was thus one of a continuous warping of the scene before my eyes.

Such 'motion after-effects', as they are called, are a subject of great interest to researchers in the field known as psychophysics, and they are the dynamical counterpart of the static adaptation (or habituation) phenomena that we encountered in the previous chapter when considering Kandel's studies of the sea hare. The existence of motion adaptation serves as a reminder that the steady state of operation of a system does not imply that all its component parts are quiescent; on the contrary, it reveals the beautifully orchestrated counterpoint that arises when the negative feedback effects which produce Mach bands in the simple illusion described earlier now have to contend with a scene that is continually changing. This better equips the eye to focus on the moving picture in front of it, but when the movement stops, the neuronal circuit takes several seconds to re-adapt and hence the temporary illusion that things are moving backwards. The detailed analysis is rather recondite, and we need not go into it here.

We ought, on the other hand, to consider the several experiments which revealed the extent of synapse modifiability, or synaptic plasticity as it is usually referred to in the scientific literature. Hubel and Wiesel, whose work on binocular vision we have already touched upon, extended their studies on monkeys to include an investigation of monocular deprivation in new-born kittens. They showed, in 1965, that the number of binocularity-serving neurons decreases if one of the eyelids is artificially held closed during the first few weeks of life. In 1970, Helmut Hirsch and D.N. Spinelli, and also Colin Blakemore and Grahame Cooper, extended this work to the rearing of kittens in conditions of severely restricted visual experience. These included confining the animals to rooms with black and white vertical stripes painted on the walls and equipping the animals with goggles which preferentially focussed on either vertical or horizontal lines.

About a decade later, Josef Rauschecker and Wolf Singer took this approach a step further and studied the visual cortex neurons of cats which had been made to wear goggles that were fitted with strongly astigmatic (i.e. distorting) lenses. The collective outcome of these brilliant pieces of experimentation has been the unequivocal demonstration that the development of the visual apparatus is influenced by visual experience; the assignment of cortical neurons to various visual specializations depends upon the tasks used in early training. A simple example of the consequences of these effects would be that kittens reared in an environment devoid of horizontal lines would become essentially blind to them; they would clumsily bump into objects decorated exclusively with lines painted in that orientation. We are aware of a similar principle in the case of the body's large externally visible features, of course. Regarding a muscle, for example, one has the saying: 'Use it or lose it'. In the case of the nerve cell there seems to be an augmenting principle of frugality because a neuron that is not used for one function tends to be commandeered for another purpose, as the experiments of Rauschecker and Singer clearly demonstrated.

Many of the well-known visual illusions involve the higher levels of our perceptual machinery, which we have not yet discussed. There is one other illusion that should be considered here, however, because it appears to be related to processes involving just a few neurons. It was discovered in 1965 by Celeste McCollough, and it is an example of what is known as a contingent after-effect. Because it involves colour, the visual detection of which has not yet been considered in this book, let me briefly review the most important facts. It turns out that there are three different types of cone cell in the retina. These receptors thus belong to one or other of the categories, red, yellow and blue, the different sensitivities arising from the presence of one of the corresponding light-sensitive pigments. These three colours are familiar to the artist, of course, and he refers to them by the adjective 'primary'. But when we turn to the subsequent processing of signals in the retina, we see that what happens in the ganglion cells bears little resemblance to what occurs on the painter's palette.

The three types of cone in our retinas (unless we are colour blind) put us in the class known as trichromats, together with monkeys and, somewhat surprisingly, goldfish. Cats are also nominally trichromats, but one of their cone types dominates the other two. Squirrels are dichromats, while birds and turtles, by dint of an oily covering to their receptors, are effectively polychromats. Credit for explaining the essentials of the mechanism of colour vision must be given to Ewald Hering. He saw pairs of colours as being in mutual competition, the groupings being red with green and blue with yellow. The circuitry which permits colour discrimination involves the feeding of the outputs of pairs of opposing receptors to what are called opponent colour cells, one synapse being excitatory and the other inhibitory. It is this arrangement which enables us to see a green colour even though we lack green-sensitive cones. The opponent colour cells have a spontaneous activity level even in the absence of signals from the receptors, and because there are both excitatory and inhibitory synapses for the latter, green can be detected as if by default, in a situation where there is incident light but light which lacks red. We have all experienced simple after-effects involving colours. Prolonged staring at a blue colour or a blue light, for example, produces a sensation of yellow for a few seconds after the blue stimulus is removed. These effects are readily explained on the basis of the above-mentioned existence of opponent cells, together with the fact that a receptor can become fatigued, and cease to emit signals, if it is subjected to protracted stimulation.

The McCollough illusion is clearly more complicated. One oscillates one's gaze between two conditioning patterns, one with alternating black and green bands drawn vertically (say) and the other with alternating black and red bands drawn horizontally. The period of imprinting should last at least three minutes and preferably as long as ten, one colour replacing the other every ten seconds or so. After the 'indoctrination', one shifts one's attention to a pattern of alternating black and white lines in which there are both vertical patches and horizontal patches. The vertical patches now appear to be faintly tinted with red while the horizontal patches seem to have taken on a tenuous green shade. The fact that this is no ordinary fatigue-related after-effect can be quickly established by rotating the test pattern through 90 degrees, thus transforming a vertical patch into a horizontal patch, and vice versa; it is still the vertical patches which appear red, and the horizontal patches green. It is as if the usual colour after-effect has become inseparably attached to the orientation of the training stimulus. When this intriguing phenomenon was first stumbled upon, it was taken to indicate the presence in the visual cortex of neurons which fire off nerve impulses only when they simultaneously receive inputs stemming from a correct orientation and a correct colour. This idea of doubly tuned neurons was later dropped when many other contingent after-effects were discovered; it was difficult to imagine so many different coincidence detectors being wired into the visual system's circuitry. The feature of the contingent after-effect which put researchers on the track of the presently favoured interpretation is its remarkable durability. An adaptive period of ten minutes produces an after-effect which can last for some hours, and the persistence can be stretched into weeks if the induction lasts half an hour or more. This is more suggestive of learning than of mere fatigue, and it appears that the training actually creates doubly tuned neurons.

Let us return to the interplay between the primary visual cortex and the lateral geniculate nuclei, and consider what could be called the visual system's *pièce de résistance*. This is the ocular–motor system, which serves us in many ways. We are, however, usually conscious of none of them and thus take them for granted. Let us demonstrate this by contrasting the performance of the eye under two different situations. Firstly, try moving your head slowly from side to side while holding your focus on a fixed object. The simplicity of this operation belies the complexity of the feedback mechanism that makes its accomplishment possible. Then let your eyes pan across the scene that you find in front of you when you look up from this text. There is no doubt in your mind that the stationary objects in your field of view are not moving, although your eyes or your head, or even both, are in motion. Now, by way of contrast, gently prod the outer corner of one of your eyes with the tip of a finger and note how easy it is to give a false impression of movement when the eye's normal mode of operation is interfered with. Finally, but this is much more difficult, because the very act of concentrating on a function that is normally achieved unconsciously will replace sublime ease by awkwardness, try to observe your eye movements as you read. The eyes scan each line in a rapid series of snatches, the associated motions being referred to as saccadic eye movements, or simply as saccades. They are accomplished by an interplay between the visual cortex, the superior colliculus, and the vestibular nuclei which lie at the top of the brain stem. And the smoothness of these movements, at least when we are unconscious of them, is the result of counteracting excitations and inhibitions.

Before we leave these feats of visual élan, we should touch on what is perhaps the most astounding of them all. Once again, fix your gaze on a convenient point in front of you and contemplate the following fact. The responses to things immediately to the right of the point on which you are focussing are channelled to the left extremity of the primary visual cortex at the rear of your left cerebral hemisphere. Things just to the left of your focal point, on the other hand, produce activity at the right edge of the primary visual cortex at the rear of your right hemisphere. Amazing! Two points in your visual field that might be separated by as little as a millimetre elicit responses in the cortex that are as far apart as they could be! How could things possibly fit so neatly together? Why do we not have a vertical seam running smack through the middle of every scene we look at, a seam reminiscent of the centre fold in a magazine's double-page spread?

The answer again lies in the two-way interplay between the lateral geniculate nuclei and the visual cortex, but there is another factor which is impressively subtle. The eyes are never perfectly stationary. They are perpetually panning from left to right and back again, over a fraction of a degree, one round trip consuming a mere tenth of a second. This effectively spreads the cortical 'image' over more neurons than would otherwise have been the case and the resulting interplay between the primary visual areas and the lateral geniculate nuclei, and between excitation and inhibition, produces perfect fusion of the two hemispherical representations and a seamless picture in the mind's eye. The small motions that help us to unconsciously achieve such a desirable result are just one component of a family of movements, the combined function of which is to stabilize vision under a variety of contingencies. Body motion, for example, elicits what is known as a vestibular reaction, which is induced by nerve signals from the semicircular canals in the ear's balance-producing centre. The outcome is called the vestibular–ocular reflex. Malfunction of this ear–eye cooperative effort can have highly disturbing consequences, as in the afflic-tion called vertigo, in which the patient experiencing an acute attack suffers a sudden loss of stimulation from the labyrinth in one of the ears.

In this chapter I have been deriding the concept of, or should one rather say the trap of, the homunculus, and the weapon of my choice has been the visual system and its lack of anything that could reasonably be looked upon as an internal screen. That the latter proposition could even be entertained is primarily due to the fact that the spatial position of objects in one's visual field is related (in an albeit distorted fashion) to the spatial position of neural responses in both the lateral geniculate nuclei and the primary visual cortex. Had I chosen the sense of hearing, the untenability of the internal-observer idea would have been more obvious, for it would have required us to put up with sounds in the head. We are fortunately spared such a burden, and when noises are heard internally they usually send us to the doctor. In the auditory cortex, it is frequencies which are 'mapped', different tones giving rise to responses in different cortical locations.

The word 'internally', as used in the preceding paragraph, reminds us of an important feature of perception: the things perceived, be they sights or sounds, are not merely registered at their points of detection, namely the receptor neurons in our eyes and ears. They seem to be observed 'out there', as an integral part of the visual and audile environment. This is a profound point, and one which, I feel, tells us much more about the mind than might at first appear to be the case. In the next chapter, indeed, I will show that much of what might be interpreted as an internal presence, somewhere up there in our heads, is better described as the ability of our nervous systems to correlate the different impressions that our senses give us of our surroundings. And we will see that a key feature of this correlation is that it relieves us of the need to internalize the things and sounds that are out there; we can get on perfectly well by leaving them where they belong.

Yet it cannot be denied that we do form pictures in our minds, and we have little difficulty in re-creating melodies and other sounds. The novelist Catherine Cookson has written of the way in which her stories are fabricated: she gives a vivid description of sessions in a darkened room in which the plots seem to unfold before her eyes. A simple mental quiz serves as a reminder that we too use such re-created images all the time. What do the following countries have in common: France, West Germany, Austria, Liechtenstein and Italy (a US equivalent of this question would ask what the states of Missouri, Illinois, Indiana, Ohio, West Virginia, Virginia and Tennessee have in common)? I hope that the reader will pause at this point and actually attempt to solve one of these questions, if the answer did not come immediately. The solution is that the five countries specified all share a border with Switzerland (and the states all impinge upon Kentucky). The point of posing this little conundrum was to demonstrate the involvement of mental images in much of our thinking, since I doubt that many will have solved it abstractly. Not only is the existence of our mental pictures beyond question, it is even the case that one can measure the rate at which we can manipulate them. In 1971, Roger Shepard and Jacqueline Metzler achieved just that by asking a number of people to compare two mutually disoriented pictures of three-dimensional objects and state whether they were the same. The answers came slower as the offset angle increased, and these experimenters reached the conclusion that we can rotate pictures in our minds at a rate of about 60 degrees per second.

How do we accomplish such a feat? What, indeed, is the mechanism of mentation? What is happening, down at the level of the neurons, when we have thoughts, when we conjure up the face of an absent friend, when we recall a piece of music, when we remember the name of something? Until recently, such speculations belonged to the realm of philosophy; these issues occupied poets more than they occupied scientists. But in the past couple of decades the situation has changed dramatically. An understanding of the processes of cognition and association now seems to lie within our grasp, as we shall discover in the next chapter.

● Summary

The brain functions in a directional manner, information flowing inward from the various senses and outward to the muscles and glands. In earlier times, the control was imagined to be exerted by a sort of inner being, the homunculus, and it is still easy to fall into the trap of invoking internal screens which provide conjectured decision-making centres with sensory pictures. We now know that there are no such intermediaries, however, and that the route from stimulus to response merely passes through a series of complex neural processors. The homunculus has been exorcised; the machine requires no internal operator, because despite its sophistication it is nevertheless simply driven by its environment.

5

The enchanted loom
Neural networks

Should we continue to watch the scheme, we should observe after a time an impressive change which suddenly accrues. In the great head-end which has been mostly darkness spring up myriads of twinkling stationary lights and myriad trains of moving lights of many different directions. It is as though activity from one of those local places which continued restless in the darkened main-mass suddenly spread far and wide and invaded all. The great topmost sheet of the mass, that where hardly a light had twinkled or moved, now becomes a sparkling field of rhythmic flashing points with trains of travelling sparks hurrying hither and thither. The brain is waking and with it the mind is returning. It is as if the Milky Way entered upon some cosmic dance. Swiftly the head-mass becomes an enchanted loom where millions of flashing shuttles weave a dissolving pattern, always a meaningful pattern though never an abiding one; a shifting harmony of subpatterns. Now as the waking body rouses, subpatterns of this great harmony of activity stretch down into the unlit tracks of the stalk-piece of the scheme. Strings of flashing and travelling sparks engage the length of it. This means that the body is up and rises to meet its waking day.

CHARLES SCOTT SHERRINGTON
Man on his Nature

It is interesting to note that two of the major areas of biological research, the study of organisms and of the brain, are currently facing similar problems. In each of these areas we now have considerable knowledge of the way things work at both the microscopic and the naked-eye scales, but what happens in between is not so well understood. Thus, in the case of organisms, we now know much about genes and the way in which they direct protein manufacture, and much about the structure of cells and tissues. And at the other end of the scale, which deals with the interactions between entire organisms, there is Darwin's competitive principle to guide us. Between these levels, however, we are confronted by the problem of development, and by a lack of understanding of how the numerous cycles of cell division lead to tissue differentiation. It is not known how a single fertilized egg cell gives rise to a whole organism, with limbs, muscles, organs and nervous system, or with roots, stem and leaves, whichever the case may be. Similarly, in the case of the brain, there is reasonably complete knowledge of the chemistry of neurotransmitters and of the structure and physiology of individual neurons. And again one sees a gratifying measure of progress in our understanding at the multi-unit level. The structure of human society has been fruitfully explored, while on a more modest scale, individual brains assist one another in the various forms of counselling. But here, too, we have met an impasse at a stage lying in between; it has proved difficult to understand the properties of assemblies of neurons, which lie at the sub-brain level of organization.

It is no accident that these two biological problems have been coupled in this way, for they are both related to the interactions between cells. And these interactions involve intercellular signalling, in both cases. A cell does not have to be a neuron in order to pass messages to its surrounding kin. The typical cell is, indeed, constantly secreting all manner of chemical molecules, and these are candidates for absorption by other cells. Moreover, such processes are not always just local affairs. Non-neuronal cells that touch one another often communicate through special junctions that can be regarded as counterparts of the synapse, but there is also evidence of long-range signalling. And the distinction becomes even more blurred by the fact that neurons, conversely, are not limited to synaptic transfer as a means of dispatching information; the main task of some neurons is to release chemicals into circulation, so that these can reach targets that might lie in relatively remote locations. (The importance of this mechanism is underlined by the psychosomatic, i.e.

brain-to-body, illnesses that can result when it malfunctions.)
In a deeper sense, therefore, the two problems are simply part
of the same broader issue. My immediate concern here, however,
is the synapse-mediated interactions between groups of neurons.

In the preceding chapters, I have described the layout of the
neural pathways which carry nerve impulses from the various
receptor neurons to the primary areas of the cortex. I have also
touched on the arrangement of the nerve fibres which constitute
the brain's white matter, but the references to that central
component were fleeting and qualitative. It is now necessary
to take a closer look, and try to discover how the cortex and its
white matter contrive to produce what we call the mind. We
have already encountered a number of cortical regions which
have been identified as the recipients of nerve fibres from the
sensory organs, and in the preceding chapter a more detailed
description was given for the case of vision. If one calculates
the total number of fibres entering the cortex from the senses,
and compares this with the total number of white-matter fibres
which carry signals from one part of the cortex to another, one
soon realizes that the latter class of connections constitutes the
great majority. As Valentino Braitenberg has remarked, the
cortex appears to expend most of its effort 'talking' to itself.
And on the basis of his own anatomical investigations, he was
able to show that the mouse cortex, for example, displays a
roughly similar distribution between internally and externally
directed connections. The mouse must also manage a fair bit
of cogitation, therefore. But if the cortex talks to itself, what on
earth is it saying?

We have arrived at the most central of all questions regarding
the brain because, as Niels Steensen had anticipated those 300
years ago, there is nothing in the nervous system that is likely
to play a more fundamental role than the cellular interactions
mediated by the white matter. It is thus clear that the path
to the understanding of the mind lies through a proper grasp
of the functioning of this vast mesh of interconnected cells,
alias Charles Sherrington's Enchanted Loom; what in today's
parlance is referred to as the neural network.

In 1969, admittedly writing about the cerebellum rather
than the cortex, John Eccles boldly compared the brain with
a computer. One often hears the comparison made the other

way around, of course, the computer being referred to as an electronic brain. But how good are these comparisons? There is no denying that there is a superficial resemblance. Both brain and computer perform the functions of information processing, storage and retrieval. But a closer look at the details reveals important differences.

The operation of the electronic digital computer, invented in the late 1930s by John Vincent Atanasoff, is based on the binary system, with its two options, one and zero, which can be thought of as representing yes and no. In terms of circuitry, or hardware as it is called, these are provided by appropriate switching elements. Although a neuron is capable of a more graduated response, let us allow that it too can be looked upon as a binary device, and its state characterized as active (i.e. impulse-emitting) or inactive. When we look at the relevant numbers, however, we see large differences between computer circuits and brain circuits. A typical large computer has about a hundred million transistors in its printed circuits, whereas the brain comprises some hundred thousand million neurons. Moreover, in a typical computer each transistor is usually joined to three or four other transistors, whereas the average neuron enters into upwards of ten thousand synaptic contacts with its brethren. Taking these two factors together, we see that the brain enjoys an advantage over the computer to the tune of about a million times as many inter-unit connections. What the digital computer loses on the roundabouts it gains on the swings, however, because the switching time of a transistor can be as brief as a thousand millionth of a second (i.e. a nanosecond), while the neuron can only manage about a thousandth of a second (i.e. a millisecond).

By far the most significant difference between the electronic digital computer and the brain lies in their mode of operation. The digital computer performs its functions in a serial fashion, consecutively following the steps encoded in the appropriate program and in the sequence thereby dictated. The operation of such a device is therefore constantly subject to a sort of bottleneck. It is this von Neumann bottleneck, which takes its name from John von Neumann who was the first to draw attention to its existence, that is now seen to be the most important characteristic of what I have been referring to as the electronic digital computer. It is interesting to note that human logic, too, is sequential, so it is not surprising that we have designed our digital computers in this manner. (The popular parlour game, *Twenty Questions*, is essentially the sequential elimination of alternatives by a series of binary choices; each question must be answered only by a 'yes' or a 'no'.) The cortex's various neural networks function in a quite different way, with numerous steps being carried out simultaneously and in parallel with one another. This enables the brain to perform its 'calculations' within as few as a hundred of its response times, or about a tenth of a second. In this respect, it leaves the digital computer standing; the computer finishes a very poor second. The brain has to perform this well, of course. If it were not able to supply answers essentially without delay, its possessor would be at a potentially lethal disadvantage. Our simian ancestors would not have lasted long without the ability to recognize instantly their predators, and any car driver is aware of the constant demands on his or her reflexes. A von Neumann bottleneck in the context of the brain's component parts could well prove to be fatal.

In citing the conjectured similarity between brain and computer, as published by Eccles, am I therefore wide of the mark? The answer is no, in fact, for there is a trump card which I will play on his behalf. The machine that he had in mind was not a digital computer but an analog computer. The mechanical version of this device, invented by Vannevar Bush in the 1930s, was known as the differential analyser. For our purposes here, we need only consider its electrical embodiment, which works in a way that is quite different from that of its digital counterpart. Its circuit represents by electrical currents and voltages, rather than by numbers, the properties being simulated. At a typical moment during such an analog computation, the great majority of the machine's wires are actually carrying currents, and the various dials and indicator lamps give one a remarkably realistic feel for the physical attributes of the system being studied. In an investigation of the weather, for example, one dial could show temperature while others display wind speed and precipitation. After using digital computation for several years, I enjoyed a brief period of analog simulation in the early 1960s, and was sorry to witness the subsequent decline of these devices. What made them obsolescent was their lack of precision; one did well to work with three significant figures on an analog computer, whereas sixteen-figure accuracy is no special achievement with a digital machine. It is ironic that the attention currently being paid to the brain's own circuits should have rekindled interest in the analog machine, albeit in a rather different form.

The digital machine, then, is accurate, incredibly fast in terms of its individual computational steps, but woefully wasteful of time because those steps have to queue up to be executed. (It would be remiss of me to imply that the designers of digital machines are not aware of this inadequacy; they are, on the contrary, now turning to massively parallel arrangements of sequentially operating units.) The analog machine, on the other hand, is not very accurate, but it is commendably efficient because many of the different steps of a calculation can be carried out in unison. The working of the cortex's various circuits resembles that of the analog machine; at any instant, millions of neurons are simultaneously carrying currents in their dendrites, and a fraction of them are, as a consequence, dispatching impulses out along their axons. It is this massive parallelism which enables the brain to 'compute' so rapidly. And the brain turns to advantage what was almost the death-knell of the analog machine. Its individual computations do not need to be particularly accurate; with so many neurons sharing the burden, the individual inaccuracies have no significance. In fact, the brain goes one better than its man-made cousin. Unlike the traditional analog machine, and indeed the von Neumann computer, it can tolerate the failure of some of its components and still continue to function. It is thus said to be robust, and to degrade gracefully. It computes reliably despite the fact that it is composed of unreliable components, whereas a serially executed program aborts the moment one of its steps fails. And the neural network is remarkably sophisticated when it comes to the making of decisions. These are the qualities that have inspired the designers of the latter-day analog computers, and they have given these machines a new lease of life. The new machines are indeed referred to as neural computers. The brain has thus become both the target and the inspiration for computer science; it has paved the way for a two-way traffic that is as vigorous as it is dedicated.

The key feature of the neural network is the manner in which it stores information. Experience is stored through the biochemical and structural changes occurring at the synaptic level, but this must not be taken to imply that a given memory is localized to a specific synapse, or even to a few synapses lying close to one another. There is actually an interesting numerical result which could lead to that erroneous conclusion. Estimates of memory capacity based on mental performance put this at about ten thousand million individual 'bits' of information. (The term 'bit', as employed here, should not be confused with the colloquial use of that word. It has a quite specific meaning, and is short for 'binary digit'; it implies a choice between yes and no.) This estimate of ten thousand million bits is not higher than the total number of neurons in the brain, and it is far less than the total number of synaptic contacts. So a memory storage system based on binary circuit elements, that is to say switching units with only two switch conditions, is a possibility. But there is plenty of evidence that memory is still retained in damaged brains, albeit with diminished resolution or definition. There is impairment of memory in these cases, but it does not appear to remove individual memories. It is rather a case of memories being somewhat harder to recall. This suggests delocalization.

One of the first penetrating studies in this topic was undertaken by Karl Lashley, who experimented with rats in the second quarter of this century. He found that ability to perform previously learned tasks diminished in rough proportion to the amount of damage to the cortex. Similarly, our mental capacities suffer a general decline, because of the inevitable daily loss of about 50,000 brain cells, but individual memories are not switched off like lights in a building. These facts have led to some speculation that memory functions in a manner analogous to holography, the photographic technique in which the record of each detail of an object is distributed across the whole of the recording film or plate, an image of the original being regenerated in response to a specific stimulating input. If part of the photographic record, called a hologram, is removed, the entire object can still be reconstructed, but with less resolution; the image is not quite as sharp as it was originally. The experiments of Wilder Penfield in the 1960s are of considerable significance in this context. He studied the initiation of memory retrieval during operations in which the temporal lobe of the brain was exposed while the patient was fully conscious. (These operations were, of course, being undertaken for medical reasons.) He found that mild activation of certain regions of the cortex by a small electrode (i.e. a small electrical conductor) caused the patient to relive a previous experience in great circumstantial detail, as if a particular memory file was being opened and a tape recording from it read out. The access key to the file, which Penfield called the experiential centre, appeared to lie in the hippocampus.

The hologram analogy is, however, only a loose one. There are no rays of light flashing around in the head. It is a useful analogy only in that it indicates how records of the past can be stored in a distributed, rather than a localized, fashion. This inspiration has in fact given birth to a family of computers known as distributed array processors. With many of its neurons similarly functioning in parallel, at any instant, the brain would seem to be a likely candidate for the role of a sophisticated version of such a device, and it is to this proposition that we now turn. But I must first forestall a possible source of confusion. The technique used to investigate this issue has frequently been what is referred to as computer simulation, by which one means numerical simulation with the aid of a digital computer. It might sound strange, not to say invalid, that one should use a computer to demonstrate that part of the brain works like a computer. There is no conflict here, however. After all, meteorology enthusiasts now study our atmosphere by computer simulation, with the hope of understanding and possibly even predicting the weather, but their activities do not imply that they believe our gaseous environment to be a massive computer. The study, by computer simulation, of brain function is now an established field of research and one could be guardedly optimistic that the brain models now being investigated are reasonable facsimiles of the genuine article. At its best, the computer software (i.e. computer programming) in this research area does a remarkably good job of mimicking what could be called, by comparison, the real brain's biological wetware. Let us therefore take a look at the way in which this field of research has developed.

REAL NEURON

IDEALIZED NEURON

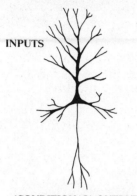

INPUTS

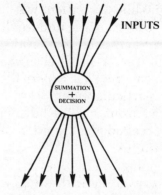

INPUTS

SUMMATION
+
DECISION

(CONDITIONAL) OUTPUTS

(CONDITIONAL) OUTPUTS

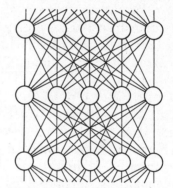

REAL NEURAL
NETWORK

IDEALIZED NEURAL
NETWORK

An individual neuron (above left) acquires information through the synaptic contacts that other neurons make with its dendrites. It sums this information at its central region, the soma, and emits one or more nerve pulses out along its axon if that sum exceeds a certain threshold value. A useful idealized picture (above right) thus sees the neuron as an integrating unit with a conditional output. The lower left figure corresponds to a microscope image of a real neural network, in which differential staining has rendered only 5 to 10 per cent of the neurons visible. The figure has been further simplified by the fact that only one type of cell (known as a pyramid neuron) is shown. In one idealized picture of such a network (lower right) the cells are imagined to populate a series of layers, with every cell in one layer being connected to every cell in the succeeding layer. Many other geometries have also been investigated. The study of such networks is still in its infancy, and it remains unclear which properties of the neural assembly are the most important.

A good starting point is the remarkably prescient work of William James, who, already at the end of the nineteenth century, was describing brain mechanisms that are hauntingly reminiscent of what today are referred to as neural networks. James had no access to a computer, of course, but this did not prevent him from making remarkably good guesses as to how the different parts of the brain interact so as to form associations. His *Psychology: A Briefer Course*, published in 1890, contains diagrams which could easily be mistaken for those used as illustrations in the numerous neural network articles which began to appear almost a hundred years later. James was a mechanist. He would have no truck with spiritual views of the mind. 'Our inner faculties', he observed, 'are adapted in advance to the features of the world in which we dwell. Mind and world, in short, have evolved together and in consequence are something of a mutual fit.' He argued, in other words, that the brain is not designed to handle abstract thoughts; it is a supremely pragmatic machine, fabricated to ensure survival. 'Objects are associated,' he wrote in another passage, 'not ideas.' James also foreshadowed the work of Donald Hebb when he concluded that 'when two brain processes are active together or in immediate succession, one of them, on reoccurring tends to propagate its excitement into the other.' We have only to replace 'brain processes' with 'neurons' to obtain a learning rule that is essentially that of Hebb.

The next important development was the seminal demonstration, by Warren McCulloch and Walter Pitts in 1943, that an assembly of neurons functioning in the on–off fashion dictated by their thresholds is capable in principle of matching any stimulus to any response. The neurons in their idealized circuits summed up the various inputs to their dendrites and sent an all-or-nothing output impulse along their axons if and only if the net input excitation attained the threshold value. In the McCulloch–Pitts model, a piece of information was represented by a pattern of ons and offs, this being the case for both the input and the output. So one of their circuits could be said to transform one pattern into another; it is what is generally referred to as an input–output machine. (Possibly the most famous non-biological example of such a device was the 'Enigma' machine built by Alan Turing and his associates for code-breaking during the

Second World War.) In the context of the real brain, the input pattern would come from the senses, of course, while the output pattern, in default of there being a homunculus to inspect it, would have to have some significance for the region to which it was dispatched.

We have already touched upon the next milepost, namely Donald Hebb's monumental guess in 1949 that synapses are modifiable and that this imbues the neural network with the capacity for remembering. Nothing is lost, therefore, when the network is deprived of input patterns and, as one could loosely put it, all the lights are turned off. Just as the path through the landscape taken by a river is not forgotten if the river dries up during a drought, so are the myriad simultaneous neural routes corresponding to a given input pattern stored for future use. And the beauty of the system is that the loss of a fraction of these routes can be tolerated, just as the clogging up of a few tributaries does not change the course of a river. The neural network computes reliably despite its dependence on unreliable components.

The 1950s saw the McCulloch–Pitts idea develop into hardware. Marvin Minsky built a neural network in 1954, its 400 vacuum tubes performing as idealized neurons, and three years later Frank Rosenblatt called his own version of the device a perceptron. One intended application of this machine reveals the reason for choosing that particular name; shown an object, the machine would ideally oblige by identifying it. It was the hope of Rosenblatt that the device would be able to perceive. The perceptron effectively had just two layers of cells, one for input and the other for output, and each cell in the input layer was electrically connected to every cell in the output layer. By analogy with the real brain, we can refer to these connections as synapses. The perceptron was 'trained' by presenting it with correlated pairs of input and output patterns and modifying the strengths (i.e. the transmission efficiencies) of the various synaptic connections, in such a way that junctions that were contributing to a correct pattern match were 'rewarded' while those that were in discord with that goal were 'punished', that is to say weakened. Adjusting the hoard of connections between the layers was a difficult and tedious undertaking, however, and in 1969 Minsky and his colleague Seymour Papert declared that the perceptron concept is intrinsically flawed; some input–output matchings lie beyond the network's capabilities, so not all logical operations can be handled, and if one tries to improve the situation by making the circuit more complicated, it loses its ability to learn from its mistakes because there is no longer an unambiguous indication as to which synapses are to be strengthened and which weakened.

It later transpired that the Minsky–Papert reasoning suffered from two important shortcomings, neither of which reflects negatively on these inspired pioneers. In choosing binary units for their circuits they were, after all, only following the McCulloch–Pitts wisdom that the essence of the nervous system lies in its ability to make decisions. But on closer inspection one finds that the typical neuron functions in a more subtle manner; although it is an undeniable fact that no impulses are emitted from a cell if the voltage at its body (somatic) region does not exceed the threshold value, it is also the case that the rate of impulse emission depends upon the amount by which that threshold is surpassed. This turns out to be of great importance; it considerably increases the network's discriminatory powers. The other critical deficit of the Rosenblatt–Minsky–Papert perceptron lay in its restriction to just a couple of cell layers. As it turned out, the remedy was emerging at about the same time, but in a different scientific discipline. In 1957, a mathematician named Andrey Kolmogorov, who had probably never even heard of neural networks, proved a theorem that nevertheless struck right at the heart of their mode of operation. Although his attention was directed towards something altogether more abstract (for the record, it was an issue known as Hilbert's Thirteenth Problem), the theorem was directly applicable to the perceptron, and it showed that the desired universality of input–output handling can always be achieved if the network comprises three or more layers of cells. Unfortunately, the theorem does not give any recipe as to how one should go about calculating which synaptic strengths would produce which pairs of input–output correlations. Kolmogorov's efforts thus appear as an isolated episode in the story, but one which, in retrospect at least, must be seen as a major milepost.

The early 1960s saw a marked increase of activity, with several people trying to find the elusive prescription for determining the synaptic strengths of a network designed to handle given sets of inputs and outputs. Their approaches are too involved to be covered here, and a full roll-call of names would require several pages. In their hands, the rules of the game gradually took shape, and in some cases machines which emulate some of the brain's functions were actually built. Igor Aleksander's 'Wisard II', for example, is a machine which can recognize complicated patterns, such as human faces. Its input field consists of a 512 by 512 field of binary pixels (i.e. picture elements rather reminiscent of the dots that make up a newspaper picture), and these are connected to a series of layers comprising tens of thousands of 'neurons'. Not surprisingly, this sort of device tends to excite the interest of the police, because once the network has been adjusted by exposing it to a large number of matching faces and names, it becomes much more than a mere filing system; shown an approximate likeness of an individual, as drawn from a description given by a witness, the device rapidly homes in on the person the sketch most closely resembles. And it does this in a manner that is totally objective. Teuvo Kohonen has demonstrated similar capacities in his extensive simulations; after it has learned a number of faces, one of his models can be shown just the eyes and nose (say) of an individual and instantly indicates to whom they belong. Such identification of the whole upon confrontation with a part is known as association. And networks of this type can even generalize; shown a novel stimulus, they can successfully categorize it. Because of this, a neural network could be said to be intuitive.

These neural networks, with their massive parallelism, function in a way that is different in virtually every respect from a von Neumann computer. They are trained rather than programmed, gradually developing expertise through exposure to typical examples of correlations, that is through matches of cause and effect. And because there is no symbolism involved, it is not easy to see where in their vast array of intercellular connections this expertise resides, for it is distributed throughout the system. But they learn from experience, which is of course the hallmark of intelligence. And their response is essentially immediate. They do not have to ruminate, as it were, the way the von Neumann bottleneck forces a sequential computer to

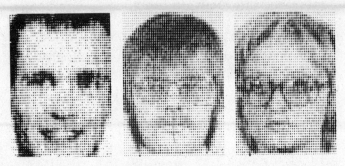

The brain's vast mesh of interconnected cells, the neural network, stores its memories by distributing each of them over many synaptic contacts. The latter are slightly modified each time a new item is deposited, and the network can thereby hold many memories superimposed on one another. The stored memories are robust in that they can survive the loss of a fraction of the synapses, and because the network functions in a parallel manner, recall is very rapid. The network can also associate; presented with a sufficiently large part of one of its stored memories, it will reconstruct the entire item. In the computer simulation of this process shown here, Teuvo Kohonen has stored digitalized versions of the pictures of fifty faces, three of which appear above. The pictures reproduced below demonstrate the ability of his 5120-element network to recall perfectly despite being presented with incomplete cues.

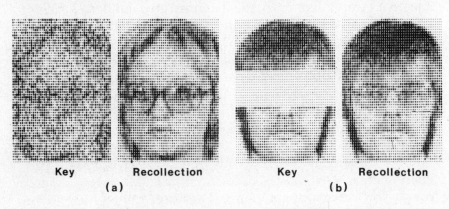

Key	Recollection	Key	Recollection
(a)		(b)	

do. The best match to incomplete information is rapidly found and it is literally produced at the bottom line, which is to say at the output layer of cells.

There is one type of model neural network that must be given special mention here. Not because it is superior to the others that have been described, for it has indeed several obvious flaws, but because it pares neural networks down to their bare essentials. And the added incentive for describing it is its possible implication in the phenomenon of dreaming, which will resurface in the next chapter. The model was first put forward by John Hopfield in 1982, and because it enjoyed the advantage of being readily understandable it won instant and massive popularity. Hopfield had, in fact, put the capstone on a succession of developments that had been underway since at least 1950, when W. Ross Ashby suggested that activity patterns in the brain's networks will always tend towards a condition of dynamical stability, which he referred to as ultrastability. A hint as to what such states might look like was provided four years later by Brian Cragg and H. Nevill Temperley when they drew an analogy between neurons in a network and atoms in a piece of crystal. Their point was that these units can be active (and emit nerve impulses) or inactive, while the tiny elementary magnet that is associated with an atom (because of certain properties of its orbiting electrons, which we need not go into here) can point in either of two opposite directions. And just as a neuron influences other neurons by passing signals to them, so does an atom exert forces on its neighbours. The overall magnetic state of a crystal is determined by the orientations of all the elementary magnets, and the strong form of magnetism known as ferromagnetism arises when they all point in the same direction. (Although this was of no concern to Cragg and Temperley, the analogous state in a neural network, when all the cells are firing, corresponds to an epileptic seizure.) Cragg and Temperley speculated that patterns resembling a patchwork quilt would arise in which some groups of neurons were active while others were quiescent, and they suggested that such a pattern, elicited by an external stimulus, should be stable against any spontaneous random activity on the part of the individual neurons, and thus provide a permanent memory of the stimulus. The existence of corresponding domain patterns in magnetic materials had already been established, and their persistence had been observed experimentally. (Some readers will recall seeing such domains revealed by iron filings.)

In 1975 David Sherrington and Scott Kirkpatrick showed that the scope for forming stable domain patterns in an assembly of atoms was much greater than had been suspected, and when Hopfield examined the neuronal counterpart he discovered that a similar thing applied. Invoking Hebb's postulate, which was considered in Chapter 3, he modified the synaptic strengths in his model cellular assembly by considering each pair of neurons in turn and making the synapse more excitatory if both neurons were active, or more inhibitory if one was active while the other was inactive. Hopfield found that this strategy produces just the sort of dynamic stability that had been hypothesized thirty years earlier. There are several obvious objections to the model, however. One concerns the interneuron interactions. They are too similar to the forces between atoms, which, because of the rules discovered by Isaac Newton, have to be symmetrical; the force on atom A due to atom B must equal A's force on B. Similarly, in Hopfield's model, each neuron sends a synaptic connection to every other neuron and receives a synaptic connection from every other neuron, and the strengths of the two connections which link any given pair of neurons are equal. Although there is anatomical evidence for a certain degree of such reciprocity of connections, it is less obvious that pairs of counter-running connections would have the same strength. And it seems doubtful, in any case, that the reciprocity could be a global feature of the cortex. Even more serious is the fact that the model requires a given neuron to make excitatory contacts with some neurons and inhibitory contacts with others; it is usually the case that all contacts made by an individual neuron are of a single type. Perhaps worst of all, synapses can be forced, during the model's learning phase, to change from being excitatory to inhibitory, or vice versa, and this is biologically quite impossible. The insights provided by Hopfield's model are nevertheless invaluable, and if his neurons are regarded as conceptual (and perhaps multicellular) entities the conflict with the brain's anatomy might turn out to be unimportant.

There is one additional characteristic of Hopfield networks which should be mentioned. They show a propensity for getting trapped into states they were not taught. These states are usually composites that are made up of fragments from various valid memories. Evocative of the chimeras one encounters in mythology, they are also reminiscent of the humorous hybrids

that arise in the popular card game 'Tops and Tails'; the upper
half of a geisha girl incongruously acquires a Scottish kilt, and so
on. Perhaps these are merely the Hopfield network's punishment
for riding roughshod over so much anatomy, but there is a more
intriguing possibility: they might be the spurious states which
Francis Crick and Graeme Mitchison suggest could provide
the motivation for the dreaming state. I will return to that
proposition in the next chapter, and consider dreaming in the
broader context of brain rhythms.

In 1986, David Rumelhart, Geoffrey Hinton and Ronald
Williams published a powerful new learning procedure for
multilayer neural networks. It was in fact simultaneously and
independently announced by these three scientists, and by David
Parker, and yet again by Yann Le Cun. (Paul Werbos had,
indeed, described essentially the same approach in his doctoral
thesis, twelve years earlier.) Known as the back-propagation
algorithm, it is simply a method of adjusting the strengths of
all the synaptic connections so as to produce the desired output
for a given input. There is a whimsical little analogy that I see
in my mind's eye every time I think of this back-propagation
scheme. The scenario has an emperor and his retinue on a golf
course, with the monarch trying gamely to get the ball into
the cup. The potentate is an utter duffer, however, because he
cannot see that he must change the strength and direction of
his putt in order to hole out. But no one dares to inform him
of his error, so the obsequious minions scurry about, changing
the landscaping of the green until one of the balls drops neatly
into the hole. This analogy fails to capture another important
feature of the neural network, however, in that the latter involves
many alternative routes that are simultaneously traversed. The
emperor would have to putt a host of balls, all at the same
time.

The Werbos–Parker–Le Cun–Rumelhart–Hinton–Williams
algorithm is essentially a prescription for such re-landscaping
in the context of an array of synaptic connections, and it is
a particularly efficient one at that. One begins by presenting
the network's input layer with a given pattern, the synapses
initially all having roughly (but not exactly) equal strengths,
and one compares the resultant output with what would have
been obtained had the input–output correlation already been

perfect. The deviations from the desired values, which of course can be regarded as errors, are then used to adjust the synaptic strengths, the degree of modification to any particular synapse being proportional not only to the error it was involved with but also to the 'current' it was carrying. The latter point is an important one; it ensures that the 'blame' for an error is apportioned according to the culpability. These error-related adjustments are made in the reverse direction, starting at the output layer of cells and working back towards the input layer, whereafter the entire process is repeated until the match is perfect. This is done for a variety of input–output pairs, and the network thereby gradually acquires its expertise.

The application of this approach to a wide variety of problems, many of them not strictly related to brain function, became extremely popular in the mid 1980s. It acquired the general designation 'Parallel distributed processing', and the back-propagation scheme is only one of several possible computational strategies. The word 'parallel' could be misleading in that it might suggest the literal interpretation of 'routes which never converge'. The most important feature of the routes involved in neural networks is, on the contrary, that they display a high degree of both divergence and convergence. It has been estimated that every cell in the human cortex can be reached from every other cell by a route which traverses as few as five or six synapses. And because each cell makes upwards of ten thousand synaptic contacts with its neighbours, the number of different possible (short) routes between any two cells is enormous. The important word is thus seen to be 'distributed', and the advantage of this arrangement is the same as that embodied in the piece of folk wisdom that advises against putting all of one's eggs in a single basket. Another useful analogy derives from what happens to the investor's capital: it diverges into a variety of financial enterprises, the actual distribution of the money being adjusted to give a hopefully optimal return, and it subsequently converges into his or her bank account. The neuronal counterpart of this principle therefore enjoys a great advantage over mere parallelism, which would only offer the lesser merit of many individual routes sharing the load.

One of the early, and certainly spectacular, successes with

this new approach was scored in 1987 by Terrence Sejnowski and Charles Rosenberg. They trained a neural network to read English text by presenting it with matched pairs of letter groupings and the phonemes of which spoken words are composed. The groups comprised strings of seven successive letters (and spaces, so that the beginnings and endings of words could also be handled). Presenting the input layer with just a single letter would not have worked, of course, because the network would then not have had a chance of distinguishing between the different sounds for (say) a, as in mate, pat, walk, and father; the letters had to be put in context. This network, which Sejnowski and Rosenberg called NETtalk, has a few thousand synaptic connections serving a few hundred neurons. The latter are distributed amongst just three layers: the input layer, a middle layer, and the output layer. Such a three-layer arrangement has rapidly established itself as the preferred configuration, and the middle level is usually referred to as the hidden layer. It is this layer that holds the key to such a network's remarkable discriminatory powers; it captures the correlations (i.e. the associations) between the various features of the input.

In NETtalk, the phoneme data appearing at the output layer are fed into a speech synthesizer. I will never forget the first time I heard a tape recording of this network's efforts to learn how to pronounce the words of a text it was presented with. During the early stages of training, the machine managed nothing better than a continuous stream of gibberish, but its performance steadily improved, and in the end it was pronouncing better than 90 per cent of the words correctly. The pitch of the synthesizer had been adjusted to mimic that of a female child's vocal cords, and listening to that surrogate tiny tot, fumbling at the outset, but with a voice that became increasingly more confident as time wore on, was a most eerie experience. It was also a most illuminating one, because it was like one of those action replays that are now a familiar feature of television sports programmes. In this case, however, the action had been speeded up rather than slowed down. As Sejnowski and Rosenberg remarked, fluency is characterized by effortlessness, but it requires long hours of effortful practice. Our expertise in communicating with language is easily taken for granted because we tend to forget how long it took to acquire this skill. Sejnowski and Rosenberg's fascinating demonstration thus also serves as a well-placed reminder.

As impressive as this application of a neural network undoubtedly was, Sejnowski had something even more exciting up his sleeve. Working with Sidney Lehky, he turned to the visual system, and tried to simulate the way this computes the curvature of an object from its shading under a given condition of illumination. Sejnowski and Lehky used a three-layer network, the input layer representing the centre-surround retinal ganglion cells that were discussed in the previous chapter. The 122-ganglion array was exposed to 2,000 images of parabolic shapes, with a variety of illumination directions, and correlated with curvature data that were required of the network's 24-cell output layer. (Once again, it is easy to imagine a child gradually learning to correlate one thing with another; this time a shape felt with the hands and an object's visual appearance.) It took 40,000 trial steps to train the network to correctly classify the shapes of the objects, but the effort was worth it. Inspection of the 27-cell hidden layer revealed something quite remarkable: its idealized neurons showed optimal responses when the input layer was exposed to bars of various lengths, widths and orientations. These are precisely the responses that Hubel and Wiesel had detected in neurons in the visual cortices of cats and monkeys, as was described in the preceding chapter. It was, to say the least, quite an encore, and it put the three-layer back-propagation network onto a new plateau of credibility. Until this point, the neural network was an interesting and useful device. But the Sejnowski–Lehky result, together with analogous work by David Zipser and Richard Andersen that makes even more intimate contact with physiological data, shows just how close the simulated network can be to the real thing.

Does it go all the way, however? Does it tell us all that we need to know about what goes on in the brain when something is learned? An obvious question concerns the interpretation of what is happening at the model network's output layer. Deviations from the desired pattern at this location, during the training period, are monitored and projected back through the network in a manner that is mathematically expedient

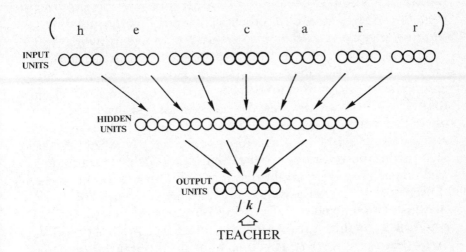

Investigations of neural networks initially aimed at understanding the brain, but networks have properties that also make them useful as computational strategies. A classical example is NETtalk, which Charles Rosenberg and Terrence Sejnowski trained to pronounce the words of written English. Their network had three layers, and its synaptic strengths were adjusted to accommodate pairs of matched strings of letters and the corresponding phonemes, of which spoken English is composed. The pronunciation of a letter depends upon the letters that surround it, and the input 'window' was chosen to be seven letters wide. There are 26 letters in the alphabet, and there are also spaces and punctuation symbols, so the input layer consisted of 203 (= 7 × 29) cells. There were 26 output units, representing the various phonemes, stresses and syllable boundaries. The strings of words, and their corresponding phonemes, were stepped through the input and output layers during training of the network on the 1000 most common English words. In the situation shown here, the network is being exposed to part of the phrase 'the carrot', and the letters currently in the window are (he carr). Appropriate pronunciation of the letter 'c' is thus the target; the surrounding letters provide the context, and show that the correct phoneme is /k/, which is voiced like the first letter in 'ken'. At the next step, the window will contain (e carro), and the central letter 'a' will correspond to the phoneme /@/, which is voiced like the central letter in 'bat'. If, after training, the network is confronted with a window containing (ur catc), during the reading of the phrase 'your catch', for example, it will correctly respond with the phoneme /k/. The arrows in the figure merely indicate direction, not the actual synaptic connections, of which the model has nearly twenty thousand. In the computer implementation of this network, an automatic 'teacher' monitors the outputs and corrects the synaptic strengths until training is complete. In the brain, this task might be managed by the internal reward system.

but as yet is supported only by rather indirect physiological evidence. And who is doing the monitoring? Is our old nemesis the homunculus threatening to return from exile, or worse still, are neural networkers preparing to hand him a free reprieve? In describing NETtalk, Sjenowski and Rosenberg unabashedly enlist the services of a 'teacher', since they make no claim that a three-layer network could possibly embrace all the neural circuitry required to correlate sight (the strings of letters seen) with hearing (the phonemes vocalized). The same limitations apply to the Sejnowski–Lehky simulation, since touch would be implicated in the determination of shape. Zipser and Andersen actually put the question explicitly when they asked themselves 'where the output units of the model could exist in the brain'. After considering, as one possibility, areas that receive synaptic connections from the primary visual region, they came to something that could be far more attractive. The final spatial output may, they speculated, only exist in the behaviour of the animal; it may not exist in any single cell in the brain, but might rather be found in the pointing of the eye or finger accurately to a location in space.

This is a most attractive idea. Taken to its logical conclusion, it suggests that the function of the cortex is to act primarily as a correlator, as a mediator for the smooth cooperation of the sensory and motor functions. There would obviously be an evolutionary advantage attached to the development of such an ability, and one might wonder whether this wouldn't be a goal of considerable priority. We noted earlier that the sounds we hear do not appear to be located at our ears, in spite of the fact that this is the point at which sound waves are converted into nerve signals. Things heard are, on the contrary, heard 'out there' as it were. And the same is true of things seen, of course. The Zipser–Andersen idea suggests that we should be content to leave them out there; there is no need for them to be pulled inside the skull, where indeed there really might then arise the problem of enlisting some agency to scrutinize them for us. The brain is an admittedly impressive building, but there is no one at home!

There are two points that ought to be considered before we pursue this thread. One concerns the tenuous physiological evidence in support of back-propagation. This reverse transmission could occur by an appropriate collection of excitatory and inhibitory neurons, arranged in a feedback loop, of course, but there is also some sign of a mechanism which permits retrograde transport of material in a single neuron. The usual state of affairs is that the flow of information is as in a one-way street, with the neurotransmitter-loaded vesicles being shunted along the axon and its branches until they reach the presynaptic membranes. But signs have been observed of a transport of chemicals in the counter direction, from the axon terminals back up towards the soma. Even if this is confirmed, it does not automatically imply that there is a mechanism for sending synapse-changing information back up the pipeline, as it were, so the proposition remains something of a long shot.

The other point concerns a central aspect of the back-propagation idea. We have seen that its implementation requires the involvement of a 'teacher', who checks the 'errors', that is to say the deviations between the current and the desired patterns at the output layer of cells, and uses them to send correcting adjustments back up the system. The Zipser–Andersen idea gives the output layer a more global interpretation, but it does not really remove the need for some sort of supervising agency. In 1954 James Olds and Peter Milner discovered something which could have a bearing on this issue. They had been experimenting with a rat which had an electrode inserted into certain areas of its brain, and they observed that it would continually press a lever to stimulate itself. It is as if these areas of the brain act as 'pleasure centres'. The phenomenon is now known as intracranial self-stimulation, and the crux of this behaviour lies in a contingent association between the response and its consequences.

There thus appears to be a system of reward operating in the brain, and Aryeh Routtenberg and Eliot Gardner have shown that it can be so powerful that higher primates, and perhaps also humans, will even indulge in self-starvation in order to obtain rewarding brain stimulation. A number of brain regions appear to be involved, including the medial forebrain bundle, which is a group of nerve fibres that pass through the hypothalamus, and also the amygdala and the hippocampus, both of which are known to play roles in the learning of goal-oriented behaviours.

I will not go into further detail here, so suffice it to say that the brain probably does have the wherewithal to reward the advantageous behavioural correlation, and thereby ease its admission to our store of memories. What this does not account for, on the other hand, is the familiar fact that we tend to remember events that are associated with something very important in our lives, whether this be positive or negative. For example, many of us who are old enough remember exactly what we were doing when we heard of the assassination of President John Kennedy; it is difficult to believe that such memories involve a reward. (At a more mundane level, the idea embodied in the maxim 'spare the rod, and spoil the child' implies a belief in the enhanced storage of behavioural correlations in the brain, caused by appropriate sanctions.) Perhaps there is another system that favours storage of memories that are especially abhorrent, since this might enable us to avoid the corresponding situations.

The gist of this chapter has been that knowledge of the properties of neural networks removes much of the mystery surrounding the working of the brain's cortex. These networks are able to discriminate, remember, associate and generalize, and through their activities they appear to imbue the organism with the ability to smoothly coordinate sensory input and motor output. Moreover, they further endorse the idea that internal representations of the external world are not scrutinized by any agency in the brain, but merely appear as stations *en route* to the ultimate goal of remembered associations. There is, however, something which seems to refute all this: we can form pictures in our minds, and we can readily conjure up sounds. Mention the name of the film actor Gene Kelly, for example, and I will immediately hear and see him 'singing, and dancing, in the rain'. Does this spoil a promising idea, or is there something which we can invoke in order to salvage it? It appears that there is indeed a resolution to this apparent paradox.

Some of the most detailed work on mental images has been carried out by Stephen Kosslyn. His is probably one of the cheapest of all forms of research, since it requires little more than a variety of simple drawings and a stop-watch. It needs, on the other hand, a lot of imagination and clear thinking. What

Kosslyn has been able to demonstrate is that the parts of the brain's neural network which are responsible for mental imagery are very likely the same as those that are involved in vision. He came to this conclusion when he noticed that mental imagery appears to be subject to the same laws as visual perception. If one closes one's eyes and pictures a scene, its spatial extent is about the same as the visual field, and the amount of detail that can be discerned rapidly decreases as one shifts one's imaginary attention from the centre of gaze to a peripheral region. Moreover, it is difficult to distinguish detail in objects imagined in small size or at large distances. Close your eyes and try to imagine someone several paces away from you, holding up a newspaper; you will not be able to imagine reading it. But as the person walks towards you, first the headlines and ultimately the normal print will become legible.

This is just what you would experience with your eyes open. And when Kosslyn timed the little journeys that he took by imagining walking to various points in the imagined scene, he found that they corresponded to what would have been the case in reality. Ronald Finke, Jennifer Freyd and Steven Pinker have corroborated many of Kosslyn's findings and have gone on to demonstrate that mental imagery influences visual-motor coordination, the effect persisting after the imagery has ceased. Amongst the practical applications of this phenomenon is the possibility of improved performance by those whose special-ties make heavy demands on motor coordination, and it was conjectured that the improvement in achievement would be proportional to the clarity and precision with which the suc-cession of limb movements was imagined. The American high jumper, Dwight Stones, who came close to taking the Olympic title at Montreal in 1976, appears to have been aware of this; he intensely rehearsed in his mind every step of each jump, his eyes slowly panning along his intended route to the bar, as if he could actually see himself performing the strides and the final leap. It seems that things might even be taken one stage farther in our brains, with mental images acquiring visual characteristics and thereby serving to modify perception itself. This could be the mechanism which causes us to miss even the most glaring typographical errors when reading quickly; once we have grasped the essence of a text, we start to form mental images that can actually influence our scrutiny of the printed words.

It is possibly the capacity for forming vivid mental images which underlies what is commonly called intelligence, although it seems likely that the implied definition ought to be extended to include hearing, at least. And in considering intelligence's travelling companion, logic, we encounter something intriguing: although the brain acquires its pattern-recognizing abilities from the parallel 'wiring' of its neural circuits, it probably achieves its reasoning by the type of sequential handling of data which occurs in a von Neumann computer. (It is tempting to speculate, further, that the two main components of such a computer, namely the memory and the central processor, might be the counterparts of memory and consciousness in the biological brain.) As James McClelland and David Rumelhart have pointed out, the prerequisite for this faculty is skill in handling symbols, and our culture has augmented the brain's internal tools with the written characters which our pattern-recognizing neural circuits help us to manipulate. One could add that these, in turn, are reinforced by the operations one acquires by rote learning, by the things we 'know by heart'. Whence the efficacy of committing to memory such elementary arithmetic as the tables for all multiplications of two numbers up to and including, say, twelve. When I multiply 623 by 517, for example, I lean heavily on things which can be recalled without thought or hesitation. But because the two numbers are, for me at least, longer than can be managed entirely in the head, the use of external symbols is also mandatory. And the sequential operations which I carry out with the aid of pencil and paper demand not only consciousness but also considerable attention.

The recent developments in the understanding of neural networks are exciting, and many believe that they constitute the decisive breakthrough regarding a proper appreciation of the way in which the brain works. These advances have been made possible by a symbiosis between computer science and brain science. It would be wise to sound a note of caution, however, because such a symbiosis has occurred earlier, and it did not live up to its original promise. I am referring to the large amount of activity in the area known as artificial intelligence, which was very popular in the 1960s and 1970s.

In essence, it was a glorified version of an approach that I alluded to earlier, namely the narrowing down of alternatives by a sequence of binary choices. This activity failed miserably to tell us anything about the brain; the gap separating the real and the artificial was simply too wide. It is already clear that the study of neural networks will produce successes which will far outstrip anything that was achieved by artificial intelligence, but it is less obvious that this new approach will be able to go all the way. To appreciate this point, one has only to bear in mind what current neural network models are ignoring: the multiplicity of neurotransmitters; long-range signalling between cells that does not involve synapses; the considerable subtlety with which real neurons are able to react to multiple inputs, and so on. Some scientists working in this area prefer to look upon each neuron as an individual computer. If this transpires to be a sound attitude, an understanding of real neural networks is going to take a great deal more time and effort than has yet been invested in the subject.

By way of demonstrating that all is indeed not yet understood, I will end here by returning to the seemingly trivial act of multiplication that I described above, and recognize just one of the remnant difficulties. There are people who have the amazing ability of multiplying ten (or more) digit numbers in their heads. And many of these people appear to be sub-normal in many other respects. These individuals are known as *idiot savants*, and some of them suffer from the syndrome known as autism. An explanation of how an otherwise impaired brain could manage such an astonishing feat would presumably bring us even closer to understanding exactly how the mind works.

● Summary

The nerve cells in the brain's cortex are linked up into a series of neural networks, which process information in a parallel and almost instantaneous fashion. The transfer of information from one cell to another involves the simultaneous passage of signals along many alternative paths, and the reinforcement of favoured routes leads to memory traces that are distributed over a large number of synapses. This mode of storage makes memories robust against deterioration of individual synapses, and even against the loss of entire cells, and it gives neural networks their remarkable abilities of associative recall and generalization. Software computational strategies and hardware computer devices based on these principles require the aid of a supervisor, but the brain possesses a reward system that might permit automatic storage of useful associations. There is thus no need for a ghost in the machine.

Perchance to dream

Brain rhythms

> If any one faculty of our nature may be called more
> wonderful than the rest, I do think it is memory.
> There seems something more speakingly incompre-
> hensible in the powers, the failures, the inequalities
> of memory, than in any other of our intelligences.
> The memory is sometimes so retentive, so
> serviceable, so obedient – at others, so bewildered
> and so weak – and at others again, so tyrannical,
> so beyond our control! – We are to be sure a
> miracle in every way – but our powers of recollecting
> and forgetting do seem peculiarly past finding out.
>
> JANE AUSTEN
> *Mansfield Park*

In view of the trouble that had been taken to set up the delicate
voltage-measuring device, and connect it to the thin pieces of
metal that he had stuck to the scalp of his son Klaus, the initial
results must have been crushingly disappointing. Realization of
a long-cherished dream was, however, just a few minutes away.
Hans Berger had tried the experiment before, but never with
an instrument of such high sensitivity. The recording pen was
barely moving, and it seemed that its minute motions might be
merely stray electrical effects. But then Klaus, becoming drowsy
during the seemingly endless adjustments, closed his eyes to
relax. One can imagine his father's surprise and excitement as
he observed the pen spring into life, and record a set of fairly
regular waves. When Klaus opened his eyes again, the waves
ceased. Berger, mystified by the way in which his observations
appeared to run exactly counter to expectations, but nevertheless

encouraged by the fact that he was now detecting something at least, examined the traces more closely. He soon realized that the recordings made while his son's eyes were open were not spurious; they were admittedly less regular, and the amplitude was much lower than when the eyes were closed, but they were real enough. Patience had been rewarded. Berger had succeeded in recording what has come to be known as an electroencephalogram (or EEG).

As so often happens in science, Berger's discovery turned out to be a rediscovery. Richard Caton had beaten him to it by some fifty-five years. Caton's observations, reported in 1875, had been limited to animals, however, and he applied his electrodes directly to the surface of the brain. He observed electrical currents, which even appeared to be related to cortical function, and the currents ceased only upon the death of the animal. But Caton's experiments aroused little interest, and even Berger was generally looked upon as a figure at the fringe of medical science, a crank almost. It was not until Edgar Adrian, already a greatly respected figure, rediscovered the phenomenon a second time, in 1934, that it won the recognition and respect it deserved.

Berger had set his sights high. He hoped that the EEG would prove to be the preferred diagnostic tool for all manner of pathological conditions, and in 1932 he had already measured the EEG corresponding to an epileptic seizure. But although the technique has had its successes, and is nowadays used to establish brain death, for example, it has not yet lived up to Berger's expectations. The situation would change, however, if the precise origin of these electrical signals could be established, for the lamentable fact is that although they are obviously related to the electrical activity of the brain's neurons, the exact connection is still nebulous. It is primarily as a monitor of the various states of consciousness that the EEG has played a role, and this is why we will concern ourselves with it here. We should also note, in passing, that it is one of the few techniques which allow one to measure what is going on inside the head in a non-invasive fashion, that is to say in a manner which involves no surgery. The only other techniques of this class are magnetoencephalography, which is the more discerning magnetic counterpart of the Caton–Berger–Adrian method, positron emission tomography, a radioactive technique which enables one to pinpoint brain activity to within a few millimetres, and the entire panoply of psychophysical investigations, touched on earlier (Chapter 4). The latter are, however, only applicable to human subjects since they invariably require some sort of evaluation or report.

Let us return to those earlier experiments carried out by Berger, and take a closer look at his results. The regular waves observed when son Klaus relaxed with his eyes closed had a frequency of about ten cycles per second. Berger called these alpha waves. The less regular, eye-open, waves had a frequency about double that of the alpha variety, and they are known as beta waves. Their occurrence and their general characteristics can be explained by assuming that the larger amplitude of the alpha waves is due to the fact that each of these is really made up of many constituent waves, all having the same frequency and all mutually in step; if these get out of step (i.e. if they become desynchronized) the result will often be partial cancellation. In fact, the situation is more complicated than this because the EEG of the active brain consists of waves of various frequencies, and these cannot all be in step, so periodic cancellation of their effect is inevitable. Two other rhythms have subsequently been discovered. One of these is the delta type, with frequencies around one to four cycles per second, which normally occur during sleep, but which are also seen during waking, in the neighbourhood of tumours and stroke damage. The other rhythm is that of the theta waves, with a frequency around four to eight cycles per second; their associations remain unclear. There are other more specialized EEG patterns such as the intermittent spikes seen with some head injuries and certain developmental disorders; the modified delta form that is characteristic of coma; and the superimposed spike and wave pattern that is the hallmark of the *petit mal* form of epilepsy.

In recent years, the use of computers to average and analyse large numbers of individual EEGs has revealed something new and important, namely the evoked potential, also known as the event-related potential or ERP. (The word 'potential' can be read as 'voltage' for our purposes here.) An ERP is triggered in association with an event in the brain, and it can be located in time with a precision of around a millisecond, which, as we have seen, is about the duration of a nerve impulse. The brain event might be related to a sensory process, or a motor command, or indeed a cognitive event. We thus see that there is scope for much complexity, and this is indeed the case. But this branch of brain science is still young and, as ingeniously devised sets of stimulative conditions are studied in detail, the pieces of the jigsaw puzzle will no doubt be put in place. The earliest ERPs are apparent within 30 or 40 milliseconds of the stimulus being applied, while later components are not seen until more than a second has elapsed. These different timings indicate that some parts of cognition are being handled in a parallel fashion while others are carried out serially. Remembering our discussion of neural networks, in the preceding chapter, where the terms parallel and serial cropped up repeatedly, we see that the study of ERPs might supply vital clues to the way in which our cortical nets actually work, and just how they apportion their computational tasks.

Meanwhile, and in default of definitive answers in that exciting research area, let us turn to another use of the EEG which appears to be altogether more prosaic: the distinction between sleep and wakefulness. This subject is fascinating because it gets to the very heart of the issues of attention and consciousness. It is, however, rather prone to misunderstanding. When openly pondering why we sleep one is likely to be told that the answer is patently obvious: one sleeps because one gets tired! And further contemplation of why one gets tired is likely to meet with even greater scorn. As I hope to explain in the rest of this chapter, such derision is quite out of place; there is much more to sleep and dreaming than might at first appear to be the case. And for a start, one could ask why it is that the great majority of people have a sleep–wake cycle that neatly fits the night–day alternation caused by the earth's rotation. How come that we all get tired at about the same time of day, give or take a couple of hours, irrespective of our occupation? People who have quickly travelled across several time zones, as well as others working on night shifts, often suffer sleep disturbances in which they doze off during the day and lie sleepless at night. This is readily explicable by the fact that they get out of step with the timing of the daylight. But there are those who are burdened with a pathological version of this syndrome. There were many of these out-of-phase unfortunates, suffering jet-lag as it were, long before the Wright brothers ever ventured aloft.

In 1952, Eugene Aserinsky and William Dement discovered that the EEG of a sleeping subject displays a period of the desynchronization first noted by Berger about once every 90 minutes. This was referred to as the paradoxical period, because although the subject remained asleep, his brain activity was more characteristic of the waking state. (A bizarre side-effect is that the penis springs to attention during the paradoxical period, in what could be called an irrelevant erection; in the female, the clitoris disgorges during the paradoxical period.) Because the paradoxical EEG pattern is accompanied by an almost frenzied motion of the eyes beneath their closed lids, as detected by electrodes taped to the latter, these episodes became known as rapid eye movement sleep, or REM sleep, and a person is actually quite difficult to awaken during this phase despite the alert EEG. This was established in 1953, by Aserinsky and Nathaniel Kleitman. Dement and Kleitman went on to discover something even more intriguing, two years later. Awakened during the REM period, a subject can usually remember having dreamt, and will frequently be able to recall the dream's content in vivid detail. Although the distinction between normal sleep and REM sleep is not ideally sharp, it does seem that the latter, and its peculiar EEG, can be identified with the dreaming state. And this state appears to be essential. People continually deprived of their REM sleep, through being disturbed at the onset of the characteristic EEG, show impaired mental capacity when awake. They find it difficult to concentrate, and their normal capacity for logical thinking appears to desert them. As if in an attempt to catch up on lost dreaming time, the sleeping brain then initiates REM periods more often. Prolonged deprivation of REM sleep can even provoke hallucinations, which are essentially waking dreams.

But why do we dream at all? This question, at least, is not likely to elicit ridicule. On the contrary, dreams are one of those things that fall within the province of all manner of self-appointed experts, and dream interpretation has been a lucrative pursuit for the phenomenon's gurus. Certain features of dreaming have tailor-made this state for charlatanism: some themes occur almost universally throughout the population,

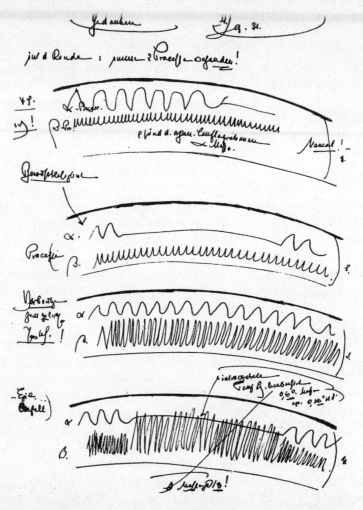

This facsimile page from Hans Berger's laboratory notebook records his observations and impressions from a day's work on the electroencephalogram of one of his subjects. His handwriting is a mixture of normal German and a type of shorthand. The heading reads as follows. Thoughts 21.9.31. In the cortex: Always 2 processes present! The English translations of the four numbered entries read: 1. Psi Phi. Psychophysical, Alpha-process. Nutrition! Beta- process. That is the organ. Conflagration of Mosso. Normal! 2. Unconsciousness. Process Alpha. Beta. 3. Preparation for epileptic seizure. Aura! Alpha. Beta. 4. Epileptic seizure. Alpha. Beta. Intercerebral temperature increase measured 0.6 degrees, Mosso 0.36 degrees in the human. According to Mosso, not always, however! (The person referred to in the final section was Angelo Mosso (1846–1910), who made the first noteworthy attempt to investigate blood circulation in the brain, in 1881.)

and this provides the possibility of unifying generalization, while other themes seem to occur more specifically, allowing the dream mandarin to offer a personalized service. Amongst the common dream elements, one could cite the feeling of falling, and also the sensation of being chased. Sigmund Freud, whose book *The Interpretation of Dreams* (published in 1900) is probably the best known work in this field, inclined towards sexual interpretations of dream events. Thus the climbing of a ladder, which is achieved by a series of rhythmical movements, and which leaves the climber breathless, was envisaged by Freud as a representation of the sexual act. Freud's sexual conception of motivation ultimately caused his closest colleague, Carl Jung, to dissociate himself from the Freud school of analysis. Jung's interpretation of the dream's ladders and staircases was far more mundane; they were, he felt, symbols of one's striving to climb the rungs of one's career or social system. Although Freud and Jung were thus divided in their deductions, they nevertheless shared the belief that the dream, if properly explained, could lay bare the secrets of the subconscious.

Given the almost ubiquitous curiosity of people about the murky depths of their inner beings, that facet of psychoanalysis was always guaranteed an enthusiastic following. But the diagnostic aspect of the dream pales in comparison with another vista which the dream has frequently been assumed to open up: the foretelling of the future. For the common man, the events foreshadowed could be as modest as that embodied in the belief that 'a duck snared means that a woman's favours will be won', but the more prominent the dreamer the more momentous the significance of what was dreamt. The dream of the leader was seen as the harbinger of good or evil for all his subordinates. Jacob's dreams, recounted in Genesis XXXVII, came close to ruining his relationship with his brethren, and Herodotus of Halikarnassos, the Greek historian, tells of the Gods leading the Persian king Xerxes to defeat at the hands of the Greeks by making him overconfident via a series of ego-boosting dreams. Even in the twentieth century, some leaders have seen prudence in retaining the services of professional dream interpreters, a notable example being the highly superstitious Adolf Hitler.

What does modern science tell us about the dreaming state? Through observations of the EEG, it is capable of revealing quite a lot. Allan Hobson and Robert McCarley were guilty of no exaggeration when they wrote that 'dreams offer a royal road to the mind and the brain'. For a start, with very rare exceptions, everyone dreams. And that does not mean once in a while; we all dream periodically throughout every night's slumber, the total amount of time spent in the dreaming state being an hour or more. Then again, dreams do not flash through our sleeping minds in the few seconds immediately prior to waking; they last for many minutes at the end of each (approximately) 90-minute inter-dream period. And if we toss and turn during our sleep, it is emphatically not because a tempestuous dream is agitating us. On the contrary, during the REM (i.e. dreaming) phase, the motor neurons that would dictate such movement are actually decommissioned, and they remain out of service until the dream period is over. People might be able to sleep-walk, but they could not possibly dream at the same time, and persons who are informed by their partner that they talk in their sleep need have no fear of revealing incriminating facts during these night-time episodes.

One could imagine two obvious pathologies related to this decoupling of the majority of the motor nerves during dreaming: failure of the decoupling during dreaming, and decoupling at times other than during dreaming. Both conditions are observed, but they are happily rare. To understand the first of these, we should consider an experiment in which the condition was deliberately induced. In 1979, Michel Jouvet destroyed the locus coeruleus alpha (which is located at the upper end of the brain stem) of an experimental cat. When subsequently asleep, the creature periodically displayed a variety of stereotyped behavioural patterns, such as licking and washing, attacking an imagined prey, and even exploring its immediate environment, but it undertook these little tasks in a desultory and disconnected fashion. This indicated that the observed behavioural fragments, which are produced by structures in the mid-brain rather than the cortex, require the mediation of the locus coeruleus to knit them into a useful fabric of behavioural events.

Shakespeare seems to have been aware of the naturally occurring counterpart of this phenomenon, for he has a court doctor say of Lady Macbeth's nocturnal rambling: 'A great perturbation in nature – to receive at once the benefit of sleep, and do the effects of watching! – In this slumbery agitation.' And the Bard was apparently in no doubt as to the deep-lying nature of the Lady's troubles, for the doctor later notes: 'More needs she the divine than the physician.'

Failure of decoupling during dreaming is disturbing enough, but the other condition, known as cataplexy, is downright dangerous because it affects the motor system during wakefulness. A cataplectic attack is triggered by a sudden inhibition which decouples the motor nerves, and the victim suffers a loss of control over his limbs and neck. An attack can last from a few seconds to several minutes, and one only has to imagine this happening on a motorway during the rush hour to gauge the potential seriousness of the situation. But let us return to the lighter side of the story.

The typical dream is characterized by its hallucinatory and delusive qualities and by the fact that it is difficult to recall even if one is woken in mid-dream. And we seem also to be able to hear and touch when in this state. The senses of taste and smell, on the other hand, are either absent or severely diminished, and in our dreams we feel no pain in spite of the multitude of imagined physical ills that can befall us. The plot of a dream is invariably bizarre because of its inconsistencies, its defiance of physical laws (as in the hair-raising falls which never end with a bump), and its discontinuities. The dreaming state appears, moreover, to be associated with a heightening of awareness, in that all manner of people, places and events from one's past are dredged up and woven into the dream's kaleidoscopic fabric. And yet, despite the richness of the montage, it is difficult to prevent a dream evaporating like dew in the morning sun. It is especially this latter feature that seems at variance with Freud's ideas; if the goal of the dream is the expurgation of our neuroses, why is it so difficult to hold on to and analyse. Moreover, how would Freud have explained the fact, which has only more recently come to light, that infant children dream even more than adults do; a newborn baby can spend as much as eight hours a day in the dreaming state, and this fraction is even exceeded by the foetus in the last three months of gestation. Although there have been the occasional claims of prenatal mental activity, as when the surrealist artist Salvador Dali attributed some of his more extreme productions to experiences in the womb, for example, it does not seem likely that the average little tot could acquire neuroses enough to warrant so much dreaming time. The Freudian ideas are on particularly thin ice in respect to this issue.

In 1886, Wolfgang Robert produced a volume entitled *Der Traum als Naturnothwendigkeit Erklärt (The Dream as a Necessity of Nature)*. In it he argued that the purpose of the dream is 'to excrete certain kinds of thoughts'. 'A person deprived of dreaming', he continued, 'would ultimately suffer mental derangement, due to the burden of his unresolved thoughts and unrationalized impressions; these would prevent assimilation of properly constructed memories.' This idea languished for almost a century. Then, in 1983, it resurfaced in a more thoroughly underpinned form, in an article published by Francis Crick and Graeme Mitchison. 'We propose', they wrote, 'that the function of dream (REM) sleep is to remove certain undesirable modes of interaction in networks of cells in the cerebral cortex. We postulate that this is done in REM sleep by a reverse learning mechanism, so that the trace in the brain of the unconscious dream is weakened, rather than strengthened, by the dream.'

Given the mechanistic view of the brain that this book is advocating, the Robert–Crick–Mitchison theory would seem to be grist to our mill. Let us take a closer look, therefore, at its details. In the previous chapter I described how the neural network stores memories through modifications to the 'strengths' of the various synapses, that is to say by alterations to the connections between the cells. The network is said to be thereby trained rather than programmed like a conventional computer. The memories are distributed over many such connections, and this makes them robust, or invulnerable to the loss of either individual synapses or indeed entire cells. Particular memories are thus not localized to a single cell, or a few cells. Our brains do not have cells which start to fire every time we see a picture of our grandmother, for example. (It has recently been demonstrated, however, that there are cells which respond to specific features, such as the shape of a hand.) The neural network has the remarkable property that it can associate. Presented with part of a previously learned memory, it will complete the picture, as it were, and recall it in its entirety. This is in accord with our everyday experience, of course. Given a few bars of a familiar tune or a commercial jingle, we have no difficulty humming the rest. And given the first stanza of a favourite limerick, we can jump to the punch line. The network does not need to label its memories in order to retrieve them, therefore, because they can be addressed by their actual content. Finally, this manner of storing memories allows them to be superimposed on one another, with no risk of mutual interference.

There, however, is the rub, for we must add the proviso that absence of interference is contingent on the system not being overloaded. If too much is stuffed into the network, unwanted patterns of activity, or parasitic modes of behaviour as Crick and Mitchison call them, will arise and, to put it bluntly, jam up the works. Crick and Mitchison mustered powerful circumstantial evidence for their theory, linking the greater amount of dreaming in childhood, for example, with the fact that the brain's neurons are establishing many new synapses at that stage of development. When a new synapse is formed, it will not 'know' what strength it is to adopt in order to harmonize with the memories that it inevitably becomes part of, and it will thus threaten to contribute to one of Crick and Mitchison's parasitic modes. They also noted that the only mammal that does not dream is the echidna, *Tachyglossus aculeatus*, commonly known as the spiny anteater. This creature happens to have unusually large cerebral hemispheres, however, and these distended regions may be able to accommodate memories without the risk of overloading.

How, then, are the detrimental effects of overloading to be corrected for? Crick and Mitchison have a surprisingly simple prescription: close the system down, excite these parasitic or spurious memories into activity, and weaken them by a process of 'unlearning'. And the activation of these modes, which by definition must have no relationship to reality, is, they argue, what gives a dream its bizarre character. The authors of this fascinating idea even went on to suggest that one should not try to 'hold on' to a fading dream, upon awakening, because it is part of a mental state that the brain would like to get rid of.

Although Crick and Mitchison do not state this explicitly, their idea of closing the system down in order to activate the putative purging mechanism implies that ordinary (i.e. non-REM) sleep serves merely as a route to REM sleep. In effect, it makes dreaming the *raison d'être* of sleep itself. In this respect, the theory is at variance with traditional views of slumber, which see this state as being one of rest and recuperation. But is that common view justified, in the light of the latest information? Let us take a closer look at the more salient features of this condition in which we spend about a third of our lives, and compare our situation with that of other creatures.

Before going into these comparative details, however, we should remind ourselves of the relative position on evolution's ladder of those that lie below us. Working our way successively downwards from the rung occupied by ourselves and the other mammals, we encounter first the birds, then the reptiles, then the amphibians, and finally (because lower creatures will not concern us) the fish. The non-REM state is seen in mammals, birds and most reptiles, while there is no substantial evidence of it in amphibians and fish. REM in adults is clearly identifiable only in mammals. There are brief REM periods in recently hatched birds, however. It thus appears that regular alternation between non-REM and REM sleep is exclusive to mammals, and it seems natural to link this cyclic regime to the higher degree of development seen in the mammalian brain.

We have already seen that the echidna, or spiny anteater, is anomalous amongst the mammals in being a non-dreamer. It must be remarked, however, that this animal belongs to the very primitive subclass known as the Monotremata, which comprises the duck-billed platypus and two genera of spiny anteater. These creatures are only distantly related to all other known mammals, from which they differ in laying eggs and in possessing many other reptilian features. These facts taken into consideration, the echidna's lack of dreaming seems far less surprising.

If the purpose of dreaming is to rehearse, or keep in trim, patterns of behaviour learned during wakefulness, as Michel Jouvet suggested in 1980, these patterns could not be related to basic life-preserving functions because, as we have just seen, many types of creature do quite well without ever dreaming. The dreaming state must be associated with what we call thought; it is an indispensable correlate of the mind. But if non-REM sleep is merely a route to REM sleep, why does the unsophisticated, and thus non-dreaming, crocodile need to sleep at all? Non-REM sleep must serve other purposes. What are they?

Aristotle believed that sleep is induced by warm vapours that rise from the stomach, an idea which probably occurred to him because of the soporific effects of heavy eating. More recently, sleep has been attributed to lack of stimulation. (This suggestion is in danger of falling prey to a circular argument: the relative paucity of stimulation during the night hours could, in turn, be explained by the fact that the majority of one's fellow human beings are asleep.) Both these theories are easily refuted. People on hunger strikes spend much of their time sleeping, thus giving the lie to Aristotle's notion. And regarding the stimulation theory, we have the twin facts of the people who manage to doze off surrounded by the din of a cocktail party, and their opposite numbers, the habitual, and ear-plugged, insomniacs who toss fitfully in their sepulchrally silent bedrooms.

At the beginning of this century, Edouard Claparede put forward a new view of sleep when he suggested that it is instinctive. Although his conjecture that it serves to rid the body of toxic humours has now been refuted, the belief in a sleep-regulating system remains valid to this day. And if such a regulatory system exists, it is natural to expect that it would function in a cyclic manner, that it would imbue life with certain basic rhythms. Why, however, should these rhythms be tied to the earth's rotation, and thus have a periodicity of twenty-four hours? Such a daily cadence is referred to as circadian rhythm, after the Latin words *circa*, which means approximately, and *dies*, which denotes a day. That sleep is subject to a circadian rhythm was demonstrated, in 1938, by two intrepid (and clearly non-claustrophobic) pioneers, Nathaniel Kleitman and Bruce Richardson. They spent thirty-two days voluntarily incarcerated in Kentucky's Mammoth Cave, isolated from the cues provided by the normal terrestrial light-dark cycle. Instead, and using artificial illumination to set a false pace, they subjected themselves to a twenty-eight-hour day consisting of nineteen hours of light and nine hours of dark. Kleitman's system obstinately refused to accommodate to the synthetically protracted day; his body temperature maintained its normal twenty-four-hour rhythm, and his sleep was particularly fitful when, every sixth day, the terrestrial and artificial times were maximally out of step; when, in other words, the bogus midnight coincided with Kentucky's high noon. Kleitman's body was, in short, revealing that it possessed a sort of inner clock.

A striking parallel is seen in the behaviour of a species of yellow-brown algae which live in the coastal regions of Cape Cod. Usually buried under the sand during high tide, they emerge as the waters recede to harvest some of the sun's energy by basking in its light. But the timing of the tides varies according to the lunar day of 24.8 hours rather than the solar day. When removed to an inland laboratory, and subjected to continuous illumination, they nevertheless continue to display their customary lunar rhythms; so faithfully, in fact, that their behaviour can be used as a tidal predictor for the Cape Cod location from which they were taken. Their lowly status notwithstanding, therefore, these creatures have an inner timepiece that is every bit as sophisticated as our own.

But what of Kleitman's colleague? He turned out to be something of a freak, because whereas the great majority of people would have shared Kleitman's distress under the unnatural conditions, Bruce Richardson's body gradually did acclimatize itself to the twenty-eight-hour day. Kleitman had unwittingly allied himself with one of Nature's rarities.

Normal creatures, then, ourselves included, have biological clocks which dictate the timing of their cyclic behavioural patterns. Let us redirect our attention to the specific issue of sleep, and ask what it is that acts as the metronome. In 1907, René Legendre and Henri Piéron extracted some of the cerebrospinal fluid from dogs which had been deprived of sleep for periods as long as two weeks. Injected into dogs which had been allowed adequate slumber, the liquid immediately induced sleep. Their conclusion was that the solution contained a sleep-provoking substance, which they called hypnotoxin. The existence of such sleep mediators was subsequently confirmed, and they were chemically identified as neuropeptides. These substances are remarkably potent. John Pappenheimer had to use 3,000 litres of human urine in order to extract a mere seven millionths of a gram of a particular neuropeptide known as muramyl peptide, but this was sufficient for 500 doses. Administered to a well-rested rabbit, a single dose is enough to induce six hours of sound sleep.

It has even proved possible to locate the sources of these trace substances. In humans, they emanate from several regions at the brain stem, including the reticular formation, the raphe nuclei, and the locus coeruleus. There is evidence of much interplay between the workings of these components, and the counterpoint enables the brain to be nudged into the various states with impressive precision, as long as nothing has happened to upset its balance. This is why our sleeping habits are normally so regular. The reticular formation appears to control arousal, while the raphe nuclei cause sleep by inhibiting the reticular formation through discharge of the neurotransmitter serotonin. This substance could be said to be in opposition to another neurotransmitter, norepinephrine, which is produced by the locus coeruleus when that structure too causes arousal. Damage to the locus coeruleus causes its owner to spend a disproportionately large amount of time in slumber. Yet another structure, the suprachiasmatic nucleus, dictates the actual timing of the onset of sleep, but not its duration. The regular alternation between the non-REM and REM phases of sleep is handled by interactions between the locus coeruleus and the reticular formation. And here we must take particular note of an important subtlety. Some of these brain stem structures exert their influence by discharging neurotransmitters of the amine family, while others use members of the choline class. Considered in this respect, the superficial similarities of the EEG traces corresponding to the waking and REM states are seen to be misleading, because the amine activity is high in waking and low in REM while that of the cholines is high in both waking and REM. Dreaming is thus not to be regarded as a sort of pseudo-waking; it is a quite distinct state and it resembles no other condition that we experience during the circadian cycle.

This brings us back to the theory of Crick and Mitchison, which proposed that a process of unlearning occurs during REM. Their implication that non-REM sleep is merely a route to the REM phase does not appear to fit the facts, as we have seen, and it seems safer to conclude that non-REM sleep arose in the natural course of evolution, and that it was favoured in the Darwinian sense because it conferred advantages such as husbanding our energy resources and keeping us out of the way of nocturnal predators better adapted to low illumination levels. The unlearning idea, however, remains intriguing and we will now consider it in greater detail. It has, in fact, been supported by the results of two computer simulation studies on neural networks of the type described in the preceding chapter. We saw that the network studied by John Hopfield has an unfortunate capacity for generating spurious memories, that is to say adventitious memories that are unwanted hybrids of memories that were intentionally imprinted on the network.

Crick and Mitchison noted the similarity between Hopfield's spurious memories and their conjectured parasitic modes, and one can imagine their excitement upon learning of an extension to Hopfield's study, carried out by David Feinstein and Richard Palmer in collaboration with Hopfield himself. In short, they discovered that they could greatly diminish the network's complement of spurious memories by subjecting it to a period of unlearning, during which the normal learning rule is simply reversed. One should recall, here, that the normal learning rule, first proposed by Donald Hebb, stipulates that a synapse that connects two cells is to have its strength increased if the presynaptic cell contributes to the firing of the postsynaptic cell, and weakened if this is not the case. In unlearning, these recipes are interchanged. In view of what was mentioned earlier regarding the striking difference between the amine level in the waking state and the amine level in REM, the idea that Hebb's learning rule could be reversed during dreaming does not seem all that far-fetched. The unlearning concept had, moreover, already received endorsement in an earlier computer study carried out by John Clark, in collaboration with Johann Rafelski and Jeffrey Winston. The details of the model differed somewhat from those employed by Hopfield, and the term 'brainwashing' was used rather than 'unlearning', but the principle was much the same.

As attractive as these ideas of spurious memories and unlearning undoubtedly are, we should not let them blind us to other possible explanations of our need to dream. Crick and Mitchison suggested that the bizarre nature of the typical dream provides a strong hint that spurious memories do exist, but one could question this point. Are dreams really so grotesque that they must perforce invoke the type of hybrid that the Hopfield model throws up, with its 50 per cent of one valid memory grafted onto 50 per cent of something entirely different? Should we not, rather, acknowledge that many features of a dream are nevertheless relatively normal? Perhaps surprisingly so, indeed, in view of the fact that they do not enjoy our conscious intervention. After all, the people in our dreams bear an impressive resemblance to real people; they, at least, are not split schizophrenically down the middle. Is it not primarily in respect to what one could call the plot that the typical dream is eccentric? This might be a natural consequence of the fact that the normal controls arising from consciousness are absent during a dream, and the latter might consequently enjoy a freedom that is normally impossible. Perhaps we have already taken too much for granted, in fact, for one could question whether it is natural for a dream to have a plot in the first place. That one thing in a dream does seem to lead on automatically to another, even though the plot occasionally flies off at a tangent, might reflect a fundamental continuity in the brain's way of handling information. One could imagine a mechanism whereby one percept strikes up a sort of associative resonance that leads the brain mechanically on to another percept. During waking, with the normal controls switched on, the train of thought is confined to the tracks as it were: the permanent way dictated by one's experiences and one's prejudices. If many such resonances are normally evoked, the lack of control during dreaming would allow the brain a freedom of choice to explore new avenues. Perhaps this is why sleeping on a problem sometimes enables us to come up with novel solutions, as in the celebrated case of Kekule's discovery of the closed-ring structure of the benzene molecule.

Ernest Hartmann published a paper in 1968 that deserves more attention than it has received. In it, he pointed to several characteristics of dreaming that appear not to be generally known. He showed, for example, that the sleep–dream cycle closely parallels the metabolism-linked cycles of the body. And in particular, a higher body temperature reduces the amount of time that elapses between REM periods, and vice versa. This is just what one would expect for a process involving chemical reactions that are controlled by the body's numerous enzymes, because the efficiency with which these proteins carry out their biological tasks increases with increasing temperature. Hartmann compared the metabolic rates and sleep–dream

cycles for the mouse, rat, rabbit, cat, human and elephant, and
the inverse relationship was very clear: the higher the metabolic
rate the shorter the period between dreams. The mouse, for
example, has a metabolic rate which exceeds that of man by
a factor of about twenty, and it enters a brief dreaming period
every five minutes or so, throughout its slumber. The elephant,
on the other hand, has a metabolic rate that is about 40 per cent
below ours, and it dreams approximately every two hours.

These findings were interesting enough, but they were overshadowed by something else that Hartmann was able to document, something that adds a quite new dimension to our picture of the dreaming state. Examination of the EEG trace of
a normal human subject, during a twenty-four-hour period,
reveals that a state bearing the usual hallmarks of dreaming
occurs approximately every ninety minutes throughout the day.
We have already seen that the view of non-REM as a mere
route to the REM phase of sleep is difficult to defend; this
new revelation, that a type of dreaming occurs even during
waking, surely delivers the *coup de grâce*. What does it tell us
about dreaming, however? Hartmann himself suggested that one
might expect a tendency towards an increase in day-dreaming
or loosening of associations every ninety minutes, or an increase
in what he called primary process thinking, by which he meant
activation of deep-lying mechanisms related to creativity. This
would be in agreement with the idea, expressed earlier, that the
dreaming state corresponds to a situation in which the normal
mental controls are not operative. But in the case of dreaming
during sleep, the controls are absent because the senses are either
switched off or, more realistically, working with a considerably
diminished efficiency. The level of consciousness, in other words,
is very low. During waking, wouldn't this pseudodreaming be
shackled with the constraints imposed by our alertness? How
could it too let the brain freewheel, as it were?

As a preliminary to pursuing this issue, one should consider
certain anatomical facts. In 1892, Friedrich Goltz showed that
when the cerebral cortex is damaged, a dog is unable to learn
from past experience. As Goltz remarked, a decerebrated dog is
essentially nothing but 'a child of the moment'. He also found,
however, that the dog's sleep–wake cycle survives intact from
such a gross surgical invasion. This is not surprising, of course,

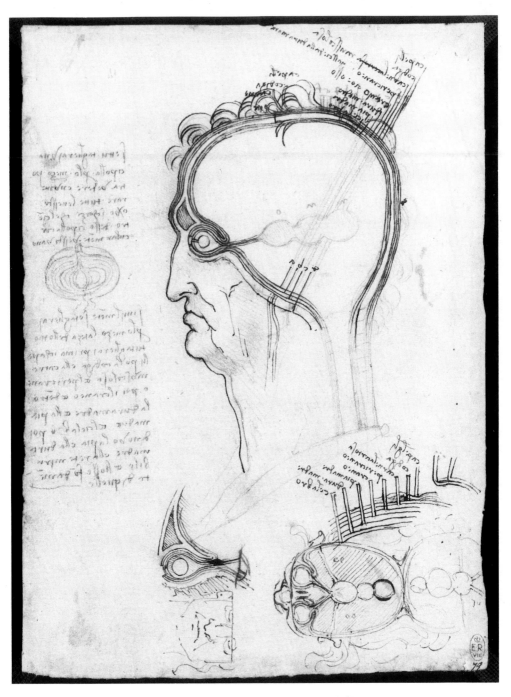

Scientists are invariably influenced by current wisdom. In Leonardo da Vinci's day, it was believed that the brain functions through its animal spirits, which were taken to reside in the four ventricles. Leonardo showed great technical resource when he determined the form of these chambers by pouring molten wax into them. When the wax had set, he was able to observe the ventricles' shape by cutting away the surrounding tissue, thereby discarding the material which really held the mind's secrets! (See Chapter 1.) (© Her Majesty the Queen)

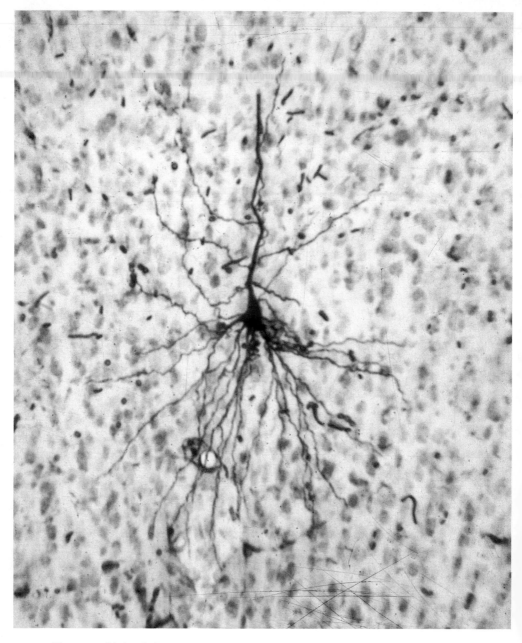

The pyramidal cell shown here was photographed by Charles Gilbert and Torsten
Wiesel during a microscopical investigation of part of a cat's visual cortex.
Rendered visible through injection with horseradish peroxidase, this neuron is
seen to possess many dendrites, through which it receives electrical signals.
The axon, via which it sends signals to other cells, is not visible at this
magnification. (See Chapter 3.)

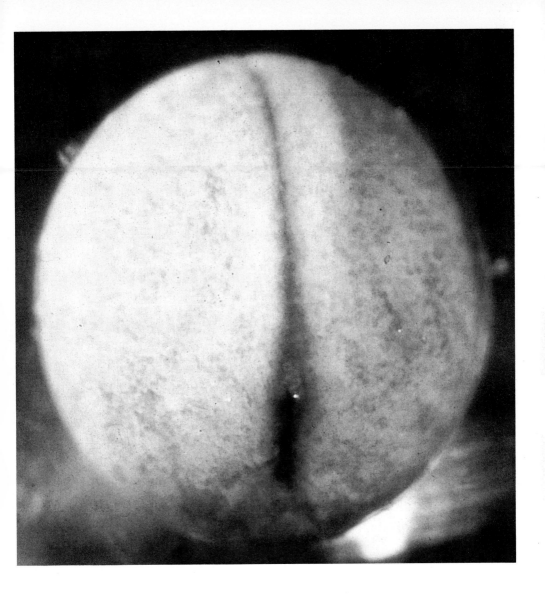

During embryonic development, the precursor of the brain and spinal cord appears as a layer of cells called the neural plate. It is visible as the dark line in this picture taken by John Gurdon of the one-day-old embryo of an African clawed frog, *Xenopus*. The roughly one millimetre diameter embryo contains about 60,000 cells at this stage. (See Chapter 7.)

Studies of various animals, including the chicken, rat, guinea pig, cat and several species of monkey, have shown that the same parts of the nervous system control attack and defence. The cat on the right, photographed by W. R. Hess and M. Brügger, displays typical defensive behaviour against a threatening dog. The cat shown below had leads implanted into its midbrain, and Richard Bandler used it to demonstrate that electrical stimulation of that region evokes a similar response. This is the case even if the midbrain has been surgically separated from the cortex, so the former is the real seat of such behaviour. (See Chapters 2 and 7.)

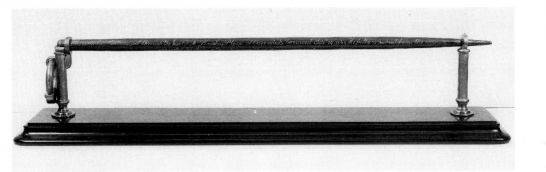

The iron rod (above) that was accidentally
shot through Phineas Gage's head, in
September 1848, is now preserved at the
Harvard Medical School. As can be seen
from his skull, and also from his life mask
(both below), it entered just above the left
eye. As it exited, it lifted away a flap of about
ten square centimetres of the cranium, which
later grew back in place. But the damage to
his frontal lobe was permanent, and it
caused a lasting change in his personality.
(See Chapters 1 and 9.)

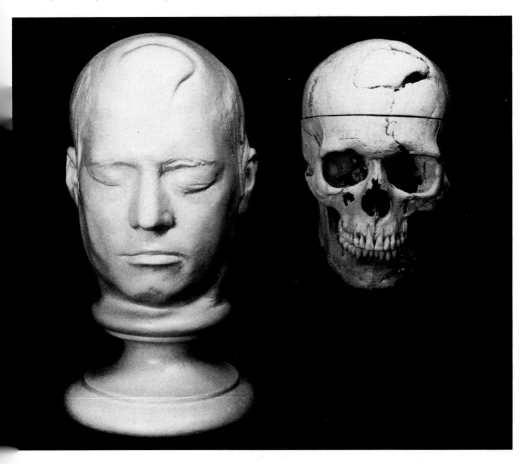

As depicted in this picture of her at Domrémy, painted by Lenepveu in 1889, Joan of Arc was prone to hearing voices, a typical symptom of schizophrenia. This delusion, and the other bizarre behavioural traits characteristic of the affliction, ultimately led to her execution. But it is now clear that her plight was attributable to an organically determined over-production of the neurotransmitter dopamine in the limbic system, which controls the emotions. (See Chapter 9.) (Courtesy of The Mansell Collection)

With a resolve suggestive of thought, a nesting killdeer will deliberately lead a potential predator away from its nest or young, often acting as if it were injured, to make itself more attractive to the intruder. The bird shown here, which was photographed by Noble Proctor, is feigning a broken wing. (See Chapter 10.)

Patients close to death whose vital systems have been resuscitated frequently report having observed a tunnel with a bright light at its end. This is not new. Hieronimus Bosch's fifteenth-century painting shows departing souls being helped toward such a tunnel by attendant angels. The illusion is probably caused by perturbations of the nervous system as its normal functioning breaks down. (See Chapter 11.)

because it has already been emphasized that the centres that control sleep and dreaming lie at the top of the brain stem, not in the cortex. The interesting point is, however, that these centres send nerve fibres (i.e. axons and axon branches) to essentially every region of the cortex. Whatever is happening during sleepful dreaming and wakeful pseudodreaming, therefore, it appears to be rather fundamental. And that it occurs every ninety minutes or so, day and night, is suggestive of a need that requires frequent attention.

Returning to the idea propounded by Crick and Mitchison, that we dream in order to unlearn spurious or parasitic memories, one could ask whether such a process would have to be carried out so often. Suppose, however, that there is a mechanism by which all recently acquired memories gradually deteriorate, a mechanism that confronts every new memory with an inevitable race against time, unless it is in the process of being actively reinforced through actual use. If such a mechanism were operative, every thought that was a potential candidate for storage would become vulnerable as soon as our attention was redirected to something else. The countdown to irretrievable erasure would begin the moment we moved on to new mental pastures. But because the whittling process would be gradual rather than abrupt, and because memories are robust, as I have stressed several times earlier, there would be a certain temporal leeway; a periodic repair of the damage would be adequate so long as this was undertaken sufficiently frequently. The damage would presumably take the form of changes at the synaptic level, and the refreshment mechanism would involve getting the strengths of the affected synapses back into conformity with the strengths of the other synapses involved in the relevant memory.

These issues are so central to the functioning of the cortex's neural networks, that they deserve fuller illustration. Let us look at a typical situation in more detail, therefore, and ask what is going on at the level of the individual synapse. We have already seen that there is now experimental evidence which supports Donald Hebb's hypothesis that memories are stored through changes in the strengths of the synapses, that is to say through changes in the efficiency with which they transmit signals from one neuron to another. These strengths can be imagined as lying between a minimum of zero and a maximum of 100 per cent. In the former case, firing of the presynaptic cell has no effect on the postsynaptic cell, while in the latter case the effect is as large as it can be, given the biochemical constraints that govern the situation. The neural network consists of billions of cells, interconnected with thousands of billions of synapses. The incorporation of a new memory into the network slightly changes a large number of the synaptic strengths. One synapse might thereby have its strength increased from 71 to 73 per cent, for example, while another underwent a decrease from 42 to 38 per cent, and so on. The important point to bear in mind, however, is that these modifications are part of an overall plan; they are highly inter-dependent. The deterioration mechanism conjectured above would, on the other hand, be a random process, in which the synapses suffered impairments that were independent of what was happening elsewhere in the network. During the putative refreshment process, the cooperativity would come into play and each synapse would be helped back towards its proper value through the collective influence of the other synapses. This would work successfully only if the deterioration had not progressed too far, however, and hence the need for the frequent recuperation that is presumed to operate during dreaming and what we have called pseudodreaming. It is important to note that such a recovery would not be possible if an individual memory were stored in a single synapse; there would be no collective reference to indicate the proper level to which a degraded synapse should be returned.

Hartmann's observation that a person dreams more frequently when the body temperature is raised, as in a fever, appears to be in accord with the idea of memory degeneration. The metabolic rate increases with increasing temperature, and it does not seem particularly far-fetched to assume that the impairment of synaptic strengths will proceed at a rate which parallels that of the metabolism. Bernard Davis and I independently proposed the memory reinforcement idea, after the theory of Crick and Mitchison appeared, and Davis suggested the interesting extension that the mechanism holds the key to the maintenance of long-term memory. He quite rightly stressed the fact that any gradual impairment of a recently acquired memory would put the transition from short-term to long-term memory at a serious disadvantage, and this would make the refreshment or reinforcement process indispensable.

My own concerns lay more in the details of the degeneration, and I was anxious to find a process that would put an additional factor that would be operating in the immature brain on an equal footing with what was described in the preceding paragraph, for the adult. This proved to be a manageable task. Let us first consider the nature of that extra item. The immature brain contains all the cells it will ever need, but its cells are still forming new synapses at a prodigious rate. When a new synapse is established, there is an obvious risk that it will barge in on a memory that has already been established by modification to the neighbouring synapses. What is there to tell the new synapse which value it should adopt in order to harmonize with its surroundings? The only possible agency is the other synapses themselves, but they will only be able to pass on their guiding advice by way of signals. Whence the need for the conjectured refreshing pulses, which might take the form of the so-called PGO waves (which take their name from the structures involved, namely the pons, the (lateral) geniculate and the occipital cortex). That the refreshment process probably involves actual nerve impulses rather than something more diffuse seems to be suggested by the work of Jean-Pierre Changeux and Antoine Danchin. They were able to show that the new synaptic connections established between still-sprouting neurons are initially unstable, but that they can be stabilized by firing of the post-synaptic cell. Synapses which do not get this stimulus simply degenerate.

The reason why the refreshing waves would have to be administered throughout the cortex lies, of course, in the fact that the conjectured synaptic deterioration would strike indiscriminately, at locations that could not be predicted. But the ubiquity thus required of these curative pulses would mean that various functions would be activated out of context. This could be the cause of those frenetic movements of the eyes beneath their closed lids, and the bizarre erection that has no purpose. One might loosely compare the situation with what happens to one's car when it has its periodic maintenance check-up in the garage. The motor is revved up, but no journey is undertaken. And the headlamps are switched on and off in broad daylight.

At present, it remains unclear which, if either, of these theories of dreaming will prove to be the most tenable. We have the hybrid-type spurious memories on the one hand, with the conjectured unlearning occurring during dreaming, and we have the synaptic-deterioration spurious memories on the other, with the hypothesized relearning, or refreshing, mechanism to correct the resulting deficiency. Time will decide. It is tempting, however, to fire off a parting shot in favour of the latter theory: subjects deprived of their dreaming sleep do seem to suffer a loss of recently acquired memory.

It might seem that this chapter which set out to celebrate the rhythms of life, has finished up by becoming bogged down in one particular cadence, namely that of the sleep–dream cycle. If we appear to have been mesmerized by that issue, however, it could be reiterated that we do, after all, spend about a third of our lives sleeping, so one chapter out of eleven, devoted to the subject, hardly seems excessive. And the possibility that the dreaming state will shed decisive light on the workings of the mind, even though the promise remains unfulfilled as yet, does make the enterprise worthwhile. So it is not because other biological rhythms have been skimped that I will close by turning my attention to something which appears, at least, to be unrelated to what I have just been considering. I am going to switch to a species that lies rather remote from us on evolution's ladder. And I will shift the scene to, of all places, sanitary plumbing.

Not just any such plumbing, however, but examples in which the level of hygiene leaves much to be desired. But why the interest in such a forbidding venue? The answer, in Latin, is *Dictyostelium discoideum*. This is the name of the green slime mould that thrives in unclean toilets (and in other places where bacteria are plentiful), and it is remarkable in that it can exist both as a single amoeboid cell and as a multicellular organism. When supplies of bacteria are abundant, individual cells can survive independently, moving about to hunt their prey. But when the bacteria are in short supply, or totally absent, some of the *Dictyostelium* cells secrete a special cyclic form of the molecule AMP (i.e. cyclic adenosine monophosphate), and this provokes the remaining cells to migrate towards the emitting members of the colony. When they reach the cyclic-AMP source, the cells cluster to form a single slug-like creature, known as a pseudoplasmodium, which can crawl around in search of nourishment, and ultimately form a stalk which is tipped with a fruiting body that sheds new spores to complete the life cycle. The point of special interest, in the present context, is that the cyclic-AMP molecules are emitted in a series of waves. In this lowly system, therefore, a few cells are responsible for imparting the *Dictyostelium*'s own rhythm of life, which keeps their brethren on their toes, as it were. At this other end of evolution's scale, therefore, we see a counterpart of what the PGO waves achieve for the brain during dreaming. For it is intriguing to note that the same chemical substance, cyclic-AMP, also plays an important signalling role in the brain.

I will close by noting just one more of these fascinating parallels, one which lies at the most fundamental of levels. In 1920, Alfred Lotka predicted that some chemical reactions might display stable oscillations; he hypothesized that they would perpetually alternate between two different distributions of their chemical components, and thus never settle down to a single quiescent state. He was, unfortunately, before his time, and the suggestion met only with ridicule. Forty years later, however, A.P. Belousov reported such oscillations in mixtures of organic fuels in water. The fuels in question were citrate and malate, both of which are involved in the energy-producing reactions in living cells. Then, in 1970, A.N. Zaikin and A.M. Zhabotinsky discovered the recipe for a chemical reaction that not only pulses but also sends sharp waves of colour out across the surface of the reacting liquids, like grass fires across a field. Such reactions have no steady stable state; they oscillate with an almost clock-like precision. And it is here that we make contact with the biological rhythms that have been discussed in this chapter, because, as Arthur Winfree has stressed, our circadian cycle appears to be produced by similar self-contained oscillations within the central nervous system.

The hub of this rhythm generator lies in the suprachiasmatic nuclei of the hypothalamus, and it has been established that the system is influenced by light. This internal clock has a natural period that is slightly longer than the earth's rotational period, and it is brought into synchrony with the latter by various clues, of which the light–dark cycle is the most obvious. Amongst the other influences that are at work, one should not overlook our knowledge of the time of day, and our usually regular ingestion of food and drink. (Rutger Wever has recorded the course of one particular experiment, in which a young male volunteer was subjected to an environment that was devoid of any pointers as to the time of day. But the young man had a sweetheart, a female laboratory assistant, who managed to persuade one of her colleagues to pass on to him a daily love-letter. Her swain's delight at receiving the illicit and regular mail was enough to keep his circadian rhythm in phase with our terrestrial time-piece.) What remains more challenging is the question of which, amongst many, is the compelling cue. And the issue is clearly not merely an academic one. The phenomenon of jet lag, for example, and the distress that it causes, provide motivation enough for research in this area.

Such things are not our concern here, however. The interesting point, in the present context, is that cyclic events at apparently quite different levels of sophistication might stem from one and the same basic type of process. The throb of the test-tube reaction, the pulsations of the slime-mould colony, and the regular alternations of our sleep–dream cycle might be governed by essentially the same type of chemical interactions. This suggestion of an underlying unity, moreover, has a direct bearing on my central thesis. For if it is a ghost that drives the palpitations of our circadian rhythms, then it would have to be a ghost that cranked the handle of Zaikin's and Zhabotinsky's reaction to produce those tremulous waves of colour. That latter ghost was exorcised long ago, however, by Friedrich Wohler, as we have already seen. It seems natural to conclude, therefore, that in life's rhythms in general, and in the brain's rhythms in particular, we observe nothing more than the inexorable tick-tock of a mechanical time-piece.

● Summary

The working of the brain can be externally monitored through a variety of physical techniques, the most common of which is electroencephalography. Electrical leads fastened to the scalp are found to carry signals in the form of waves, reflecting the state of brain activity. The various stages during the body's daily rhythms have thus been identified, and it has been shown that there is periodic activity even during sleep. This is the dreaming state, which appears to be a form of memory preservation and husbanding; as with any other machine, the brain thus requires periodic maintenance.

Chips off old blocks
Genesis of the brain

> The evolution of the horse was certainly a most
> tortuous process. None of your seven day nonsense!
> Seven days' labour wouldn't evolve one primitive
> earthworm.
>
> JOHN MORTIMER
> *Voyage Round my Father*

'Hard and prolonged training will turn even the average distance runner into a champion', I recall my favourite sports manual proclaiming, long ago, 'but great sprinters are born, not made.' Anyone who has been a spectator at an athletics competition, particularly a top-level international contest, would surely feel that the facts bear out this dictum. Good distance runners come in all manner of shapes and sizes, but the top sprinters do appear to conform with a rather standard pattern: they tend to be taller than average, and very well proportioned. There are other sports in which the demand for physical peculiarity is even more pronounced. In basketball, for example, the competitors are usually very tall indeed. These lofty individuals have, of course, acquired their unusual height through genetic endowment. It is all in the genes, as the saying goes, and few would challenge the idea. What about the brain and the mind, however? Do the same principles apply? Has fate also written our mental make-up into our chromosomes, and thus ordained beforehand whether we are to be clever or dim-witted, intellectually scintillating or dull? Were the geniuses amongst us born or made?

The message of this book is that the functioning of the brain, and what we call the mind, can be explained in mechanical terms. This does not automatically imply, however, that the workings of the brain were predetermined. We are still confronted with the task of deciding whether to attach most importance to nature or nurture, and these two sides of the question will be considered, respectively, in the present chapter and the one that follows it. Here, therefore, my immediate concern will be the question of how much of behaviour is, as it were, programmed in.

Of all the recent developments in biological research, none has been more spectacular than that seen in genetics. We now have a molecular-level picture of the genes that dictate the way in which the body is put together, and we are getting a feel for the principles which govern the division of the earth's flora and fauna into the various species. The hopelessly prejudiced discount the evidence, of course, but one upshot of this new knowledge is the confirmation of Darwin's surmise that we descended from the apes. Ninety-nine per cent of the chimpanzee's genes are also found in our own chromosomes, indeed. This seems almost indecent, but one must bear in mind that biological development involves what the mathematician calls non-linearity. We can look upon this as meaning lack of simple proportionality, and an example exposes its essential feature. In a tug-of-war competition for teams of twelve men, a fifteen-man team (assuming they were similarly sized to their adversaries) would not merely win 25 per cent more of its matches; it would win all of them. In an analogous fashion, our 1 per cent genetic difference from our chimpanzee cousins gives us a decisive advantage.

How are the genetic difference and the advantage related, however? The most familiar answer to this puzzle really only scratches the surface, because it concentrates on the macroscopic scale; it invokes what almost seems like a common-sense fact, namely that the bigger the brain, relative to the size of the body, the more clever the possessor. But even this seemingly obvious observation must be treated with caution, because *Homo sapiens neanderthalensis*, who appears to have existed at the same time as our species, *Homo sapiens sapiens*, had a brain that was not smaller than our own. His heavy brow ridges, low forehead, and somewhat crouched stance are suggestive of intellectual inferiority, as gauged by current social norms at least, and the fact that he is no longer around could be assumed to bolster that conclusion. The issue is not so clear cut, however, because it is not known whether the Neanderthals became extinct or were merely re-absorbed by our own species, about 50,000 years ago. This somewhat marginal example does not invalidate the idea that a larger brain gives a more accomplished species, of course, but it does indicate that one might be able to make a more balanced judgement by considering things at a smaller scale. This I will now proceed to do, and I will start with what has been referred to as the central dogma of molecular biology.

Ever since the pioneering discovery, by Robert Hooke, that organisms are composed of cells, it has been clear that an explanation of physiological function requires an understanding of what goes on at the cellular level. We now know that the working of an individual cell is primarily dictated by the behaviour of its proteins, each cell possessing hundreds of thousands of these little molecular machines. The proteins come in about a hundred thousand different versions, each brand being able to carry out one specific biological task. Just what a particular protein can do is determined by the way its constituent atoms are arranged, and that arrangement, in turn, is dictated by a specific gene on one of the cell's chromosomes. A typical human chromosome, of which we possess twenty-three pairs, comprises several thousand genes. If a gene is absent, or simply faulty, the corresponding protein either will not be available to the organism or it will be present in a mutated form. This can have dire consequences, if the protein's task is a vital one, and even if the absence or mutation is not life-threatening it can still cause serious departures from the ideal. Our concern is primarily with the way in which these principles govern the wiring up of the brain, as it were, and there is one thing which is already clear. If the chromosomes in a given cell (and thus every other cell, because their complements are identical) contain a total of about a hundred thousand genes, whereas there are roughly a hundred thousand million cells in the brain, each cell can not be distinct. And if there is insufficient potential for genetic diversity to permit individual neurons to be tailor-made, then the individual synapses, which are about ten thousand times more numerous than the neurons, could not possibly be designed to this degree of specificity. The myriad intercellular connections merely follow a general trend that is predetermined by the chromosomes; as with the branches of trees, no two of which are precisely alike, it is only important for the overall structure to be correct.

Such latitude is not seen in lowly species. Richard Goldschmidt, who in 1912 proposed that neurons are unique in their properties of electrochemical interaction, made detailed observations on the intestinal parasite, *Ascaris*. He found that the solid masses of nervous tissue known as the ganglia, in the brains of these small worms, always contain 162 neurons, in a standard arrangement. In the 1970s, Sydney Brenner and his colleagues established that the brain of the nematode worm *Caenorhabditis elegans* has exactly 279 neurons, which are connected to one another in essentially the same fashion in every individual. So these lowly worms, on the one hand, have brains with precisely defined circuits, while we and our evolutionary relatives, on the other, possess brains characterized by a certain variability in their structure. Is this, then, the origin of human individuality? Does the nebulous quality of the brain's blueprint give us freedom of will?

If unequivocal answers cannot be given to such questions, it is primarily because the different facets of a person's mental make-up cannot be pinpointed with the same accuracy as some of the brain's other attributes. In an earlier chapter, we saw how several of the brain's primary functions, such as hearing, touch and vision, can indeed be localized to specific regions of cerebral tissue. But in Chapter 5, when considering the neural networks which provide the brain with a sort of inner sanctum, I stated that distribution is the governing principle. A given memory is not stored in one specific synapse; it is spread over a large number of these modifiable junctions. To appreciate what this implies, one has to develop a frame of mind that contrasts sharply with that of our ancient forebears. When we speak of someone having a lot of gall, for example, we do not mean that his impudence really stems from the secretions of a minor organ located near his liver. But in earlier times this was actually taken to be the case. Galen of Bergama, the Greek physician encountered near the beginning of this book, tried to squeeze us all into just four temperamental pigeon-holes: sanguine, choleric, phlegmatic and melancholy. These, he decreed, are related to the four bodily fluids: blood, green bile, lymph and black bile. We may soon, more accurately, be linking these categories of personality to constellations of genes. Evidence

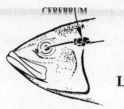

STRIPED BASS

LEOPARD FROG

GRASS SNAKE

PIGEON

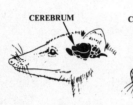

OPOSSUM

CAT

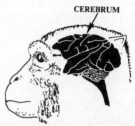

MACAQUE MONKEY

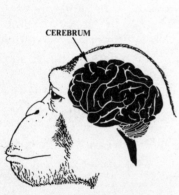

CHIMPANZEE

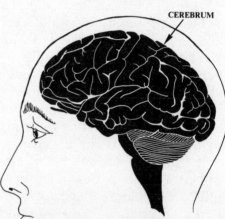

HUMAN

The average mental ability of members of a particular species is determined by the ratio of brain weight to body weight, rather than by brain weight alone. Thus although elephants, whales and even dolphins, have larger brains than ours, they cannot match us in mental capacity. Within a given class, the brain–body ratio is approximately constant, but the ratio increases as one progresses up the evolutionary ladder. The dinosaurs had rather small ratios, which were exceeded, in turn, by the amphibians, fish, reptiles, birds, mammals, and most recently by the primates. An impression of this gradual increase in the brain–body ratio can be gained by comparing the species depicted in this figure.

that some behavioural traits are genetically dictated at the sub-chromosomal level is, in fact, beginning to accumulate; some elements of a person's psyche might be related to just a few specific genes. As an example, I could cite the recent announcement, by Roy King, that even such an innocuous quality as shyness can be traced to abnormally low levels of the neurotransmitter dopamine, presumably caused by a genetic factor.

Dopamine, however, is found in many parts of the brain, and the same is true of most of the other several dozens of neurotransmitters that have now been identified. We should not fall into the trap, therefore, of taking the above link between shyness and dopamine to indicate the existence of a sort of shyness centre somewhere up in the head. That would almost be tantamount to reinstating Franz Gall's phrenology, which was disposed of in Chapter 2. We should rather conclude that the nature–nurture problem is compounded by the delocalization of all but the simplest of brain functions. And this brings me back to the question of the brain's development. It is, in fact, just one aspect of the broader issue of developmental biology, which has still to be given a satisfactory explanation. The central question, however, does at least have the merit of being well defined. It is simply this: in a multicellular organism, what is it that causes cellular differentiation? It is paradoxical that our knowledge is so full at the microscopic level, beyond the reach of unaided human vision, and yet so incomplete concerning what is manifestly apparent to the naked eye, namely that cells develop in different ways so as to produce hand and heart, and lung and lip and liver. In spite of this diversification, every cell carries in its nucleus the same chromosomes, consisting of the same genes, which are composed of DNA (i.e. deoxyribonucleic acid) having precisely the same sequence of base pairs, which are DNA's fundamental units. Something must dictate that only part of the information is translated, allowing different cells to produce the various tissues, organs and systems of the ultimately adult animal. And the differentiating mechanism is doubly mysterious because it does not appear consistent in its demands for precision; the fingers of the hand are subject to a rigid numerical constraint, while the alveoli of the lung, and, as we have already seen, the branching patterns of the brain's neurons, are merely required to follow the correct general arrangement.

Differentiation has an obvious spatial dimension because cells in different parts of the body develop in different ways. In our own bodies, this specialization produces about 200 different types of tissue. There is also a less obvious temporal dimension to the process. Proper development requires that certain cells must die at the correct time. This occurs to a marked degree in the modelling of the limbs. The fingers and toes are joined during early development, but they subsequently separate when the connecting tissue disappears. (A more spectacular temporal effect is seen in the transition from caterpillar to butterfly. It is astonishing to realize that the chromosomes in the cells of both forms of this creature are identical!) It has become clear, in recent years, that these spatial and temporal features of differentiation arise from the switching on and off of the various genes that are located in each cell's chromosomes, and it seems that the agencies which give the cell the green or red light, as it were, are hormones. These signalling substances, which are obviously vital members of the body's chemical inventory, are produced in minute quantities by the endocrine glands, and they are transported in the blood stream to other locations, where they have a profound influence on cell function.

Just how important these control mechanisms are can best be judged by the consequences when they go awry. Amongst the more familiar glandular malfunctions, I should mention the case of Cushing's disease. This is traceable to a faulty adrenal gland, and it is characterized by limbs that are thinner than normal, and a distended abdomen. Insufficient activity of the thyroid gland, on the other hand, produces the condition known as myxoedema, in which the face becomes puffy and the limbs swollen. There is another aspect of this story which we must not overlook, however. It stems from the fact that tissue differentiation has already set in well before these, and all the other, glands have finished developing. In order not to miss anything essential, therefore, I have no recourse but to return to the earliest stage of development: embryogenesis.

The fertilized egg cell is known as the zygote, and it grows not by getting larger, but by subdividing. When it has thus multiplied itself a couple of times, the resultant cells, then known as blastomeres, are still of a single type. If the embryo is, by chance, separated at this very early stage, each portion of

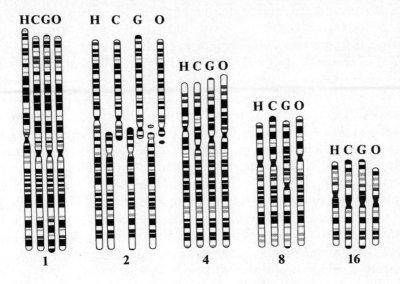

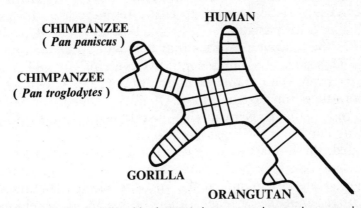

The close genealogical relationships between humans and several ape species is revealed by the similarities of the banding patterns seen in their respective chromosomes, when these are appropriately stained (upper part of the figure). One chromosome from each of five of the twenty-three chromosome pairs is shown, for the human (H), chimpanzee (C), gorilla (G) and orangutan (O). The largest difference is seen in the second chromosome, which is composed of two parts in the chimpanzee, gorilla and orangutan. The lower figure is an ancestral tree for the same species, this time differentiating between two species of chimpanzee. Each of the transverse lines represents a chromosomal change. The human, gorilla and chimpanzee probably shared an ancestor in whom the fine genetic organization of the chromosomes was similar to that found in the present human. Indeed, eighteen of the twenty-three modern human chromosomes are virtually identical to those of our common hominoid forebear.

cells is capable of developing into a complete individual. Such a fissioning thus gives rise to identical twins. (Non-identical twins are produced when two different egg cells are each fertilized by a separate sperm cell.) At the third division, or cleavage as it is called, differentiation sets in. Each blastomere produces two unlike cells, so the eight-blastomere embryo is divided into two distinct regions, one light coloured and the other somewhat darker. The former group, destined to become what is called the endoderm, will ultimately give rise to the alimentary system, that is to say the food-pipe, the stomach and the intestines. The latter four-cell region goes on to produce the ectoderm, which forms the skin, nervous system and sense organs. After a few more cell divisions, a small hollow ball of cells, known as the blastula, is formed, and the cells at its inside are already easily distinguished from those lying on the outer surface. Further growth leads to relative movement of differentiated cells and a cleft forms down one side of the ball. This produces a shape something like a clenched fist. It bears an even closer resemblance to a cowrie shell. This is the gastrula, and the different types of cell are essentially in the relative positions that they will occupy in the final body. This is true only in general, however, and we will soon see that the brain is a notable exception to the rule. The movement that produces the gastrula is known, quite logically, as gastrulation, and it effectively turns the blastula inside out, through an opening known as the blastopore. In many mammals, ourselves included, the latter subsequently develops into the anus.

Gastrulation brings the various types of cell into transitory contact. Hans Spemann, in the 1920s, showed that they exert a mutual influence on each other's subsequent development. This is known as induction, and the outcome seems to be that the various cells become committed to a particular mode of evolution even though they appear indistinguishable at this stage. If one compares the embryo of a chicken three days after conception, for example, with a three-week-old human embryo, the similarity is quite striking. As the gestation period proceeds, however, the differences between embryos of different species become more pronounced, and a human foetus at fifteen weeks is clearly recognizable as an incipient person.

Having established the foundations of this aspect of the story, we are ready to return to the part of the body which is our main concern. Small clusters of cells ultimately destined to develop into the brain's major parts are identifiable early in embryonic growth. The brain's precursors are located near that cleft in the blastula, and in the balance of the prenatal period, the developing brain acquires new neurons at the rate of hundreds of thousands per minute. The frenetic activity during this period includes not only growth and proliferation, but also differentiation of immature neurons, migration of entire neurons, the establishment of myriad synaptic connections, and the selective elimination of certain cells that play only a formative role. There is a second, non-neuron, class of cells that is very well represented in the brain. These are the so-called glial cells, and they appear to serve as structural guides for the developing neurons. Maturity achieved (after about two years) and that marshalling job therefore completed, the glial cells do not become mere spectators. On the contrary, their job is then to provide the neurons with both physical support and nourishment. It is interesting to note, parenthetically, that a post-mortem examination of the brain of Albert Einstein revealed nothing remarkable about that genius's neurons, but he does seem to have been particularly well endowed with glial cells.

In the human, around the time of birth, the brain contains all the neurons it will ever possess, but these continue to sprout new extensions (or processes, as we called them earlier) and form new synapses for the balance of the maturative period. Retention of its increasingly complex structure during growth puts certain limitations on the plasticity of the overall brain, and at birth the head is closer to its final adult size than is the rest of the body. Major discoveries regarding neural interconnections were made by Roger Sperry in the 1940s. They involved surgical rotation of the eyes of newts, and it is difficult to see how the highly important information that Sperry's work yielded could have been obtained in any other, less invasive, manner. Sperry severed the optic nerves of an embryonic newt and rotated the eyes through 180 degrees, that is through half a turn. The eyes were then re-inserted into their sockets and held in place by suitable bindings, until the connections between the cleaved nerve endings had been re-established. The important question centred on just how these connections would be made. The half-turn rotation would place fibres that could previously have been designated as being 'up', but were now 'down', in juxtaposition with fibres on the other side of the cut that were, and always had been, 'down'. Similarly, there were 'down' fibres that now found themselves looking across the cut at 'up' fibres. To the retinas of the rotated eyes, meanwhile, what used to be up in the outside world would now appear to be down, and vice versa. If the healing process in the severed and rotated optic fibres simply involved the fusion of a fibre ending with the other severed stumps that it found lying closest to it, the two reversals, one at the retina and the other at the site of the cut on the optic fibre, would have compensated each other. Sperry's experimental newts, once recovered, would then have behaved normally. But they did not. On the contrary, they lunged downwards every time prey flew overhead and leaped upwards when a potential meal passed under their noses. Their brains were receiving signals that were 180 degrees wrong regarding their environment. Since it was easy to show that the eyes had not rotated in their sockets, back to their original positions, Sperry's conclusion was inescapable: the truncated fibres were not joining up with those lying closest to hand; they were finding their way back to their original other halfs, and re-establishing contact with them!

Sperry's work was of paramount importance because it demonstrated the specificity of connections between the retina and the relevant region of the brain, which is known as the tectum. Not to be overlooked was the fact that the experiments also proved that surgical damage can be fully repaired. But the major result was that the incision and rotation at the embryonic stage still produced an adult newt displaying the bizarre behaviour. The developing neural fibres and their connections to the tectum are apparently predestined; they seem to possess some sort of biochemical marker or hormone which directs them to grow in a certain direction and link up with certain other neurons (though this precision is at the level of groups of cells rather than individual cells). The nature of the biochemical mechanism that permits this astonishing feat has not yet been fully elucidated. One important piece of the puzzle has been provided, however, by the work of Rita Levi-Montalcini. She has demonstrated that the presence of a complex of proteins, collectively known as the nerve growth factor, is vital to the development and routing of several types of neuron. It appears to manage this by inducing growth of the neuron in just the right direction for it to make its programmed synaptic contacts. But we must bear in mind that this programming is not specific right down to the level of a single synapse; it is sufficient for the tentacle-like extensions of the growing neuron to reach a goal that consists of a group of neurons in the appropriate region of the brain, and make contact with one or a few of them.

Given these few ingredients, that is to say the hormones, the selective death of certain cells when their job is done, and the nerve growth factor or factors, there is ample scope for the brain to develop the complexity of structure that we know it has. For we must not forget the capacity of even simple systems for the non-linear, or disproportionate, behaviour that was earlier exemplified by the tug-of-war analogy. Lewis Wolpert has emphasized that differentiation is further complicated by the fact that development is determined by the length of time a cell spends in a particular growth zone, so the developmental fate of a cell is determined not only by its location, but also by the time at which it occupies a given position. He compared the basic positional situation to the French flag, in which a slight change in location can cause a radical change in colour if a boundary is traversed; unless the manufacturer has made a sloppy job of printing the colours on the fabric, some white fibres and some blue fibres, say, will lie within a minute fraction of a millimetre of each other. We need not burden ourselves, here, by trying to imagine a French flag effect simultaneously in space and time. Suffice it to say that the architecture of the brain seems less mysterious when one recognizes how many different factors are at work during its sculpturing.

Complexity of structure, then, is something we do not find difficult to accept, when contemplating the brain. But where, in all this, are the roots of individuality? Each of us has his or her own unique set of genetic instructions, but this does not mean that the selection of genes displays the sort of variety one would see, for example, in the shopping baskets of the various customers in a supermarket. If the patterns along our chromosomes were that haphazard, life as we know it would be impossible. What variety we do possess, at the level of the genes, is more subtle. The situation could be compared to the unlikely event of every one of the supermarket's customers purchasing the same types of items, bread, butter, meat, milk, peas, and so on, but with different individuals selecting different brands of these groceries. And in very rare cases, we would find that the customer had forgotten to buy one particular item, because in the genetic counterpart of the shopping basket (i.e. the collective chromosomes) some unfortunate individuals do in fact lack a gene. Because human reproduction is sexual, and thus involves the consolidation of genetic components from two people into a single set of chromosomes, each act of fertilization effectively reshuffles the genetic dice. The odds against any two individuals, even close relatives, having precisely the same variants of all the human genes are astronomic. Each of us is therefore unique. There will never be another Pablo Picasso (ignoring the irrelevant fact of namesakes), another Isaac Newton, another Wolfgang Amadeus Mozart, another you, or another me. Offspring might be referred to as chips off old blocks, but in genetic terms we are emphatically not carbon copies of either of our parents.

The question remains, however, as to the degree to which genetic variety carries over into variety of mental make-up. Or do different brains, in spite of the uniqueness of the chromosomes in their constituent cells, all function in essentially the same manner, just as do all cars of a given model, say, in spite of minor variations in their components? The answer to this latter question must be a qualified yes. All brains, unless they are impaired by sickness or injury, possess about the same level of cognitive and interpretive abilities. Our criteria in this evaluation are, however, limited to the most basic of faculties. The great majority of people learn to speak, and a large fraction master a variety of skills in manipulating the multifarious products of technology. And although this might smack of rather modest aspirations, on behalf of humanity, it must be remembered that even these simple achievements put us way ahead of our nearest competitors in the animal world. To a first approximation, therefore, we do not need the uniqueness with which Nature has endowed us. The system is robust against the genetic variability that we know is present in our chromosomes. But the development of humanity has long since passed the stage at which one was satisfied by the bare essentials. The structure of society has, for the most recent many centuries, been based on the special abilities of the individual person. We tend to be subjected to a sorting process at a fairly early age, so that our contributions to the common cause can be as effective as possible. And even when we are not on the job, as it were, our interactions with our human environment are strongly influenced by our personal strengths and weaknesses. Where would our culture be, indeed, without the fact of our individual idiosyncrasies, our metiers, and our foibles? It is for this reason that curiosity drives us back to this chapter's central issue: how much do we inherit from our biological parents? For although it is true that we are not an exact copy of either our mother or our father, we are, at least, genetically closer to them than to anyone else (unless we happen to have an identical twin). To what extent, then, are our mental possibilities predestined by our genetic endowment?

There are some cases in which an unequivocal answer can be given to this question, and the answer is: to a great extent, and with devastating consequences. Down's syndrome, also known as mongolism, is a familiar example. Patients with this syndrome, named after J. Langdon Down, are severely retarded, and they have characteristically gross facial features. The condition occurs in people who have inherited three copies, rather than the normal two, of the twenty-first chromosome. New techniques of genetic analysis are helping to pinpoint genes that are related to other mental handicaps. Prominent amongst these new methods is one called restriction-fragment length polymorphism. Its acronym, RFLP, is usually pronounced 'riflip'. RFLP has led to the identification of genetic markers associated with Huntington's disease, one form of Alzheimer's disease, and phenylketonuria, a metabolic defect which leads to brain damage if not corrected for shortly after birth. The RFLP technique is made possible by the way genes are inherited. Because we receive only one copy of each chromosome from each parent, and because there is a swapping of parts of the material in each pair of chromosomes, the chromosome that is passed on carries a new combination of genes. But the number of such swaps is far fewer than the number of genes, so there is a high probability that a given gene will remain adjacent to its original neighbour on the new hybrid chromosome. If an easily detected stretch of DNA can be found that is a neighbour of a disease-causing gene, therefore, it will serve as a marker for tracing the inheritance of that gene. There is the additional requirement, that the said stretch should come in several variants, because the region of DNA immediately adjacent to the disease gene is then likely to differ in a readily detectable manner from the corresponding region associated with the normal version of the gene.

James Gusella succeeded in isolating such a marker for Huntington's disease in 1983, and he went on to map the chromosomal locations of familial Alzheimer's disease and von Recklinghausen's neurofibromatosis. This latter affliction, also known as elephant man's disease, is a disorder that manifests itself in multiple skin tumours and also tumours in the peripheral nerves. It affects about one in every 21,000 individuals. Other diseases which have subsequently proved amenable to the RFLP technique include one form of manic depression. The availability of a powerful diagnostic tool such as this inevitably raises thorny ethical and moral questions. It is becoming possible to reveal flaws in the genetic material of a person years, and even decades, before the corresponding disease will develop, and the current quest to map the entire human genome will further sharpen this difficult issue. Should the carrier of a faulty gene be informed of what the future inevitably holds?

I will leave this sombre problem, and return to that question of inherited behavioural traits. But I should, in passing, note the danger of over-interpreting observed genetic correlations. It would be too facile to imagine a given facet of a person's conduct as being necessarily coded for by a single gene. Conversely, one gene could influence different aspects of behaviour. Indeed, sets of apparently associated genes can even influence things that seem to have very little to do with each other. A case in point is the bizarre fact that males suffering from some forms of mental retardation possess remarkably large testicles. With that caveat in mind, therefore, let us look at a few interesting examples.

One does not have to be a cat expert to be aware of the fact that some cats are friendlier (towards humans) than others. Dennis Turner, Julie Feaver, Michael Mendl and Patrick Bateson have carried out a survey in which subjective evaluations of friendliness were compared with more scientific measurements of cat behaviour, such as their propensity for approaching and investigating an observer. They found that the assessments were remarkably consistent, and they discovered a suggestive genealogical factor. The cats they studied spent the first few weeks in individual pens with their mothers, prior to being admitted into larger social groups. There was no clear indication that friendly mothers tend to have friendly kittens. But the friendly offspring showed a definite bias towards having the same fathers. Oddly enough, not all these fathers were themselves friendly, and Turner and his colleagues concluded that genes were being passed on that influence personality only indirectly.

These cat studies merely hint at the possibility of genetically determined behaviour. Recent work on colonies of bees has gone farther than this; it has actually demonstrated that the link exists. This important advance was made possible by the social conditions that prevail in the typical hive. It is not unusual for a number of queens to be present, and for them to share the same husband, as it were. The situation is known as polygamy, and it naturally does not imply that only one male is being called upon to do all the fertilizing. Far from it, indeed, for there is always a simultaneous current of polyandry, which is the term used to denote that a given female (in this case a queen bee) has a plurality of mates. These circumstances provide those who study bees with a variety of types of individual, and the way in which this variety arises is only now beginning to be elucidated. It had earlier been assumed that the caste system that exists in a beehive is the product of a complicated set of social interactions. But it is now possible to genetically label individual bees, and this has yielded some startling results. Interest focussed on worker patrilines, in particular, these being worker offspring of different fathers but the same mother, and the genetic identification was carried out by pinpointing certain enzymes through the technique known as electrophoresis.

It has long been known that some of the hive's workers serve all their lives as guards, repelling marauders when the need arises, while others are undertakers. These latter individuals efficiently remove the corpses of their fallen comrades. These two behavioural patterns are vital to the colony's viability, but they are displayed by relatively few of the hive's company. Using the enzyme markers, Gene Robinson and Robert Page Jr looked for correlations between genetic endowment and behaviour in the species of bee known as *Apis mellifera*, and they obtained a positive result. They were able to rule out the element of chance from their observations, and their conclusion was that the guards and the undertakers had neither chosen their careers nor had them forced upon them by their worker peers; they were what they were because they possessed certain rare genes. Remarkably, the results of a related study, on the same species, were announced at the same time by Peter Frumhoff and Jayne Baker. They had been intrigued by two other types of behaviour, namely mutual grooming between workers and mutual feeding. The genetic markers in this case also differed from those employed by Robinson and Page, because Frumhoff and Baker differentiated between patrilines through the colours of their cuticles. Some were black, while the others were cordovan, which is a reddish-brown colour reminiscent of leather. It transpired that cordovan patrilines indulge in substantially more grooming than the black variety, whereas no bias was observed in feeding behaviour. Again, therefore, there were indications of a genetically dictated proclivity.

Aldous Huxley's *Brave New World*, published in 1932, foresaw a situation in which different classes of human being were produced by genetic manipulation and reared artificially for the balance of the gestation period. The categories in his novel, in order of decreasing mental ability, were called alphas, betas, gammas and deltas, and many readers must have been daunted by the book's thesis. This was probably Huxley's intention. The fascinating thing about these recent discoveries in connection with the caste system in bee colonies is that they seem to have anticipated Huxley's scenario; the bees have apparently already separated themselves into alphas, betas and so on. Not of their own volition, however, and not through the complexities of social interaction; it has been foisted upon them through genetic endowment.

Does this make the bee society different from our own? India, for example, has a well-developed caste structure, and it has a marked hereditary component. But this is not a genetic phenomenon; the strata of Indian society are held in place by social traditions and taboos, not by anything present in Indian chromosomes. The Indian caste system is but one small corner of human culture, however, and the question remains as to whether any of our behavioural traits or propensities, ill-defined as they might be, are somehow dictated by our genes. The intriguing fact is that there has recently appeared evidence which does indeed support that proposition. I will round out this chapter, therefore, by taking a closer look at a couple of human attributes that seem to have a genetic dimension, two facets of our mental make-up which we acquire by nature rather than nurture.

There are certain types of activity that I find absolutely terrifying, even though many people indulge in them of their own choice, and for apparent pleasure. Parachuting and mountain climbing top this list of dangerous pursuits, and they are closely followed by automobile and motorcycle racing, bull-fighting, hang-gliding, diving from high platforms, performing somersaults from trapezes, and taking the more violent rides at fairgrounds. Such things are anathema to me, and no doubt to the majority of my fellow human beings, because they involve too high a risk factor. But although I do not deliberately court danger, I am equally put off by the prospect of too dull an existence. A soupçon of risk does seem to put a bit of spice into life, especially when one is in the mood for it. There are, however, people who clearly thrive in circumstances that I would find utterly boring. Some of them spend a large fraction of their time in front of their television sets, deriving vicarious pleasure from interminable soap operas, game shows and situation comedies. Risk is just not these people's cup of tea.

There are, then, risk-seekers and risk-avoiders, and a broad spectrum of people lying between these extremes, and the question naturally arises as to what pushes us into a particular category. Recent research has indicated that the issue has a marked genetic component. Marvin Zuckerman, for example, has demonstrated that identical twins show a distinct tendency to fall into the same division, whereas this is not the case for non-identical twins. The daredevil with a thirst for thrills that can only be satiated on the North Wall of the Eiger or behind the wheel of a Formula 1 racer is not likely to have an identical twin who prefers the Readers' Room of the British Museum. Hans Eysenck has suggested that our attitude towards risk is governed by the degree of general activity in the brain, and that the normal tendency is for this to be regulated to an intermediate level. If the environment provides us with insufficient stimulation, at a given time, the brain automatically drives us to seek more excitement.

Too much activity going on around us, on the other hand, causes us to shy away, and to withdraw to a situation we can more readily manage. The part of the brain that exercises this control is the reticular formation, which we have already encountered in the context of attention, and it is another example of what was one of our concerns in Chapter 2, namely the governor. People who constantly crave thrills might have reticular formations that are sluggish; greater levels of danger and excitement would then be required to get their control centres performing up to par. Conversely, the quiet types amongst us might have reticular formations that are naturally overactive, and thus in need of being dampened down.

A related theory pins the blame for foolhardiness on the sex hormones oestrogen and androgen, and it suggests that, in the case of the male at least, there really is a connection between having hair on one's chest and being the bold and fearless type. These hormones apparently lead the body to produce the supernormal amounts of the neurotransmitter noradrenalin that have been shown to be present in people who display a pronounced degree of daring. And evaluation of the latter quality is no longer merely subjective; it can be measured by laboratory experiment. The volunteer is fitted with a pair of electrodes on one finger and told to expect an electric shock of undisclosed intensity. Automatic monitoring of the subject's heart beat and the moisture level at the palms of the hands clearly reveals which people suffer anxiety during the waiting period. The results show that those who naturally avoid excitement develop a racing pulse and clammy hands while anticipating the shock, whereas the daredevils are free of both symptoms.

It thus seems that what one could call the spirit of adventure is susceptible to quantitative measurement, and that it is at least partly determined by what one has in one's chromosomes. Some as yet elusive combination of genes appears to hold the key to processes which, through the mediating agencies of the reticular formation and certain hormones and neurotransmitters, can drive one individual to seek out the dangerous challenge and another to shun it. But this genetic factor could only dictate a person's propensities; it alone cannot determine what they will lead to, for that depends upon what opportunities present themselves. And it is here that nurture steps in, to play what will often prove to be the decisive role. Frank Farley has carried out an exhaustive investigation of the environmental factor in the development of risk-loving males, and his findings are of singular sociological importance. He established that those risk-seekers who grew up in impoverished urban areas, and downright slums, had a much larger than average chance of ending up in criminality of the more daring type: safe-breaking, armed robbery, and the like. Their counterparts from the choicer suburbs, on the other hand, enjoyed a greater than average measure of success in high-risk businesses, such as playing the stock market. And these Yuppies, as they are now called, displayed a distinct preference, in their leisure periods, for such sports as mountaineering, downhill skiing and parachute jumping. What one has in one's chromosomes thus dictates an individual's relationship to risk, but it is what one has in one's pocket that will determine how that relationship will express itself. And in the case of the disadvantaged risk-lover, with his regrettably high probability of winding up in gaol, there is an obvious moral to this story. Merely incarcerating one of these unfortunates in a penitentiary, and condemning him to a life of inactivity, is not only grossly unjust; it is biologically unsound. The more appropriate way to rehabilitate such individuals is to present them with exciting and socially acceptable challenges. Properly handled, these same people could, when they are returned to society, be given the sorts of task that would cause most citizens to demur because of the associated danger. Many a re-directed risk-lover could find himself the recipient of an award for bravery.

I will now turn to another human attribute that has also been shown to be determined by genetic endowment. It belongs, in fact, to the same class of behavioural characteristics as our previous example, but it has implications and consequences that are more far-reaching: it is motivation. Recent investigations have shown that an individual's level of motivation, his get up and go, as one says these days, is under the decisive influence of what are referred to as opioid drugs. Because of the customary application of the word drug to something that is externally administered, let me hastily add that the substances in question are produced by the body itself, and for exclusively internal consumption, as it were. Much recent attention has been directed towards an opioid known as beta endorphin. It is chemically related to both heroin and morphine, and the term endorphin literally means 'the morphine within'. Beta-endorphin has been observed to induce a variety of effects, including analgesia (i.e. an absence of pain), euphoria, respiratory depression and, oddly enough, constipation. It appears that this substance is released into the blood from the pituitary gland. (This controls the other endocrine glands, and should not be confused with the pineal gland, which Descartes saw as the mind–soul junction, but the implication of the pituitary gland in something so central as motivation seems to suggest reinstatement of that ancient idea.) Within the brain, beta-endorphin predominantly turns up in part of the hypothalamus, the amygdala, and in the pons.

Of course, the main interest centres on the conditions under which beta-endorphin does its job, and on the exact nature of that job. Regarding the former issue, the simplest answer seems to be that it goes into action when the level of stress or provocation becomes sufficiently high. In an experimental rat, for example, a release of beta-endorphin can be achieved simply by pinching the creature's tail. And a common result of this is that the rat starts to eat, even though it has shown no signs of hunger immediately prior to the stimulation. The eating seems to be symptomatic of a sudden and general desire for comfort or consolation. Substances which chemically oppose beta-endorphin have been identified, one of the most frequently used being naloxone. If such an opioid antagonist is administered, the tail-pinching no longer elicits comfort seeking.

These observations might seem to be of modest scope, not to mention dubious utility. After all, we are not, on the basis of these results, going to advocate wholesale pinching of rats' tails in order to induce them to eat the grain in our silos. The point of such rat experiments was, however, that they suggested extensions to broader and deeper insights. The outcome has been a linking of beta-endorphin to something we encountered when considering neural networks in Chapter 5. I remarked there how easy it is to slip into the fallacy of invoking an internal teacher, to monitor the development of our vast mesh of interconnected neurons, and to ensure that it always evolved in the direction of increasing wisdom. Such an internal *alter ego* does not exist, of course, and we saw that the need for it was bypassed by what was referred to as the brain's reward system. It is now becoming clear, as Jane Dum and Albert Herz have emphasized, that the emotional and motivational effects of beta-endorphin and the other so-called opioids stems from their influence on that reward system. Moreover, the genes which direct the production of opioids in the body have now been identified, and the structures of some of the corresponding receptor proteins have been elucidated. Given the well-established link between mutant forms of genes and the resultant mutations of the proteins they code for, one can begin to glimpse a hierarchical set of connections which lead from the genes right up to an individual's capacity for taking the initiative. But this path becomes fuzzy because of the fact that the emotions are at the mercy of a multiplicity of types of opioids.

It is such biochemical diversity which inevitably clouds the issue of genetic determinism, and it denies to the proponent of a strong hereditary factor the chance of making as good a case as the situation really deserves. That nurture also plays a major role cannot be denied, of course, as we shall see in the next chapter, but it is probably true to say that the degree of genetic determination is currently being underestimated. And in my final examples of initiative, or lack of it, two extremes can be identified which are at least not incompatible with the idea of a genetic origin. The one concerns the syndrome known as autism. As is made abundantly clear in Clara Claiborne Park's book *The Siege*, the most striking feature of the autistic patient is his or her lack of desire to originate any activity, however modest. And a hereditary factor in this affliction has recently been demonstrated. The other end of the scale brings us full circle, back to the question with which this chapter started, namely the origin of genius. (The special case of mathematical genius has now been linked with exposure in the womb to high levels of the male hormone testosterone, this being the outcome of an analysis, undertaken by Camilla Benbow, of 10,000 American children.) As Thomas Edison once said of genius: it is 1 per cent inspiration and 99 per cent perspiration. Because there is at least a loose connection between initiative and a willingness to perspire, geniuses might indeed be born rather than made.

● Summary

The layout of the brain is genetically determined, and the structures ultimately destined to form this crucial part of the central nervous system are discernible at an early stage in the embryo's development. The myriad intercellular connections follow a predetermined pattern dictated by the chromosomes. This is only a general trend, however, since there is insufficient genetic material to individually code for every synaptic contact; as with the branches of trees, no two of which are precisely alike, it is merely important for the overall structure to be correct. But because there are such vast numbers of cells involved, this strategy for construction appears to be sufficient to guarantee proper functioning. Some attributes of a person's mental make-up appear to be dictated by genetically related surfeits or deficits of certain neurotransmitters. The brain machine is fabricated according to a blueprint which allows for some flexibility; no two machines are exactly the same.

8

Old dogs and new tricks
Nature and nurture

There is no long-distance target, no final perfection
to serve as a criterion for selection, although human
vanity cherishes the absurd notion that our species
is the final goal of evolution.

RICHARD DAWKINS
The Blind Watchmaker

The case for a genetic component in personality does seem reasonably strong, and the dyed in the wool reductionist might even
find facts like those presented in the previous chapter positively
seductive. Heredity cannot be the whole story, however. After
all, no child was ever born spoiled, and no child was ever born
brainwashed either. It is thus patently clear that the development of any particular human mind is at least partially dictated
by the stimulation it receives from other humans. My task here
is to try to quantify the degree to which this is so. We will find
that studies of identical twins reared in separate environments
demonstrate the importance of external influence. And we will
learn how the work of ethologists (i.e. those who study animal
behaviour) has revealed the extent to which the infant animal
can be imprinted, as the process is called. The extreme inference
from such observations would be that the mind at birth is like
what John Locke called a *tabula rasa*, or blank tablet. But those
same twin studies provide a necessary counterweight, because
identical pairs show a statistically significant tendency to have
similar intelligence levels.

Religion has always had a strangely ambivalent attitude to
the nature–nurture issue. Professing an interest in bringing

children up in the ways of God, though as often as not simultaneously concealing its own interest in recruitment and the collection plate, the Church has invariably subjected young minds to
intense doses of rote learning while nevertheless insisting that the
individual has free will. It has to, of course, because the concepts
of heaven and hell would otherwise be nonsense. If anything, the
general acceptance of the concepts of heaven and hell reveals
more about the mind than it does about anything supernatural,
and it exposes our intellectual limitations; it betrays our poverty
of conceptual nuance. For it has always been implicit that there
is a roughly fifty-fifty chance of our eternal soul taking an upward
or downward journey upon departing from our mortal remains.
Were the cards to be stacked against us, ninety-nine to one,
say, resignation would prevail, and we would be inclined to
salvage what we could from the situation by at least deriving
the maximum pleasure and advantage from our sins. And if,
contrariwise, all but one per cent were, willy-nilly, destined for
paradise, wouldn't there be a great danger of laxness and a general taking of things for granted. Whence the balance between
the probabilities of eternal bliss and eternal damnation. So we
have heaven or hell, just as we have good or evil, up or down,
white or black; a pair of equally weighted alternatives is what
our minds feel most comfortable with. But in the case of this
division that religion has thrust upon us, it is all predicated on
our enjoying freedom of will. As we consider the role of nurture,
therefore, we will naturally bear in the backs of our minds that
supreme question which will have to be faced squarely in the
final chapter: are we or are we not free agents?

We are not yet ready for that issue, however. There are things
of more immediate concern, and one of these is that question
of imprinting, because it is relevant to nurture's very earliest
stage. In the 1930s, Konrad Lorenz observed that newly hatched
chicks, ducklings and goslings will become socially attached to
the first object that catches their gaze. They can be tricked, for
example, into assuming that a coloured ball is their mother if it
is the first thing they see moving. Lorenz even fooled one flock of
ducklings into believing that he was their mother. In subsequent
investigations, he showed that any object could fill the same role
provided that it was conspicuous, his definition of that adjective
being that the item was larger than a matchbox and that it was

in motion. This left the process of imprinting with wide scope, exact colour and shape being irrelevant. Lorenz believed that the imprinted association is permanent once it has become fully established. Later studies have tended to undermine the Lorenzian conclusions, both regarding the nature of imprinting and its assumed permanence. It is now clear, for example, that one of these young creatures will transfer its filial allegiance to a second object after repeated exposure to it. And there does seem to be a marked preference for particular types of object.

Johan Bolhuis, Gabriel Horn and Mark Johnson have probed this latter aspect of the issue, in the context of chicks, and have gradually homed in on its essentials. To begin with, they found that a stuffed hen, mechanically agitated, attracted more attention than a similarly moved red box. Then they showed that it was not the overall form of the hen that was eliciting the response, because a mutilated stuffed hen with its limbs reassembled higgledy-piggledy proved to arouse just as much interest as its undefiled counterpart. When the head too was cut up and jumbled, however, the composite creature was far less successful as a mother surrogate. Indeed, young chicks prefer the isolated head to the entire hen. And what is more, the head does not even have to be that of a hen in order to arouse chick curiosity; a stuffed duck's head, and even the head of a stuffed polecat, will do just as nicely. It is as if sensitivity to a certain standard pattern is genetically programmed into a chick's visual, or perhaps cognitive machinery, and the question naturally arises as to how the creature acquires just the right neuronal circuitry to imbue it with the undeniably useful faculty of recognizing its mother. The answer must ultimately lie in the usual Darwinian argument that such an ability to recognize a dual protector and provider confers a decisive advantage in terms of survival. So those members of the species which came to possess the right versions of the necessary genes simply dominated the scene, and secured the inside track when it came to having successful offspring.

But what exactly is this neural wiring that allows a tiny fowl to be so aware of Mum? A strong hint was provided by work on a different type of species, namely our own. It was carried out in 1975 by Carolyn Goren, who investigated the reactions of babies just a few minutes after birth. Mothers of newborn babies usually believe that their infants cannot really see until they are about two months old, but Goren's study refuted this myth. She showed that the eyes and head of a newborn child will follow more or less any slowly moving object for a brief period, but the child generally tends to lose interest quite quickly. If the object possesses a face-like pattern, however, the interest is preserved over a markedly longer period and the child will often track it until it is out of sight. Follow-up studies by Mark Johnson and John Morton pared the process down to its barest essentials. They demonstrated that a very strong response, on the part of a newborn baby, can be elicited by a 'face' that is very primitive indeed. One of their test patterns that proved to be particularly popular amongst their diminutive subjects merely consisted of three black rectangles on a white background. Two were in the positions usually occupied by the eyes, while the third was located where the mouth normally lies. (When the manufacturers of cheap dolls produce faces composed of just three dots, similarly arranged in a triangle, they are thus not really wide of the mark.)

Such a starkly geometrical arrangement brings to mind the pioneering work of David Hubel and Torsten Wiesel, which I described in an earlier chapter. We recall that they established the presence, in the visual pathway, of cells that respond preferentially to lines of a given orientation and direction of motion. They also discovered cells which display peak sensitivity to patterns that can be regarded as composites of these simple line configurations, such as a bar that abruptly terminates or a sharp corner. The Johnson–Morton three rectangle array can, in turn, be looked upon as lying on a yet higher level of organization, a sort of composite of composites. The fact that it is nevertheless a far cry from a real face makes one realize just how sophisticated our visual systems are. But the point here is that if on the one hand we have cells that are tuned to respond to specific lines, while at the other extreme we can develop intercellular synaptic connections that enable us to recognize actual faces, it is perhaps not so surprising that even the youngest amongst us can possess the circuitry necessary to make them relate to three rectangles or dots, appropriately juxtaposed. In fact, because the key to all types of perception lies in abstracting the essence from the mere background, the conceptual wheat from the conceptual chaff as it were, we see that the infant's primary need is for an adequate filtering system. It might get this for free, in effect, because of the initial lack of fine tuning in its visual system. A virtue is thus made out of necessity, and the baby probably makes nothing more out of its mother's face than something resembling those three dark patches.

The other senses show similar evidence of genetic pre-wiring. Jacob Steiner has studied the infant's powers of taste discrimination, for example, and has come up with evidence of a surprisingly sophisticated system. A baby as young as twelve hours, with no taste experience whatsoever, not even its mother's milk, will gurgle contentedly if a drop of sugar solution is placed on its tongue, and screw up its face in annoyance if the drop is followed by another of lemon juice. Positive responses are also produced by banana and vanilla essences, while the smells of both rotten eggs and shrimps produce an irritated recoil.

The difficulties inherent in trying to gauge what a baby knows and what it does not know would not exist, of course, if babies could talk. (The word infant comes from the Latin *infans*, which indeed means incapable of speech.) But this lack of communication has been circumvented by cleverly devised techniques and procedures in recent years. A particularly noteworthy example is known as the visual preference method. Invented in 1958 by Robert Fantz, it presents the infant with a visual choice of just two objects and involves measurement of the time the youngster looks at each of them. A marked temporal bias in favour of one of the objects reveals that the infant can discriminate between members of the pair. By a judicious choice of a variety of pairings, the resourceful researcher can in effect put questions to the baby and receive unequivocal answers. Davida Teller used this approach to demonstrate that some children can differentiate between red and green squares (on a yellow background) before they are one month old. By the end of the second month, the fraction with this skill had climbed to around a half, while virtually all three-month-olds were capable of successfully distinguishing between the colours. It had earlier been believed that colour perception was part of a complicated socio-cultural phenomenon with an unavoidable linguistic component, but the Teller studies exposed this for the fallacy it was; colour vision is an integral part of early visual organization, and it is at least partially 'wired in'. Another remote measuring technique known as photorefraction allows the experimenter to determine the eye's accommodation, that is its ability to focus, and Janette Atkinson and Oliver Braddick used it to show that at least half of all newborn babies can focus on objects up to about 150 centimetres away. The visual acuity at this tender age would give the typical child an optometrist's rating of around 20/500, which corresponds to legal blindness, and this puts the child at a twenty to thirty-fold disadvantage compared with the average adult. But this rudimentary resolving power is nevertheless sufficient to enable the child to accomplish such tasks as distinguishing its fingers when they are held at arm's length.

The photorefraction technique involves photographing the subject's eye with a combination of lenses suitably placed so as to reveal the point of focus. Its ability to yield precise information on the state of the eye without the subject's participation has found an important application that has nothing to do with these investigations of newborn infants. Retarded patients, for example, often suffer from multiple handicaps, including seriously impaired vision. The optician can use the photorefraction method to fit spectacles to a patient who is quite oblivious of the fact that the eyes are being tested.

Returning to my main theme, and by way of summarizing the evidence reviewed thus far, one could say that a baby is born with certain reflexes and that these are gradually augmented by learned behaviour. The division between instinct and the capacity for learning is generally taken to depend upon which species one is considering, and a predominance of instinctive behaviour has usually been regarded as the hallmark of a lowly rung on the evolutionary ladder. A modicum of instinct and a great propensity for learning, on the other hand, is generally supposed to be a sign of intelligence and evolutionary sophistication. It is certainly the case that the newborn of some modestly endowed species are capable of prodigious instinctive feats. The infant kangaroo, for example, with its surprisingly small birth size, has to undertake a long journey crawling up the fur of its mother's abdomen in order to reach the nipples that are hidden in her pouch. (Watching a film of this performance is a nail-biting experience; until the goal is reached it seems that the little mite has virtually no chance of succeeding. And one feels like cheering when the mission is finally accomplished.) Conversely, the infant human's instincts can be precariously fragile. The newborn child has an instinctive ability to avoid suffocation, for example, by pushing away items such as bedclothes that threaten to smother it. But this respiratory occlusion reflex, as it is called, is gradually replaced by a more comprehensive set of learned reactions. Some children encounter difficulties during the transitional period, and in extreme cases the tragic result is the 'sudden cot death' which strikes during the child's first year.

But it is now becoming clear that this neat division between instinct and learning is not really tenable. We are beginning to realize that learning is frequently guided by instinct, and this has tended to blur the distinction between nature and nurture. In order to appreciate the way in which the picture has changed in recent years, we should first review the situation that prevailed before this particular intellectual edifice began to crumble. Instinct was the province of the academic field known as ethology, which reached a new pinnacle of respectability when its founders, Konrad Lorenz, Nikolaas Tinbergen and Karl von Frisch were awarded the Nobel Prize in 1973. From an ethological point of view, behaviour has four major facets: sign stimuli, which are instinctively recognized cues; motor programmes, which are the innate responses to those cues; drive, which controls the motivational impulses; and imprinting, which we have already encountered, and which is a relatively uncommon and somewhat spurious form of learning. The assumed opposite to instinct, namely learning, traditionally lay in the domain of the different academic discipline of behavioural psychology. Its standard-bearer was Ivan Pavlov, whose work on conditioning was briefly discussed in an earlier chapter.

Let us take a closer look at what the two fields represent by considering examples of the above categories in action. We have already contemplated one aspect of ethology in discussing Lorenz's imprinting of young fowl. The other three aspects are nicely illustrated by something that a brooding goose is often observed to do. An egg will occasionally roll down the side of the mound-shaped nest, and the sitting goose retrieves it in what at first appears to be a thoughtful response. The goose catches sight of the wayward egg, stretches out its neck so as to get a closer look at it, and then rolls the egg gently back up the slope with its bill. 'Wise and clever' might be our judgement of the goose in this accomplishment. But wait. The creature has just noticed a nearby empty beer bottle and it is rolling this too up into the nest. Our illusions shattered, the ethologist points out that the curves on the egg and the bottle are the sign stimuli (which the goose failed to distinguish between), while the act of rolling is the motor programme. The drive, which provokes the recovery operation, is not a permanent attribute of the goose. It is related to the incubation period, and the creature possesses it from a couple of weeks before the eggs are laid until a similar amount of time has elapsed after they are hatched.

Turning to the other field of scientific enquiry, behavioural psychology, we note that its stocks-in-trade are classical conditioning on the one hand, and operant conditioning on the other. There are three components to classical conditioning: the unconditioned stimulus; the unconditioned response; and the conditioned stimulus. These various pieces of the story were presented earlier, in the context of Pavlov's conditioned dog, which is of course the classic example. This brings me back to an example, drawn from my own experience, that I touched on earlier; let us now take a closer look at it. I frequently find myself emulating Pavlov's hound when I eat lunch in our local Faculty Club. Fish and chips, one of my weaknesses, is available only as a special order, and one has to wait while the dish is prepared. The cooking complete, the cashier rings a small bell and one trots up to the counter to be rewarded for one's patience. On those days when I have chosen a different item on the menu, I find myself nevertheless salivating (the unconditioned response, which is the counterpart of the ethologist's motor programme) at the sound of the bell summoning someone else to the counter (the conditioned stimulus) because this strikes up in me an association with the fish and chips (the unconditioned stimulus, which is equivalent to the ethologist's sign stimulus). Operant conditioning is quite different, and it is epitomized by the laboratory rat running his maze and pushing at his levers, in order to achieve a reward or avoid a punishment. The performing circus animal is another example. Mention of operant conditioning usually makes me recall a cartoon I once came across in a popular science magazine. It showed two laboratory rats in an experimental cage, and one is saying to the other: 'I've got that fellow in the white coat perfectly trained; every time I press this right-hand lever, he responds by giving me a pellet of food.'

The cartoon's humour lay in its hinted reversal of the normal man–rat relationship, of course, and it acquired extra bite because there is something odious in the suggestion that a human can be operant conditioned. In the 1968 US presidential campaign, Michigan governor George Romney carelessly let drop a gratuitous remark to the effect that he had been brainwashed on a particular minor issue. He did not seem to appreciate the implications of what he was admitting, for one who aspired to be the leader of a nation. The point was not missed by the attending journalists, however, and the remark ruined Romney's political career. The nefarious overtones inherent in conditioning provided the basis for Richard Condon's novel *The Manchurian Candidate*. The story recounts how an American prisoner of war is trained to murder the president of his country, after his release from captivity, in response to a specific conditioned stimulus.

Behavioural psychologists used to believe that operant conditioning could be used to train an animal to perform any task which lay within its physical and cognitive abilities, but recent developments have made them change their minds. The first cloud on the horizon was perceived by John Garcia when he discovered that rats cannot associate visual and auditory cues with food that induces nausea, even though their sight and hearing is excellent. They can, on the other hand, associate signals based on taste and smell with such food. Turning to quail, he found that associations with bad foodstuffs could be established through visual signals, namely colours, but that taste and smell cues were ineffective. Similar inadequacies have since turned up in other species. The much-vaunted rat, for example, with its prowess for pressing levers, will do so to obtain food but is apparently incapable of repeating the performance in order to preclude being given an electric shock. Conversely, it can learn to avoid the shock by jumping at the right moment, but it is unable to establish a mental link between jumping and being rewarded with food. There are, it seems, serious chinks in the rat's intellectual armour, and this appears to apply to all animal species that have been thoroughly investigated. The natural conclusion is that a given type of animal is predisposed to make certain types of association while being innately incapable of detecting other correlations that are no more demanding of its sensory machinery. There are, in other words, biases that are 'wired in' to the creature's mental circuitry. And the 'programming' clearly has an adaptive logic. The rat, for example, is nocturnal, and odour is therefore more significant than colour. It is thus not surprising that olfactory cues are much more effective than visual cues in the conditioning of that species.

The important lesson to be learned from such observations is that learning has a strong instinctive component, and this indicates that the division between ethology and behaviourism is not as watertight as it was formerly taken to be. It shows, moreover, that imprinting is not so anomalous as once thought; it is, on the contrary, actually made possible by this bridge between instinct and learning.

The origin of instinct must lie in an animal's nervous system, of course, and there are cases where the neuronal circuitry related to a particular behavioural trait is not difficult to guess at. We have already considered a human baby's inborn sensitivity to those triangularly-arranged black rectangles, and a similar agency appears to be at play in the visual system of the bee. This insect seems to be most adept at recognizing objects possessing what is known as a high spatial frequency. If the object was black and it was observed against a white background, this term would merely refer to the degree of alternation between black and white, as perceived by the bee. A good one-dimensional example would be the alternations caused by black railings situated in front of a white façade. The fact that flowers are coloured is only a minor complication, and the important feature in this context is the way in which space is divided up by the pattern of the petals. It is this which provides the sign stimulus, which we now realize must be simultaneously thought of as an unconditioned stimulus. It provokes the motor programme (and unconditioned response) of alighting on the flower and investigating its nectar-bearing regions. If these recompense the insect sufficiently, the flower's physical characteristics will be learned. These will thus become the conditioned stimuli. The early recordings of these aspects of bee behaviour were the work of Karl von Frisch, and they again revealed a bias in that bees have a hard time learning non-floral odours. Their olfactory systems must be quite prejudiced.

There is another aspect of learning in bees that is both surprising and impressive: they appear to be almost bureaucratic in their ability to organize information. There is clear evidence that they allocate different priorities to cues of odour, colour and visual appearance, and these are inserted ledger-like into a sort of mental hierarchy. Odour is most important, and attention is paid to colour and shape only if several alternatives have the same smell. This reflects what could be called a realistic relationship with the environment, in that odour is usually a more reliable cue than colour, the perception of which depends upon illumination, and shape, which depends upon the angle of view. As impressive as this pigeon-holing is, on the part of our pettifogging bee, it pales in comparison to the importance the creature attaches to the time of day at which a flower provides it with a rewarding forage. Franz Bogdany investigated this factor with a set of artificial feeding stations having different shapes and colours, and equipped with different odours. During the period 10:00–11:00 hours, he one day provided bees with food at a peppermint-scented feeder station in the shape of a blue triangle. Then he replaced the feeder station with an orange-scented one in the form of a circular yellow disc, and continued to make food available for one more hour (i.e. from 11:00 to 12:00). After a few days of training, Bogdany made both stations available at 9:00, each liberally supplied with food. The bees started to show up at the blue station around 9:45, and seemed quite oblivious of the yellow station even though this was close at hand. Then around 10:45 some of the bees started to transfer to the yellow station, and all had done so by 11:15 even though the blue triangle was still laden with food. Bees thus appear to keep a mental diary, with their flower appointments scheduled to a precision of about fifteen minutes. It has since been established that a 'page' of this symbolic book has space enough for at least nine different assignations in one eight-hour working day! The neuronal circuitry of the bee brain that permits such an astonishing feat of learning must be one of the most impressive pieces of instinctive machinery in the insect class.

Animals have to learn other skills than those involved in acquiring nourishment. They must know how to avoid predators and recognize their own species, to learn how to distinguish friend from foe. One of the best-studied mechanisms of kin recognition is that of bird song, the science of which owes much to the pioneering efforts of William Thorpe. There are approximately 8,000 different species of birds on our planet, and about half of these are songbirds. Generally speaking, only the males of any species produce song. A newly hatched bird can make a variety of sounds, and the ability to generate them is retained irrespective of the bird's subsequent environment and experiences. For some species, this is as far as it goes. The chicken, turkey, ring dove and many other types of bird are apparently lacking the flexibility that is required to develop these rudimentary vocalizations into anything that could be called melodic. But in singing species, the young learn from adults the skill of producing the species-specific songs that are used for attracting a mate and defending its territory. Each species of songbird has a unique song. Peter Marler established this in 1957 by playing back recordings of song in the field. Male birds defending their territories during the breeding season respond only to the song of their own species. A particularly well-documented case history has been compiled for the white-crowned sparrow, *Zonotrichia leucophrys*, particularly through the efforts of Masakazu Konishi and Marler himself. The song of this species is quite distinctive. It begins with a whistle, which is followed by a second whistle or a sort of buzz. Thereafter, a trill of notes is sounded, the tone being gradually swept from high to low. The interesting thing is that although different individual members of this species sing songs that are a variation on this general theme, the song is usually similar to others heard in the geographical area where the bird was reared. There are, in other words, white-crowned sparrow dialects. (The same is true for several other species.)

In considering just how a young white-crowned sparrow acquires the local dialect, we find all the characteristics of classical conditioning. Even if it is initially reared in isolation, the newly hatched bird experiments with its repertoire of sounds, and after about three months this suddenly gels into a rudimentary song. It is halting and unpolished compared with that of the mature adult, but it is unmistakably a white-crowned sparrow song. The bird is thus born with the ability to produce the type of song characteristic of its species. The primitive song matures only if the young bird is exposed to the expert version before it is about seven weeks old. The existence of such a sensitivity threshold parallels what Lorenz observed with his young fowls, as described earlier, and it is the hallmark of classical imprinting. If the bird is deafened before its own elementary version of the song has crystallized, it never becomes capable of producing the adult song, whereas deafening after it has acquired an adult level of proficiency has no influence on its singing performance.

There are interesting comparisons to be made between bird song and human language. Indeed songbirds and humans are the only creatures in which the young mimic the voices of the adults. We have seen that the former have an inborn predisposition to string together certain vocal elements so as to produce a song. Babies learn to speak in a similar fashion, seeming to know instinctively which types of sound, in their larger sound repertoire, will be acceptable language elements. Then again, we have seen that there are well-defined dialects in bird song, just as there are in human language. The temporal pattern in the acquisition of bird song also parallels the human experience. The young bird listens to the adult, breaks the latter's song down into groups of tones, and essays an imitation. An infant child adopts the same approach. And for both, the initial attempts at mimicry produce only an indistinct babble. For both birds and humans, moreover, the ability to learn declines with increasing age. In our own species, we see this most clearly through our fumbling efforts to learn a foreign language in adult life.

The newborn human, on the other hand, is capable of learning any language, given sufficient exposure to it. Although *Homo sapiens sapiens* now has several sub-species, the young of all these can form the same phonemes. Only some of the latter are actually employed in any given language, and the others tend to become more difficult to articulate as time passes, because of disuse. The classic example of this is the inability of most adult Japanese to distinguish between the spoken forms of 'r' and 'l'. A Japanese child who matures in the United States, for example, encounters no such difficulty. His counterpart who grows up in Japan will, on the other hand, become the victim of the biological principle, 'Use it or lose it'.

We must not lose sight of the fact that human language is far more sophisticated than bird song. In drawing the above analogies, is one then saying that at the deepest level, that is to say in the cellular arrangement of the neural network, the structure of human language is innate, permanently wired in fact, in spite of its greater complexity? There is a school of opinion, of which Noam Chomsky has been the most forthright spokesman, which subscribes to just such a view. And the proponents of this attitude can muster an impressive array of supporting evidence. Let us consider some of the main arguments.

For a start, we should note how lopsided is the average child's performance with the scholastic tasks encountered during early formal training. These are often referred to as the 'three Rs', namely reading, writing and arithmetic. Even those who have a gift for mathematics learn language skills far more easily than they do arithmetic manipulations. So readily are words assimilated into the young person's vocabulary, indeed, that there is a natural tendency to take them for granted. The facts are, however, very impressive. The reading vocabulary of the typical school-leaver, at seventeen years of age, is about 80,000 words, if one includes all proper names of people and places as well as all the various idiomatic expressions. Assuming that these words have been learned at a steady rate throughout life, the young person will have acquired about 5,000 new words a year, which is equivalent to thirteen new words every day. Even the most ambitious teacher would shy away from attempting to inculcate words at such a high rate, and this is not the way it happens. Reading is one of the main methods, of course, but this is emphatically not a question of scanning dictionary entries. Dictionaries, indeed, appear to be one of the pet aversions of the normal child. The key aspect of learning a new word is that it is seen in context, and this is why conversation is an even richer source than reading; it is usually heavy with contextual supplements, including visual prompts. It is not surprising that this should be the case, given the distributed nature of memory traces, as discussed in Chapter 5. Each new word will thus not be inserted into an otherwise empty cerebral pigeon-hole. It will simply be added to the memory's already existing mesh of interconnected pathways.

There is more to language than mere vocabulary, however, and the conclusions of Chomsky and his peers were more specifically directed towards syntax and sentence construction. Chomsky illustrates the nature of the issue by considering a sentence such as: The dog in the corner is hungry. This can easily be turned into a question by shifting the word 'is', thus: Is the dog in the corner hungry? So far so good, but what about the slightly more complicated sentence: The dog that is in the corner is hungry. We see that a rule for question-making based on shifting the word 'is' now fails us because there are two such words. It is not difficult for us to turn the sentence into a question, of course, but we do not accomplish this by the application of any such simple rule. Our knowledge of sentence construction enables us to see instantly that the subject phrase 'The dog that is in the corner' masquerades as a sort of composite noun. This ability of ours is very deep-seated, however, as is attested to by the fact that even the most powerful present-day electronic computer would have a hard time doing what to us is almost second nature. Our easy fluency with such linguistic manipulations stems from an intuition that Chomsky argues must be innate. To bolster that proposition, he cites the fact that children rapidly acquire this expertise irrespective of the language environment in which they operate. The Parisian child has no more or less difficulty with French than the child in Moscow has with Russian. The underlying structure of language, and the rules of its grammar, Chomsky believes, must be universal.

What, then, is the neural origin of this universality? As has so often been the case in our story, a clue comes through the sad route of brain damage. We have already encountered Broca's area, which controls the spoken word, and Wernicke's area, from which we derive our understanding of language. These are both located in the left cerebral hemisphere. Damage to that side of the brain very early in life, before two years have elapsed in fact, results in a shifting of the responsibility for language over to the right hemisphere. But this refugee language, as it were, is lacking in several important respects. It does not enjoy the full range of grammatical expression. Often impoverished with respect to prepositions, or even devoid of them, the migrated language also scores badly with case-inflexions; speech becomes a parsimoniously worded telegram. These observations suggest that language is mediated by intrinsic neural circuitry which normally resides in the left hemisphere.

The currently favoured model for this circuitry was primarily championed by Norman Geschwind, who built on the earlier work of Wernicke. It does not provide a very detailed picture, but it does at least tackle the question of the route taken by the neural signals as they develop into the spoken word. Let us see what this model says of the process by which we recognize an object and speak its name. Visual information arrives at the primary visual cortex (which Brodmann designated as area 17 – see the figures in Chapter 2), in the usual manner, and it then passes on, suitably modified but in a way we still do not understand, to the higher visual cortex (Brodmann's area 18). It then travels to the angular gyrus (Brodmann's area 39) of the occipital–parietal–temporal association cortex. This area manages association of inputs from the auditory, tactile and visual senses, although just how this is accomplished we again do not know. It presumably involves an elaboration of the simple mechanisms we considered in the earlier chapter on neural networks. The signals then impinge upon Wernicke's area (Brodmann's area 22), where the auditory perception of the name in question is created. This must involve the evoking of memory components associated with both the read and spoken name, but again the exact details remain a mystery. The product of this still-nebulous process is then projected via the arcuate fasciculus to Broca's area, where the associations are stored which link the perception of the name with the motor programmes that guide the mouth and the larynx into articulating it. All these steps have been checked out against observations of patients with very localized brain damage.

Although this picture is far from complete regarding the finer details, it nevertheless contributes a strong case for an innate ability for handling language. It would take the hardest of skins, in the face of such evidence, to still maintain that our ability to speak has more to do with nurture than with nature. But although language provides a fairly reliable indication as to the importance of genetic endowment, it must be admitted that it is a rather general sort of gift. One's voice is about as unique as one's fingerprints, but the innate language structures described above are possessed by all except those who are unfortunate enough to have a speech impediment. What about all those other aspects of personality and character which have such a strong bearing on an individual's fate? Are those inherited or are they acquired? In an attempt to get decisive information on that fundamental issue, let us, finally, turn to something which ought to provide us with an acid test: data on identical twins.

The general idea behind studies of identical twins is, of course, that because they have exactly the same genetic endowment, any behavioural traits that are dictated by hereditary factors rather than by the environment will appear equally in both. The cases that are of particular interest are those in which the twins have been raised separately, for this produces a situation in which the nurture factors are different while the nature factors are identical.

Because behaviour and personality are complex attributes, to say the least, one would not expect observations on people, identical twins or otherwise, to produce mathematically exact results. One would be looking for statistically significant trends, and the laborious compilation of data by scientists working in this area is as commendable as it is indispensable. But although one must understand from the outset the danger of attaching too much importance to isolated examples, I cannot resist recounting the most intriguing case of identical twins that I have come across. It concerned Lizzie and Edith Hope, who lived all their lives in the small English town of Barnoldswick. In contrast to the twins who will otherwise be of interest to us here, Lizzie and Edith were not separated at an early age. Indeed they were not separated at all, ever! They lived together, ate identical diets, wore the same clothes, experienced the same things in every respect, and after they were married, on the same day and to two quite similar men, they lived in adjacent terraced houses that had identical exteriors and internal furnishings. That their habits remained closely parallel could be seen, amongst other things, from the fact that they drew their identical sets of curtains at nine o'clock each night, and their reading lamps were usually doused within minutes of each other. On one such occasion, this turned out to be the last thing they would ever do, because they both died (at the age of 84) of heart attacks that came in their sleep – the same night!

This fascinating case is a mere isolated statistic, of course, and as such it proves nothing. But it does at least suggest that there is no capricious third factor that subjects individual destinies to the whimsical throw of what could be called fate's dice. When nature and nurture are both identical, the outcome might not be negotiable.

Our interest, however, is primarily with the cases of identical twins reared apart, and we can draw on the results of a number of admirably detailed studies. Because there has always been a premium on the gathering of large amounts of data, these have invariably involved teams of researchers, armed with question-naires and address lists. A notable exception was the case of Niels Juel-Nielsen, who made twin studies his life's work, and whose *Individual and Environment* (published in 1965) has become one of the cornerstones of this branch of science. Prominent amongst the earlier investigations were those reported on by H.H. Newman, F.N. Freeman and K.J. Holzinger in 1937, and by J. Shields in 1962. These studies were based on the records of nineteen and forty-four sets of identical twins, respectively, while the Juel-Nielsen work was based on a further twelve pairs. Seen against the background of these relatively modest numbers, the recent University of Minnesota investigation, with its data collected on 348 pairs of twins, obviously sets a new standard in statistical reliability, and we will consider its findings shortly.

Shields had initiated his project in connection with a BBC television programme on the subject of twin research. During the transmission, an appeal was made to identical twins reared apart to come forward and fill in a questionnaire. Forty-one such pairs subsequently contacted the BBC, and their number was augmented by three pairs procured by other means. The ages of the total sample lay in the range 8–59 years, and thirty of the pairs had been separated in the first year of life. Of these, the majority had in fact been living apart essentially since birth. Shields compared these people with forty-four pairs of identical twins and thirty-two pairs of non-identical twins, both these control sets being matched to the primary set with respect to age and sex. All pairs were given intelligence tests, both verbal and non-verbal, and their personalities were probed for such qualities as extroversion and neuroticism.

In the intelligence tests, it transpired that the separated identical twins were less alike than the non-separated identical controls, while both were markedly more similar than the non-separated non-identical controls. The personality tests, on the other hand, were able to reveal no statistically significant differences between the separated and non-separated identical twins. In fact, the results suggested that the separated pairs tend, in some respects, to be more similar in their personality and behavioural characteristics than their non-separated counterparts. This was particularly noticeable in respect to the capacity for extroversion. The main conclusion of the Shields investigation was, however, that there is a significant genetic factor in the development of both intelligence and personality, and that 'family environments can vary quite a lot without obscuring basic similarity in a pair of genetically identical twins'.

My main concern, in describing studies of individuals reared remote from their biological origins, is to probe the relative strengths of the genetic and environmental influences on the broad variety of attributes that collectively define personality. But it is interesting, in passing, to consider what this approach has been able to reveal about one particular aspect of an individual's character, namely the relationship to alcohol. I have not arbitrarily settled on this specific facet of mental make-up, for it is invariably coupled with one of this book's chief preoccupations, namely the will. It is, indeed, lack of will-power that is often cited as the reason for a person's failure to resist the temptation of intoxicating beverages; in the popular view, the drunk is quite simply a moral backslider. Seen in this light, the recent emergence of evidence for a genetic factor in alcoholism is a major event. It has transpired that about 95 per cent of all alcoholics have an alcoholic relative, and Donald Goodwin, in the early 1970s, set about finding out why this should be so. Studying 133 Danish men raised by non-alcoholic foster parents, he found that those with an alcoholic biological parent were four times more likely to run foul of liquor than those without such a parent. An even larger Swedish study, carried out by Michael Bohman and C. Robert Cloninger in the early 1980s, revealed further details. Examining data on 1,775 adopted men and women, they were able to differentiate between two types of alcoholic. Members of the first group, which accounted for about a quarter of the cases, tended to drink heavily before the age of 25 years, and their rehabilitation record was very poor. A related statistic was quite depressing: the sons of men in this group are themselves nine times more likely to become alcoholics than the average person. This form of the affliction does, in fact, appear predominantly in men, and Bohman and Cloninger dubbed it 'male limited alcoholism'. The remainder of the alcoholics in the test group comprised both men and women. Labelled 'milieu-limited', they took to drink later in life and enjoyed an excellent recovery rate. Probing deeper into the underlying factor in the male limited variety, Henri Begleiter has found that their electroencephalographs show a much diminished amplitude for one of the constituent brain waves (called the P-three wave), and their sons' waves followed the same pattern. Biochemical indicators of a genetic factor are now also surfacing. Marc Schuckit has discovered that imbibing several drinks leads to less of a change in prolactin and cortisol levels in sons of alcoholics than in sons of non-alcoholics. In summary, then, there is growing evidence that heredity, and not lack of moral fibre, underlies one form of alcoholism. But let me now return to the more general issues, and describe what twin studies have recently shown.

The Minnesota project, completed in 1986, easily outstripped anything of its kind that had been undertaken before. An impression of its thoroughness can be gained from the fact that it employed a questionnaire comprising no less than 15,000 items, on subjects ranging from personal interests and values, phobias and aesthetic judgement, to television and reading propensities. The 348 pairs of identical twins, which included forty-four pairs that had been reared separately, were also subjected to medical examinations (which included such physical factors as the electrical conductance of the skin and refractive aberrations in the eyes) and intelligence tests, and they were queried on details of their life histories, including stressful episodes. Not surprisingly, the large research team, which included Thomas Bouchard, David Lykken, Stephen Rich, Nancy Segal, Auke Tellegen and Kimerly Wilcox, observed considerable variation amongst the individual pairs. Perhaps the most intriguing case was that of Jim Springer and Jim Lewis, who had been separated four weeks after their birth in 1940. They grew up just 45 miles apart, in Ohio, and were not reunited until 1979. Comparing notes, they were astonished to discover that they both drove the same model blue Chevrolet, both chain-smoked Salems, both bit their fingernails, and both owned dogs which they had named Toy! On the basis of their returned questionnaires, plus the results of the other tests, the investigators also found them indistinguishable in respect to such personality traits as flexibility, self-control and sociability. At the other end of the scale, there were pairs in which the members displayed only superficial similarities.

The Minnesota study confirmed the previous finding, mentioned earlier, that identical twins reared apart are, on average, actually more alike than their counterparts who grew up together. Sandra Scarr has suggested that the reason for this seemingly anomalous fact might be that parents of identical twins tend to stress differences between these offspring, in an effort to give them separate personalities. There would, of course, be no such differentiating pressure on identical twins raised apart. Another factor could be sibling rivalry, which is invariably present irrespective of whether children are twins.

The most significant results of this investigation were, however, the numerical values that the research team were able to put on various aspects of personality, with respect to their links to heredity or environment. What the team called social potency, that is to say leadership or dominance, proved to be about 60 per cent inherited, and similarly high genetic factors were observed for respect for authority, moral judgement, dedication to hard work, and a penchant for taking the initiative. Notable amongst the traits which appear to owe little to inheritance was the need for intimacy, comfort and help, or what the team referred to collectively as social closeness. All in all, the team's answer to the question of how much of an individual's personality is due to heredity was: about half.

That such twin studies do not produce a more biased answer, either way, should not surprise us. It has already been stressed that the patterns of genes in an individual's chromosomes dictate only the general trends of his body's structure. We see this through the fact, for example, that identical twins do not have the same fingerprints. But although the results demonstrate the clear presence of environmental factors in a person's mental make-up, the existence of a genetic component is equally undeniable. Whatever the mind of the newborn child is, an empty page it is not.

● Summary

The brain of a newborn child contains all the cells it will ever possess, and many which it will gradually lose, but the number of cell contacts continues to increase during the first few years of life. This permits the growing infant to store and remember experiences at a rate which far exceeds what can be accomplished in its mature years. Early training is thus crucial to the formation of the personality. Observations on identical twins, separated at an early age and reared in different environments, indicate that part of a person's mental make-up is also inherited. The performance of the machine thus appears to be dictated both by its manufacture and how it is treated during the running-in period.

The mind unhinged

Brain malfunction

All theory is against the freedom of will; all experience for it.

SAMUEL JOHNSON
Letter to Boswell

Only two possibilities exist: either one must believe in determinism and regard free will as a subjective illusion, or one must become a mystic and regard the discovery of natural laws as a meaningless intellectual game.

MAX BORN
My Life

The signs were all bad, and it seemed clear that another human tragedy was in the making. Admittedly, the divers were down, and their expertise in rapidly locating bodies and returning them to the surface was well documented. But four-year-old Jimmy Tontlewicz had disappeared through that same hole in the ice almost twenty minutes ago, and survival after such a prolonged period in freezing water would have been remarkable even if Jimmy had been on the surface. To suggest that he could still be alive *under* such water would have been to invoke a miracle. And yet this was the truth of the situation. The divers re-emerged, with Jimmy's apparently lifeless body, as gauged by his ashen face and absence of heart beat. But within the hour, warmed back to his normal temperature, Jimmy was very much alive.

The 'miracle' of Jimmy's survival was attributable to what is known as the mammalian dive reflex. Most adults have lost this instinctive reaction, and it is not equally strong in all young children. It is common amongst aquatic animals, such as beavers and seals, however, and it enables these creatures to stay submerged for impressive lengths of time in very cold conditions. The reflex first automatically stops the animal's breathing, and then it cuts the heart's pulse from a hundred beats a minute to less than ten. The blood flow is simultaneously directed away from the less essential parts of the body, giving almost all the circulation's attention to what is known as the body's vital core, which is to say the brain, the spinal cord, the lungs, and the heart itself. This is what had saved Jimmy from succumbing to hypothermia, the symptoms of which seem to mimic death itself. But fortunately, as experts in this area assure us, a person is not dead until he is warm and dead. This is why Jimmy's body, seemingly bereft of life, was able to make its astonishing recovery.

Why, however, should we be interested in this example of a dramatic recovery from hypothermia, remarkable as it undoubtedly was, in a book about the brain, the mind and the soul. In fact hypothermia has recently proved to be a most unexpected source of information about the working of the brain. Let us look at a few more facts about the phenomenon. The normal temperature of the human body is 37 degrees Celsius. The typical adult is unable to maintain that temperature in water below about 29 degrees, because the circulatory system cannot compensate adequately for the loss of heat. Hypothermia sets in when the temperature of the vital core has fallen approximately 1.7 degrees below the normal level. As the body cools further, consciousness in general and alertness in particular gradually diminish. When the vital core temperature has dropped to about 34.5 degrees, the memory starts to show signs of impairment, and by the time it reaches 33.4 degrees, the brain's recall function is operating at only around a third of its normal level. If the cooling of the core is continued down to about 32 degrees, the person starts to slip into unconsciousness.

During investigations undertaken by Richard Hoffman and his colleagues, carefully controlled examinations shed important light on several brain phenomena. The overall effect of hypothermia, they found, is to induce a state which resembles anaesthesia, but they also observed more bizarre behaviour on the part of some of their chilled volunteers. Amongst these, the strongest is paradoxical undressing. The last thing that a freezing person ought to do is to disrobe, and yet this is precisely what some hypothermia sufferers do.

In run-down urban areas, people are sometimes found unconscious or wandering about delirious, in various stages of undress, and they have sometimes been mistakenly assumed to be victims of sexual molestation. Hoffman believes that such people might have experienced a sudden reversal of the blood re-routing mentioned earlier. The renewed gushing of blood through their bodies' peripheral areas immediately below the skin would give them a sensation of uncomfortable warmth, causing them to throw off their clothes. (The Court Jester in Shakespeare's *King Lear* seems to have been aware of the phenomenon, because in the fourth scene of the third act he notes that 'This cold night will turn us all to fools and madmen'.)

Even more interesting are the effects produced by hypothermia on the brain's biochemistry. For example, when the temperature falls, an increased amount of epinephrine (also known as adrenaline) is released into the bloodstream. This is a common reaction of the brain to any threat of danger, and amongst other things it increases the heart rate. Another result of the lowering temperature is changes in the receptors for the neurotransmitter dopamine, and the upshot of this is that the chilled person experiences vivid hallucinations, quite similar to those reported by schizophrenic patients. And here we establish contact with something that was discussed at length earlier, in that dopamine is also associated with the dreaming state, while hallucinations can be regarded as dreams that occur during waking. These results, when taken together, suggest the beginning of a rationalization for the schizophrenic state. It is simply that the brain of a schizophrenic person possesses a faulty biochemistry which might make the effective operating temperature a couple of degrees lower than the actual body temperature. For the schizophrenic, therefore, the prevailing situation might be the same as that experienced by a normal patient who is suffering from hypothermia. If that were the case, raising the temperature of the schizophrenic's vital core to 39 degrees, say, should lead to more normal behaviour, just as warming the chilled normal person back to 37 degrees should restore normality. The exciting thing is that there is indeed evidence of just such an effect in some schizophrenics; their symptoms appear to be alleviated when they have a fever, this remarkable amelioration being reversed when the temperature subsides back to its normal level. This fascinating discovery is yet another example of what so often happens in scientific enquiry; work directed towards one phenomenon stumbles across a second, the existence of which was unsuspected.

It is now high time that we consider the entire panoply of conditions to which schizophrenia belongs, namely mental disorder. Let us look at the mind when it becomes unhinged, and ask whether here too one sees evidence of machine-like functioning on the part of the brain. The chronicling of brain injuries and brain-related dysfunctions has a venerable history. It appears to have begun around 3000 BC, in Ancient Egypt, for although it is true that no written records survive from that time, several papyri dating from the early second millennium BC bear signs of having been copied from much earlier documents. Three of the best-known of these are the Kahun Papyrus (from about 1850 BC), the Luxor Papyrus (1600 BC) and the Ebers Papyrus (1550 BC). Not surprisingly, the medical knowledge documented in these writings is of a rather primitive type, full of references to evil spirits, and the like, as explanations for a variety of pathologies that would now be identified as depression, senile dementia, and even alcoholic intoxication. But the Luxor Papyrus is special because it is uncharacteristically methodical and scientific in its approach. It could easily have been lost to posterity, because it was salvaged from a junk shop in that city by an antique collector, Edwin Smith, in 1862. The hieroglyphs, of which the fragmentary papyrus contained just seventeen surviving columns, remained undeciphered until they attracted the attention of James Breasted. His translation, published in 1930, included mention of the word brain six times, which, according to Breasted, is only two less than in all of recorded Ancient Egyptian. This gives one a good indication of the document's value. In all, the treatise describes the case histories of forty-eight injuries, and it provides the reader with a description of the damage, the diagnosis and the treatment. Of the many things that clearly enthralled the ancient medical observer, none seems to have made a larger impact than the fact that a lesion in the head could influence regions of the body remote from that site. The hieroglyphs reveal the physician's surprise at observing paralysis of the lower limbs following an injury in what we now know is the motor cortex, and in another case the patient is seen to suffer a permanent erection following dislocation of his uppermost vertebrae.

Before that ancient medical wisdom was being transcribed onto what was destined to become the Edwin Smith surgical papyrus, another type of investigation into brain function was already well underway, a few hundred miles to the north-east of Egypt. It represented mankind's earliest encounter with the brain's bio-chemistry, which of course lies at a much finer scale of size than the head and spine injuries described in Smith's antique scroll. But the investigators in this case deserved no special accolade, for their discoveries were made unwittingly. With the recent rise in the use of hallucinogenic drugs, amongst which LSD is a particularly notorious example, knowledge of vision-inducing agents is of course now widespread. It is thus enlightening to note that such substances first found a foothold about 4,000 years ago, amongst the Assyrian priesthood. So enthusiastic were these ancient clerics about the effects of chewing on blushing agaric (*Amanita rubescens*), and its even more potent cousin fly agaric (*Amanita muscaria*), that they elevated these red toadstools to the deity, the only members of the mycophyta division to be thus honoured. The archaic priests gnawed on the fungus in such large doses that a high concentration of the drug muscarine was even present in their urine. Quite how they discovered this must remain a mystery, but the fact is that they treated the liquor with great reverence, and even regarded it as being fit for consumption. As with most human institutions, the Assyrian priesthood was hierarchical, so the senior members passed the drug on to their subordinates in more senses than one.

We can thus identify the early awakenings of the science of brain impairment, and note that the situation then was just as it is today; any aspect of nature is amenable to serious and systematic study if there is sufficient motivation and enthusiasm, but as often as not the same natural phenomenon will also become the object of myth and superstition. On the one hand there were the pains-taking observations that were recorded in the Smith scroll, and on the other there were the occult shenanigans of the Assyrian clergy. And yet it is the latter line that I must follow in this chapter, because in spite of its dubious antecedents, the study of brain malfunction at the biochemical level lies closer to the

MUSCARINE

CARBON ●
OXYGEN ◉
NITROGEN ○
HYDROGEN ○

The toadstool known as fly agaric (*Amanita muscaria*) contains the organic compound muscarine, the molecular structure of which is shown by the schematic diagram on the left of this figure. Molecules of muscarine can interact with certain nerve cell receptors, and produce hallucinations. Chewing small quantities of the poisonous, but seldom lethal, tissue of the scarlet fungus was popular amongst the Assyrian priesthood, about four thousand years ago.

fundamental scene which we must explore in order to get at the heart of our putative machine. I can, in any event, leave the question of gross injuries to the brain in good conscience, since they were cited so heavily when I was describing the brain's anatomy.

Confronted with the seeming impasse of the brain's complexity, the brain scientist often favours the tactic of studying the system under biochemical malfunction, so let us see what that approach has exposed in recent years. Although they can be dangerous enough if taken to the extreme, self-imposed malfunctions are usually relatively mild, and we can learn a lot from them. It turns out that a number of artificial substances are composed of molecules which bear a striking resemblance to the brain's neurotransmitters; studied by the keen eye of X-ray analysis, their atoms are found to be arranged in much the same way as that observed in the native molecules which make the short voyage across a synapse. The alien molecules are thus able to mimic the action of their natural counterparts, but because the atomic patterns of the bogus and bona fide versions do not match precisely, the former provoke mental aberrations. The substances in question are, of course, the hallucinogenic drugs referred to earlier.

The naturally occurring impairments of the synapse are

uniformly grim. In myasthenia gravis, for example, the skeletal muscles become gradually weaker and more prone to fatigue. The early signs of trouble are drooping eyelids, double vision, and difficulties with speech and swallowing. Left untreated, the weakness spreads to the respiratory system, and at this stage it is potentially lethal. The underlying cause of this affliction is a decrease in the number of receptors for the neurotransmitter acetylcholine, at the neuromuscular junctions. This decrease, in turn, is brought about by what is known as an autoimmune reaction, in which the system generates antibodies against some of its own molecules (in this case, the receptors). First reported on in 1672, by Thomas Willis, myasthenia gravis was associated with an approximately one-in-three mortality rate as recently as 1960, but treatment with steroid drugs, and in some severe cases removal of the thymus gland, have reduced this ratio considerably.

Another neuromuscular disease was discovered in 1817 by James Parkinson. It now bears his name, of course, and it is estimated that there are 50,000 new cases each year in the United States alone. Its characteristics are a lack of facial expression and diminished eye blinking; muscular rigidity, which leads to jerky movements of the limbs; a rhythmic tremor of the limbs when they are at rest; a marked lethargy in the initiation of movement, which amongst other things manifests itself in a tendency to shuffle when the patient gets up from a chair; and pronounced postural abnormalities. In biochemical terms, Parkinsonism is primarily caused by a deficiency of the neurotransmitter dopamine. This inhibitory substance usually balances the excitatory effects of acetylcholine, and when that equilibrium is disturbed the acetylcholine's influence on the system predominates (particularly in the regions of the substantia nigra, the striatum and the locus coeruleus) and upsets the smooth flow of muscular function. Attempts to replenish the supply of dopamine to those critical regions of the brain simply by admitting quantities of that substance to the bloodstream would be doomed to fail, because dopamine is unable to cross what is known as the blood–brain barrier. But a substance that can be converted into dopamine within the brain (i.e. what is known as a dopamine precursor), namely the amino acid 3,4-dihydroxyphenylalanine (DOPA), can penetrate this hurdle. Although it merely ameliorates the symptoms, rather than producing an actual cure, DOPA's arrival on the scene has been a most welcome development for Parkinson patients.

Although myasthenia gravis and Parkinson's disease implicitly involve the brain, in that the neuromuscular signals emanate from that organ, they are not afflictions of the mind as such. Having considered two different impairments of the synapse, therefore, let me now move on to how such departures from the ideal can, under certain circumstances, actually influence a person's mental make-up. If ever there was a disease that deserved to be associated with a particular surname, it is Huntington's disease (earlier known as Huntington's chorea). When George Huntington first described its symptoms in 1872, he was drawing on not only his own observations but also those of his father and grandfather. It is characterized by involuntary dance-like movements, a gradual change of personality, and progressive mental deterioration towards a state of dementia. It is clearly genetic, being caused by what is known as single factor inheritance. The root cause is a single dominant gene. This means that if one parent suffers from the disease, half the children (on average) of both sexes will inherit it, and be capable of passing it on to their own offspring, while the remaining children will neither suffer from it nor transmit it. Huntington's disease is relatively rare, attacking about one in 15,000 people of Aryan descent and a far smaller fraction of orientals and blacks. But it has the unfortunate aspect that its first symptoms, which can be as unobtrusive as clumsiness, a twitching of the face or a slight awkwardness of gait, first begin to make themselves felt towards the end of the fourth decade. This is admittedly about twenty years earlier than the typical age for the onset of Parkinson's disease, but one could say that it is not early enough. That might sound callous, but the point is that a person will usually become aware of the Huntington symptoms after having had children, to whom the disease may thus already have been passed on.

Huntington's disease is caused by the local loss of neurons through what appears to be genetically programmed death of certain cells. The loss is most marked in the striatum, but depletion also occurs in the cortex. It is possible that the deterioration initially affects just one type of cell, and that other types then degenerate through lack of stimulation: the 'use it or lose it' principle that we encountered earlier. Such a repercussive effect may also underlie the multiplicity of neurotransmitters that are implicated, including gamma-aminobutyric acid (GABA), acetylcholine and several enkephalins. The implication of a single gene in a mental disease is not particularly common. The more usual situation is a faulty group of genes, or even, as in the case of mongolism, a malformed chromosome. But the pinpointing of a single rogue gene does make for ready identification. In 1983, Huntington's disease was mapped to the short arm of the fourth chromosome, using the RFLP (DNA-fragmenting) technique described in Chapter 7. Such accurate and reliable genetic diagnosis is a mixed blessing, however, because it puts the doctor in a moral dilemma. Should a young person be told that he or she will inevitably develop a fatal disease between the ages of 35 and 40, when there are no prospects for a cure? The threat of the disease being passed on to possible children forces one's hand in this case, of course, but the present goal of mapping the entire human genome is going to throw up many more harrowing decisions of this type. Offsetting the anguish of this predicament is the anticipation that the newly won precision with which such genetic frailties can be identified will also promote their cures.

My aim in describing these afflictions of the mind is not to recite an inventory of woes, even though all these conditions are undeniably sad. The intention is rather to show how impairments of the mind are related to causes that must be termed natural, even though they are not, thank goodness, inevitable. The malfunction that comes closest to being natural is possibly Alzheimer's disease. When it occurs, it appears as a sort of accelerated aging, and it produces a premature form of dementia. Its early symptoms are relatively innocuous; they include forgetfulness, which amongst other things manifests itself in untidiness, and a diminution in the power of judgement. As the condition worsens, the patient's memory is often not even up to recognizing familiar faces and the written word. Nonsense words begin to crop up in the victim's speech, and there may be mindless repetition of what others are saying (i.e. the victim may display what is termed echolalia). In the final stages, the mind appears to be almost empty. Even the most basic functions of daily life are beyond the scope of the patient, who ends his or her days bedridden and mute. As William Wordsworth wrote in *The Fountain*: 'The wiser mind mourns less for what age takes away than what it leaves behind'. The majority of people retain their intellectual powers into old age, but between 3 and 5 per cent of individuals over 65 fall prey to Alzheimer's disease. In the 1980s it was estimated that, in the United States alone, this statistic represents a cost of about ten billion dollars a year in nursing-home care.

In recent years a well-defined biochemical pattern has been identified with this disease. The cortex, the hippocampus and parts of the limbic system become depleted of chemical components that lead to the production of the neurotransmitter acetylcholine. Donald Price and his colleagues showed, in 1982, that one part of the brain, the nucleus basalis, actually suffers a 75 per cent loss of its neurons because of the biochemical disturbance. It is becoming clear that the inheritance factor was earlier underestimated for the disease, and it now appears that siblings of Alzheimer victims have about a fifty–fifty chance of developing it themselves. The case for a genetic factor is even further strengthened by the fact that individuals with Down's syndrome (i.e. mongolism) invariably develop the cellular and neurotransmitter deficiencies of Alzheimer's disease if they survive into their fourth decade.

There has been an underlying purpose, some might even say an ulterior motive, in going into so much detail with these illnesses. It is that the course the infirmity takes makes it difficult to reconcile with the concept of dualism, which in this book has always loomed as something of a *bête noire*. Take Alzheimer's disease, for example, and consider its later stages in the context of the dualist paradigm. That theory has it that the mind is related to the brain and yet is somehow distinct from it. As the faculties of the Alzheimer victim gradually fail, and as the brain accumulates its undeniable deficits, we can hardly believe that the mind remains inviolate because of its aloof position, for this is demonstrably not the case. But the other alternative would seem to be even less palatable to the dualist, for it would see the brain and the mind, separated as they are purported to be, gradually being eclipsed at precisely the same rate. What then is the merit of such a separate mind, when it thus reveals itself as nothing better than a camp follower, aspiring to ghost-like independence but exposing itself as being at the dictates of earthly biochemistry nevertheless?

The ethical, moral and legal overtones are no less worrying. What is one to say, for example, of the possible culpability of a sufferer from one of these diseases when the sickness is in its embryonic stage. When the patient is confined to bed by the affliction, the scope for criminal acts is limited to say the least, but what about that early phase of Alzheimer's disease with its mere 'errors of judgement'. In decades past, when the justice for even the pettiest forms of larceny was swift and hard, an error of judgement could lose a person his or her life. And we have seen that this particular disease can be regarded as a premature (and admittedly severe) form of aging. What then of the normal person and his or her errors of judgement? Can they too not be regarded, almost by definition indeed, as the very early stages of a condition which is foisted upon an individual by the inexorable slide down biochemistry's slippery slope?

Perhaps it is such issues which tend to make us turn our backs on sicknesses of the mind. Finding them impossible to squeeze into the patterns of our moral norms, we simply shut them out. Only the most squeamish are unable to stomach visits to normal hospitals, but for the majority of people the mental asylum remains strictly off limits. And there is even a tendency on the part of some to acquire further insulation from the entire concept of mental illness by rationalizing the condition of the unfortunate patients into a sort of self-inflicted guilt. Thus Bedlam was the name of a well-known London asylum but the word also became synonymous with a rowdy din, the implication being that it was pandemonium generated of the inmates' own volition. (The building was originally a priory, built in 1247. It became a hospital, and was given the name St Mary of Bethlehem. Conversion to an asylum occurred in 1547, and the name was corrupted first to Bethlem, and ultimately to Bedlam. The application of that name to something noisy and unruly did not occur until 1663.)

The quintessential example of a mental disorder formerly attributed to the sufferer's own responsibility was a syndrome first identified by Georges Gilles de la Tourette in 1885. Characterized by a variety of bizarre vocalizations (some of which resemble hybrid grunts and coughs), tics, gesticulations, and a liberal supply of curses and obscenities, the condition typically begins to manifest itself in childhood or early adolescence. It is not associated with any marked impairment of mental ability, but the patient's impulsive behaviour can tend to inhibit educational progress. In others, the result is quite the opposite in that the patient learns to harness the impulses and the innate flair for the unconventional. A Tourette patient in the arts may even gain advantage from a capacity for improvisation, while the almost mercurial repartee that is another of the condition's hallmarks makes its possessor popular in some social contexts. The patient is the born court jester. Not surprisingly, people with this disease were earlier considered either to be guilty of flagrant disregard for societal norms or to be actually possessed by the devil. In earlier centuries, victims of Tourette's syndrome have no doubt been burned as witches, although it should be added that the disease is more common amongst males (so they would have been regarded as warlocks). The origins of the disease are unknown, but the occasional occurrence of several sufferers in a single family is suggestive of a heredity factor. In fact, the evidence points towards the Mediterranean area as the most likely geographical origin. The sickness appears to be caused by overactivity in a series of brain structures that employ dopamine as their chief neurotransmitter. These structures include the thalamus, amygdala and the limbic system, all parts I have earlier identified as the collective seat of the personality. The symptoms can be alleviated by administering an agent that blocks the receptors for dopamine, such as haloperidol or primozide. Recalling the earlier comparison of a neurotransmitter molecule and its receptor molecule with a key and a lock, we could say that the drug functions by placing its hand over the keyhole. About half of all Tourette sufferers seem to grow out of the disease as they mature into adulthood. This was no doubt earlier regarded as a self-induced improvement, a coming to one's senses. In those cases where the person had been put under the care of a man of God, the cure was of course put down to a successful exorcism of the evil spirits.

A type of syndrome that was even less likely to elicit sympathy from the spiritual fathers of earlier centuries was that related to sex. Given the taboos that surrounded even the most forthright aspects of the subject, any suggestion of deviation from the perceived norm was obviously going to meet with condemnation. The mind boggles over what the church elders of any faith would have made of priapism, for example, which is persistent erection of the penis. This permanent tumescence takes its name from the Greek god of procreation, Priapos, and it is now known to stem from a disorder of the nervous system. Most clerics would not have encountered it, in fact, because the condition is blessedly rare, but it is a fair bet that it too would have been attributed to possession by the devil, and the sufferer would no doubt have been assumed to be preoccupied with sex to the exclusion of everything else. The patient's painful predicament would thus have been compounded by the lack of understanding on the part of those in authority. (Priapism had actually already been identified as a pathological condition by the time that the Edwin Smith papyrus was written, as mentioned earlier, but that ancient script was still awaiting rediscovery.) Such lack of understanding is consistent with the general picture, of course; well into the nineteenth century, the average inmate in a mental asylum knew only of a life restrained by a strait-jacket or chains.

As unpleasant as priapism undoubtedly is for the person cursed with it, its significance pales in comparison with what until recently was the major sex-related mental scourge, namely syphilis, for in that case the numbers affected were legion. (Well into the twentieth century, a third of all asylum patients suffered from the disease.) And it must be cited here for it was another sickness that was all too easy to identify with the soul rather than the body. After all, it was contracted through an act which could hardly be called involuntary (except in the case of rape, that is). Syphilis rates inclusion in a book about the brain because this is the organ that is chiefly affected in the latter phase of the disease. That stage is known as dementia paralytica (general paralysis of the insane, or simply GPI). The disease is transmitted by the spirochaete *Treponema pallidum* and it is now, thank goodness, essentially a thing of the past, due to the advent of penicillin in 1940. Until that happy victory for medical science, however, GPI was looked upon, even by some people in the medical profession itself, as the just deserts for a wayward life. The soul was in error, clearly, because of its failure to withstand temptation, so what fate could be more fitting than that the soul itself should ultimately appear to evaporate as the paralysis tightened its grip, a comeuppance richly deserved for wanton and unbridled venery. And even if there had been just the merest remnant of compassion for the victim, this was quickly forgotten upon the first appearance of one of GPI's oddest characteristics: delusions of grandeur. The patient, already devoid of remorse, was now seen to add a defiant arrogance to his or her sins.

It is sad that an understanding of this disease came so late. First identified as a disease not related to any other malady, in 1798, by John Haslam, it was puzzling because the patient displayed a distinct feeling of euphoria and elation in spite of the concomitant deterioration in general health. Jean Esquirol noted the association of paralysis with the disease, in 1805, and this paralysis was erroneously conjectured to attack the meninges (i.e. the brain's membranous envelope) by Antoine Bayle seventeen years later. Louis Calmeil correctly located the trouble as arising in the brain itself, in 1826, but it was not until another eighty years had passed that the responsibility for the disease could be pinned on syphilis.

This came with the development, by August von Wassermann, of a blood test that exposed the presence of the affliction, if it had been in the body about six weeks or more. And the definitive linking of syphilis with the impairment to the brain was achieved by Simon Flexner and Hideyo Noguchi, in 1913, when they demonstrated the presence of the spirochetes in cerebral tissue. The first definitive cure was the therapy which won Julius Wagner von Jauregg the Nobel Prize in 1927, just over a decade before penicillin supplied the story with a fitting capstone. Von Jauregg's solution to the problem was as daring as it was resourceful; the patient was deliberately infected with malaria, to induce a spirochaete-killing fever, and subsequently treated with quinine to remove the malaria.

The hospital beds no longer occupied by people with GPI do not stand idle. They, and many more besides, are needed for the group of people who suffer from one of the present time's most widespread mental illnesses, namely schizophrenia. And because schizophrenia, of all conditions, is a brain malfunction that derives from biochemical faults, it is an appropriate subject for the balance of this chapter. Its organic origins won recognition only after a period in which the trouble was thought to lie with the patient's mind rather than with the body. This attitude has its roots in dualism, of course, and it is still very much with us. When a person is said to have 'bad nerves', this is seldom interpreted literally; the term does not conjure up a picture of faulty neurons, or even a malfunctioning neural network. In order to appreciate the revolutionary change in medicine's attitude towards schizophrenia in particular, and mental illness in general, it is therefore appropriate that we briefly recall the efforts of some of the forerunners of psychiatry. We will see that their contributions were laudable, when one considers the paucity of detailed biochemical knowledge during those pioneering days a century ago. They were, moreover, operating in a climate that could hardly be deemed conducive to scientific thinking, when it came to man's psyche. Physics and chemistry were charging along, but the mind and soul were still very much intertwined, and the soul was the province of the Church. Not surprisingly, therefore, even medical practitioners looked towards sin as the origin of mental illness. A hundred and fifty years ago, one could read in a medical textbook by J. Heinroth that all such afflictions were the sinner's retribution at the hands of God, and were caused by deprivation of free will. In the light of such dogmatic bigotry, the small band of gifted people that formed itself around Sigmund Freud is seen to be brave indeed.

Mention of Sigmund Freud might conjure up a vignette of a bearded and bespectacled sage, sitting with his note pad while a patient lies on a couch recalling the traumas of an unhappy childhood. The name is also suggestive of the very antithesis of today's laboratory experimenters, with their electronic gadgetry and high-flown neurophysical theories. But the fact is that both these pictures are quite misleading. The person who really discovered the cathartic value of helping a patient to dredge remote memories up into consciousness was Pierre Janet, even though he stopped short of realizing that the repository of those mental relics must be what we now call the subconscious part of the mind. And Freud came surprisingly close to divining the way in which the brain serves the senses, and the manner in which it stores the records of experiences. Amongst his clairvoyant conjectures, mention should be made of his belief that nerve fibres carry signals to the brain, where the body's outer surface is appropriately represented; that the brain possesses a region that monitors the body's physiological status; and that part of the nervous system works through a chemical feedback system. These speculations, impressive as they were, are overshadowed by his hypotheses regarding the brain's electrical activities. He saw the brain's neural elements as being capable of discharging when sufficiently excited, an idea which anticipated the discovery of the action potential, with its all-or-nothing response. And he guessed that the neural elements are mutually separated by what he called contact barriers and what we would now call synapses. Finally, he argued that neural elements can be excited to a level that does not lead to discharge, an idea that foreshadowed our present knowledge of what goes on in a neuron's dendrites. There were, indeed, things in Freud's writings that could be identified as harbingers of synaptic modification. He was brilliantly prescient, and one could even say he anticipated the idea of Donald Hebb: that when one cell persistently contributes to the activity of another, the synapse (or synapses) via which they are connected becomes (become) more effective.

Freud put the science of psychiatry onto the map by defining a series of basic concepts which are still in use today. The instinctive impulses of an individual were referred to collectively as the 'id', while 'ego' was the term used to denote the conscious thinking subject, that is to say the mental agency through which the id seeks fulfilment of its aims. The job of the ego is thus to know both the instinctive needs and the constraints that the environment puts on their being satisfied. A third entity was actually identified and defined by one of Freud's acolytes, Carl Jung. It is called the 'libido', and it can be looked upon as the psychological energy which the ego utilizes to bring the goals of the id to fruition.

Freud was especially concerned with the need to explain emotions and he never gave up the hope of accounting for these in terms of the brain's electrical activity. But in that quest he was unfortunately too far ahead of his time. He had to settle for explanations at a grosser level, but this did at least carry the advantage that he was able to perceive the importance of the subconscious. He saw this as residing in the low-level excitement of the brain's neural elements. Although, as noted earlier, this excitement was insufficient to produce what Freud called a discharge, it could nevertheless transmit the corresponding (subconscious) needs to the cortex, and this would activate motor processes such as eating or copulation. These acts would produce a sense of satisfaction which would be relayed back to the subconscious, and lower what he had termed the contact barriers. Repetition of such reinforcement would leave the barriers more permanently lowered, and this would in effect be learning. Short of actually equating his barriers to synapses, Freud had thus foreshadowed Hebb's hypothesis by about half a century.

Freud regarded the totality of the reinforced pathways, and the ones that were weakened, as constituting a person's ego. The reinforced pathways themselves were seen as motives, which, when consciously experienced, became wishes. Freud believed thought to arise from an internal comparison of these wishes with the person's perception of the actual status, and any mismatch between the two was seen as being the source of the emotions. His further contemplations of the nature of the subconscious led him to speculate on the origin of dreams, and his *Interpretation of Dreams*, published in 1900, remains a monument to his powers of analysis. But Freud's credibility started to crumble, nevertheless, because of his increasing preoccupation with infantile sexuality and the notorious Oedipus Complex. We can still see a remnant of the effects of this unilateralism in the tendency to associate the word 'libido' with specifically sexual cravings. Freud's crew began to abandon ship. (Even Freud's wife vouchsafed the opinion that psychiatry was essentially pornography.) Albert Adler took a broader view than his former mentor, and saw the inferiority complex as arising from the frustration associated with the libido's goals remaining unattained. Jung was more concerned with reinterpreting the nature of what he felt was Freud's most significant innovation, namely the subconscious. He believed that this is not merely the product of a person's childhood experiences, as conceived by Freud, but rather a deep-lying mental level with a content essentially common to all individuals. Jung saw the libido as a more general mental energy, or psychic tension, whose strength determined the degree to which the ego could develop. In this picture, neuroses spring from a weak libido's inability to grow beyond the confines of childhood fantasy, and Jung believed that the cure lay in making a patient face up to the realities of the present rather than in brow-beating him or her with a gruelling analysis of early sexual life.

Karl Kahlbaum seems to have been the first to realize that there are several different manifestations of schizophrenia. He identified hebephrenia in 1863, noting that it was characterized by impulsiveness, progressive withdrawal, and by thoughts and emotions that would best be described as haphazard. Six years later, he defined another facet, catatonia, in which the patient displays impaired motor and postural patterns, and seems to suffer from a diminution of volition, often to the point of stupor. Emil Kraepelin consolidated these together with paranoia, whose tell-tale delusions and hallucinations he himself had studied, into what he called dementia praecox. This reflected his belief that the condition was already present in childhood (one is reminded of the word precocious). Kraepelin was a confirmed mechanist. He was convinced that mental illness stems from anatomical and biochemical disturbances, and that psychological factors have only a minor influence. Eugen Bleuler, who had been Jung's supervisor, felt obliged to correct Kraepelin on two important points, which effectively invalidated both words with which his contemporary had labelled the disease. For a start, he demonstrated that the sickness cannot always be traced to the patient's early years, so the term praecox is not universally appropriate. More importantly, he showed that the condition does not inevitably lead to an erosion of the mental faculties. Dementia was thus not really a fitting term either, and Bleuler favoured a word which epitomized what he perceived to be the defining characteristic of the disease, namely a splitting of the personality. He therefore coined the name 'schizophrenia', which has survived to this day (here we might be reminded of the word schism). Bleuler believed that this cleaving of the ego lay at the root of the trouble, and that the delusions, hallucinations and various other behavioural traits were merely by-products.

Armed with these bare essentials, let us see how Freud and some of his contemporaries variously attempted to explain schizophrenia. Freud's theory, as we have already noted, was based on sexual development and its aberrations. The first contribution to what Freud called a child's libidinal organization is the act of sucking. This constitutes the oral phase of what is known as the auto-erotic period, with the mouth acting as the primary source of erotic pleasure; psychologists refer to the mouth as the first erotogenic zone. But the infant does not distinguish between self and non-self at this early stage, the mother's breast being regarded as an extension of the child's own body. This is why thumb-sucking can be such a viable alternative. The independent status of the breast gradually establishes itself, however, and the child begins to learn the value of aggression, in order to fulfil its needs. By the end of the second year of life the oral phase should have been replaced by the anal stage, with evacuation now providing erotic satisfaction, although a minor portion of the libido remains fixated on oral gratification; hence the prominence of kissing, later in life, as a preliminary in lovemaking.

As strange as it may seem, evacuation is another of the child's early means of interacting with its surroundings, for a nappy (diaper) soiled but not changed can be a source of considerable irritation; the child quickly learns to correlate the act of evacuating with the possibility of a sore bottom, and the positive role played by the obliging parent also strikes up strong associations. Failure to make the transition to the anal stage is known as oral fixation, one symptom of which is self-centredness. In the extreme form, this can lead to narcissism. The normal course of affairs is for the child to become increasingly aware of its environment, and hence to develop its ego. If, for some reason, the ego remains weak, the child can revert to a state that is dominated by the id, with all drives springing solely from the instincts. This, the psychiatric pioneers believed, opens the door for schizophrenia, because the child is unable to distinguish between stimuli emanating from inside and outside the body. They felt that it could be the reason why the schizophrenic has hallucinations, in which voices are heard in the head, voices which seem to exercise considerable control over the victim.

As resourceful and persuasive as these ideas undoubtedly are, they do not provide an answer as to the ultimate source of schizophrenia. For that, we must look elsewhere, and an obvious candidate is heredity. What do the records indicate regarding the possibility that schizophrenia, too, is provoked by something in the genes? They tell us quite a lot in fact, even though they fall somewhat short of supplying us with a watertight case. The incidence of the disease in the population as a whole is just below one per cent. But if either of one's parents is a schizophrenic, the chance of developing the disease jumps almost tenfold. For half siblings and full siblings, the percentages are about seven and fourteen, respectively. As might be expected, the figure for fraternal twins is no higher than for full siblings, but in the case of identical twins, there is an 86 per cent chance of both being schizophrenic if either of them suffers from the disease.

The existence of a genetic factor might thus seem beyond question, even though some researchers in this field still entertain the possibility of influences stemming from the common environment within a family circle; agents such as slow viruses and psychological stress are still under investigation. The identification of schizophrenia genes was reported by several groups of scientists in the summer of 1988. That this is not the entire story is quite clear, however, for if that were the case the correlation amongst identical twins would be 100 per cent; either both would be schizophrenic or neither of them. It thus seems that schizophrenics have inherited something that predisposes them to the manifestation of the disease, and that the latter will be expressed if certain other factors are present, or other conditions fulfilled. Just what these are is not yet known; they could be related to dietary factors, but it seems just as likely that the social environment does indeed play a role.

The reported discovery of schizophrenia genes, mentioned above, is obviously a major event. And although the work still awaits confirmation, it deserves extra comment here. The story began when Hugh Gurling and eight colleagues (whose names appear in the notes at the end of this book) claimed firm evidence for a schizophrenia gene located on chromosome 5, their results having been obtained by the RFLP (DNA-fragmenting) technique that was described in Chapter 7. The studies started with the observation that a schizophrenic Chinese man and his schizophrenic nephew both also suffered from the same facial deformity. This suggested a chromosomal linkage of the two defects, and Gurling's team went on to study 104 members of seven families (five Icelandic and two British) prone to the mental disorder, including 39 who actually have schizophrenia. They found that the above single dominant gene is strongly implicated in the affliction, but that it is not what is referred to as fully penetrant. This means that expression of the gene is dependent on other genetic or environmental factors, or both of these, so not all individuals carrying the gene develop the illness. Another implication of the lack of full penetration is that different forms of schizophrenia can occur in different members of a single family.

The findings of Gurling and his colleagues were challenged by Douglas Blackwood, Walter Nuir and David St Clair, who failed to confirm the observed chromosomal linkage in ten schizophrenia-prone Scottish families. Further evidence against linkage to chromosome 5 was published by Kenneth Kidd and his nine colleagues (whose names also appear in the notes at the end of this book). Their work was based on observations of 157 individuals in the seven branches of three related Swedish families. These people all live in a relatively isolated location above the Arctic Circle, and their non-use of alcohol or drugs, coupled, of course, with their susceptibility to schizophrenia, made them ideal subjects. Thirty-one of them actually suffer from the illness. This study's main conclusion was that the genetic factors that underlie the disease must be heterogeneous. Yet another piece of the puzzle has been supplied by Timothy Crow, who found evidence of a schizophrenia gene on the sex chromosomes. He suggested that this explains the connection between the affliction and gender; pairs of schizophrenic siblings are more likely to be of the same sex than would be expected from pure chance, and schizophrenia is particularly common amongst people who possess an extra sex chromosome.

It is clear that this story is still only in its infancy. Psychiatry stands to profit enormously from the availability of the new biochemical techniques, but a great deal of fundamental work remains to be done. And regarding these studies of schizophrenia, it might transpire that the gene on chromosome 5 is only a minor cause of the disease. (If this proves to be so, the case will have become a parallel to the discovery, announced in 1987, of a genetic basis for manic depression amongst the members of a large Amish family; the linkage of that disease to chromosome 11 has yet to be confirmed in any other pedigree.) These studies are nevertheless of singular importance, because they have set things in motion regarding the genetic mapping of schizophrenia. Also, the discovery that a single chromosomal location can be responsible for various types of the affliction within a single family, with some members being hebephrenic while others are paranoid, and so on, suggests that the traditional classification might be ripe for revision. As Eric Lander has remarked, the study of such variable manifestations may ultimately provide more reliable and useful diagnostic demarcations.

As to the nature of the inherited component in schizophrenia, there is evidence of a malfunction in the dopamine neurotransmitter system. This comes partly from the fact that amphetamine, a drug which has a molecular structure similar to that of dopamine, provokes hallucinations reminiscent of those experienced by schizophrenics. Furthermore, Parkinson's disease patients who are administered L-dopamine to assuage their symptoms have also been found to be prone to hallucinations and delusions, and in some cases even to paranoias. And post-mortems on schizophrenics have revealed somewhat elevated levels of dopamine in some of the regions of the brain known to employ that neurotransmitter. Finally, it is interesting to note that part of the above-mentioned chromosome 5 (for the record, it is region 5q) is known to code for what is referred to as the glucocorticoid receptor, and disturbances in the metabolism of this protein have been observed to induce psychotic symptoms.

This picture is still incomplete, however. That there is more to schizophrenia can be seen from the fact that anti-schizophrenia drugs, whose use is based on the above findings, ameliorate the symptoms in some patients but not in others. It is thus encouraging to note that the story has recently developed a new twist, one that implicates the brain's frontal lobes. There are actually several independent pieces of evidence that point to this connection, but I plan to consider just one of them. It is provided by a technique that differs markedly from those cited above, and this fact serves to show how broad an arsenal of approaches the modern brain researcher has at his disposal. The typical schizophrenic scores just as well in intelligence tests as those not subject to the affliction, but he or she displays a surprising inability to cope with tasks that require mental flexibility. There is difficulty with problems in which experience would normally provide the decisive guidance. A case in point is the so-called Wisconsin card sort test, which the neuropsychologist regards as the acid test for cognitive dysfunction arising from the frontal lobes. The patient is asked to match cards on the basis of simple displayed features such as colour, shape, or number of items, and gains experience through corrective prompting by the supervisor of the test. Once the performance reaches a certain level, the rules for matching are changed without warning. People with damage in the frontal lobe region have pronounced difficulty adjusting to the new conditions. It was earlier believed that this inertia stemmed from the patient's behaviour, and it was variously attributed to inattention, poor motivation or even downright stubbornness. But a series of cleverly arranged examinations have eliminated all such factors, and it is now clear that the indifferent performance really does arise from frontal lobe deficits. What is especially interesting here is that the patient's poor showing occurs only when a specific type of demand is being made on the mental powers. This could be the reason why schizophrenics seem to vary so much in their reaction to the standard forms of therapy; how they behave depends upon what mental demands are being made of them.

We have now considered a variety of infirmities of the brain, all of which can be accounted for at the molecular level, and some can even be further traced back to errors in the genes. The implications of these advances in our knowledge, for speculations about the mind and the soul, could hardly be exaggerated. We see that the mind cannot be a mere adjunct of the brain. It is an integral and inseparable part of that organ. Its strengths and weaknesses are the brain's strengths and weaknesses. And this intimate connection is not confined to pathological conditions; it has been demonstrated to extend into the realm of personality. A case in point is the presence of a third X chromosome in a small fraction of human males. These individuals display a marked tendency to violence, and many of them wind up in prison. Their guilt and responsibility would earlier have been deemed obvious, and their incarceration manifestly just, but such attitudes are now being questioned.

We will return to that grave issue in the final chapter. The point to be made here, from the several sad conditions we have considered, is that they are now understandable on the basis of the brain's chemistry; they are totally bereft of anything mystical. But the die-hard dualist, not to mention the out and out spiritualist, would probably regard such scourges as mere disorders of the supporting machinery, ailments which by

The acquisition of language by young children seems to occur so naturally, and apparently with such little effort, that we are understandably inclined to take it for granted. There are some, however, who never learn this skill. Amongst these, autistic children are particularly puzzling because they usually seem to be normal in almost every other respect. Many of them, indeed, are extraordinarily gifted in other ways, the most common of these involving music. Stephen Wiltshire, a young autistic, is somewhat unusual in that his forte is drawing. He requires only a brief period of inspection of a scene in order to subsequently reproduce it from memory, in a sketch that is made at considerable speed, and with remarkable accuracy of detail. The subject of one of his drawings, reproduced above, provides the opening of the second chapter of this book: the statue of Eros in Piccadilly Circus.

definition lie below the level of the soul. And when the soul is invoked, free will and total responsibility for one's actions are inevitable travelling companions. So let me close this chapter by returning to a type of case where the soul itself appeared to be drawn into an imperfection at the level of the synapse.

Joan of Arc was, as we all know, burned at the stake. At about the age of thirteen, she started to hear voices, these being attributed to direct contact with heaven. She credited the divine inspiration with having led her to military victory over the English at Orléans in 1429. But when, through no fault of her own, the French were defeated at Compiègne a year later, she fell from grace and was convicted of heresy. A signed confession temporarily saved her, but two days later she withdrew the document and was promptly executed. Her auditory hallucinations and the fatal vacillation, together with other recorded behavioural traits, have led neuroscientists to conclude that she was in fact a schizophrenic. As we have just seen, this disease is related to a pathology of the dopamine neurotransmitter system in the forebrain, an area which controls emotion (as witnessed by Phineas Gage's accident, which we considered in the first chapter of this book). The court which tried Joan of Arc acted in the belief that she was responsible for her actions, but the biological evidence would now throw serious doubts against this assumption.

In the beginning of this chapter, we saw that a new aspect of schizophrenia has come to light: a marked improvement in the condition of some of the patients during the period of a fever. A similar effect has been observed in autistics, who otherwise seem to live within an invisible shell, incapable of interacting with their surroundings. Studies of these temporary ameliorations have again been suggestive of molecular origins. What, on the other hand, would the spiritually inclined make of such fever-provoked effects? Would the refractory soul be imagined as being sporadically replaced by a more acceptable counterpart?

● Summary

The connection between brain lesions and mind impairment has now been massively documented. Minor local damage causes partial or total loss of individual faculties, while more general injury can lead to pronounced changes in behaviour and even personality. The nature of the disturbances connected with a number of specific diseases is understood right down to the molecular level; the malfunctioning of the brain and its associated mind can now be explained in terms of the machine's nuts and bolts.

If we could talk to the animals
Thought in other species

Our organ of thought may be superior, and we may
play it better, but it is surely vain to believe that
other possessors of similar instruments leave them
quite untouched.

STEPHEN WALKER
Animal Thought

Man: 'Hello, my boy. And what is your dog's
name?'
Boy: 'I don't know. We call him Rover.'

STAFFORD BEER
New Scientist, 3 October 1974

If it had not been for the fact that he had seen the same thing
happen four or five times during the past fortnight, the train
driver would have blinked in disbelief. By now, however, the
occurrence was becoming almost routine, and it would have
been disappointing not to see the flock of crows dotted over
the tracks less than a hundred metres in front of him. There
was nothing unusual about the birds being there, of course,
but what they were doing was nothing less than astonishing.
As the train approached, some of the birds would pick stones
up with their beaks and lay them on the rails, right in the path
of the train. Now why would they do such a thing? Daphne du
Maurier's *The Birds* notwithstanding, this was surely no avian
terrorist plot aimed at derailment, and the sense of purpose with
which the crows went about their self-imposed task suggested

that one could rule out whim or caprice. No, there had to be a purpose in this extraordinary behaviour. The train driver had now had several opportunities to witness the performance, and speculate about it as his vehicle repeated the journey on that branch line just north of Copenhagen. And his rationalization was that the birds wanted the stones to be crushed to a powdery grit, which they could use in much the same way as chickens employ minute stones to help them fabricate viable eggshells. But the chicken's consumption of fine gravel had always been taken to be an unwitting act, a favourable result of inaccurate pecking for grain and other titbits. In the case of these Danish birds, however, there seemed to be no escaping the conclusion that their behaviour was a product of planning, that it was a manifestation of that still-disputed phenomenon: animal thought.

In Britain at about the same time, namely the late autumn of 1987, the human preoccupation with animals was expressing itself in a quite different form. One of the newspapers had carried out a poll amongst its readership, to probe the manner in which the Christmas season was being approached. The results were primarily a bunch of unimpressive statistics, such as those on presents, which revealed that a majority of wives would be giving their husbands ties or books, and that 41 per cent of them would be receiving lingerie in return. But there was one result of this head count that was a real eye opener. No less than 72 per cent of all British dog owners believed that their pets would be aware of the fact that it was Christmas, while for cat fanciers the corresponding percentage was just over forty.

Just what it is about the holiday season that might prove exciting for a dog, and why its feline counterpart finds it almost twice as difficult to get into the Christmas spirit, were questions that fell outside the scope of the poll, but the figures do expose our tendency to credit animals with a fair amount of intelligence. Is this justified, or is it merely wishful thinking? There is certainly no shortage of evidence that we like to believe that animals are capable of thought. Our literature is full of anthropomorphic animals, which think, act and speak as we do, and many of them even seem to have human motives and foibles. Consider the case of Mr Toad in Kenneth Grahame's *The Wind in the Willows*, for example, and A.A. Milne's lovable

Winnie-the-Pooh. The humanized animal has been with us at least since the days of Aesop, and it has continued to be almost taken for granted, up through the writings of Hans Christian Andersen and Beatrix Potter, and into the twentieth century. Walt Disney managed to found a vast commercial enterprise on the concept. And the descendants of Bambi, Dumbo and Jiminy Cricket, not to mention Garfield the Cat, will no doubt continue to titillate us with their all-too-human mores in the years to come.

It is interesting to note, in this context, that we are somewhat biased when it comes to our choice of species. We are quite prepared to confer human attributes on all manner of creatures, irrespective of how close to or remote from *Homo sapiens* they might be, a good example of this variety being seen in Rudyard Kipling's *Jungle Book*. But there is one group that has traditionally been under-represented, and this comprises the creatures we consume for food. Although there is not actually a taboo against humanizing beef cattle, sheep, pigs and poultry, they seem to appear less frequently in our fables than do those creatures that never wind up in the larder. It is true that George Orwell had a porcine leading character in his *Animal Farm*, but the message of that book was political. Richard Adams' *Watership Down*, in which the word is given to another edible species, namely the rabbit, is a not-so-distant relative. The reticence to credit familiar emotions and capacities to such animals presumably has something to do with the fact that we do not like to think of them as having feelings about being led off to slaughter. But there are signs of a change in attitude on our part. There is growing concern for the mental well-being of the beasts that provide us with a fraction of our diet, and things are happening these days which a decade ago would have been unthinkable. A case in point was a court trial that took place in West Germany in the autumn of 1987. Close scrutiny of the televised record of a fishing competition convinced the jury that the fish were experiencing pain, and the outcome was a 1,200 Deutschmark fine for the organizers of the event.

It is undeniably convenient to regard all non-human animals as being incapable of thought, and this attitude is reflected in the biblical picture of creation. As one can read in Genesis (Chapter I verses 20–27), all the other species arrived on earth earlier than us, and those people who adamantly credit only *Homo sapiens* with the capacity for thought need merely interpret the Bible literally to establish their case. It is interesting to speculate on what the adherents of this point of view would nevertheless concede. At the very least, the other animals must have nervous systems, since limb movement is evident. And the movement is well coordinated, so there must be a controlling unit, a brain in fact. What this view is not prepared to accord to the other species is a mind. Non-human animal behaviour is regarded as a set of reflexes, sometimes admittedly quite sophisticated ones, but nevertheless just reflexes. All these other creatures are thus regarded as being incapable of the emotions which define the human psyche: joy, sorrow, fear, tranquillity, boredom, excitement, anticipation, and so on.

There is no anatomical support for such an extreme view. For although it is true that no other species possesses a brain that can compete with that of a human, in terms of the number of neurons and their degree of interconnectedness, the brains of lower creatures do at least bear a qualitative resemblance to ours. On the basis of what one can observe under the microscope, one would expect other mammals, at least, to experience emotions that are impoverished counterparts of our own, rather than no emotions at all. And sometimes the impoverishment seems not even to be particularly pronounced. In early October 1987, the population of Italy was absorbed by a case that involved a kangaroo family. The mother, young baby in pouch, had strayed through a hole in a wire fence at the zoo in Brescia, and had then fallen several metres into the dry moat that surrounds the park. Both creatures were killed instantly. The father kangaroo, apparently stricken with remorse, paced to and fro along the edge of the precipitous drop the best part of a day, and then suddenly flung itself over the brink in a suicidal plunge. What captured the public imagination was, of course, the almost human reaction of the father, and particularly the fact that it was a delayed reaction. It is difficult to see how it could justly be labelled as a reflex.

There have been times when it was popular to go to the other extreme, and give animals so much credit for human-like powers of thought that they were then held just as responsible for their actions as any person. In the ultimate examples of this attitude, animals have even been tried, condemned, and publicly executed. A pig was hanged in a Normandy market-place in 1396, for severely lacerating the face and upper body of a child, and the same fate befell a cat in London on 8 April, 1554. The latter was actually a case of religious persecution, because the poor creature had become an unwitting symbol of Catholicism. It appears that the most recent animal execution occurred in Delémont, Switzerland, in 1906. The victim was a dog, convicted of homicide. A particularly bizarre, not to mention cruel, aspect of some of the associated criminal proceedings was that they were followed by torture, in an effort to extract a confession. No less peculiar was the fact that some of the animals dispatched through these weird goings-on were actually given the benefit of a defending counsel.

The supreme examples of mankind's willingness to exaggerate the mental abilities of at least some animals must be those which led to the creatures' deification. This was especially prominent in the religion of early Egypt. The most important animal god appears to have been Horus, the falcon-god, whose name means the Distant One, because many of the Pharaohs were depicted in close association with this figure. The largest temple to Horus was located at Edfu, and it is the best preserved of all Ancient Egyptian places of worship. Amongst the other animal holinesses were the jackal-god Anubis, who was the traditional protector of the dead, the cat-goddess Bastet, whose cult centre was at Bubastic in the Nile Delta, the crocodile-god Sebek, the ram-god Khnum, the cow-god Hathor and the bull-god Apis. It seems possible, however, that there was some reticence to go all the way in according human-like powers of thought to these creatures, because they frequently appear as animal–human amalgamations, the animal head being grafted onto a human body. This is especially true of Horus, Anubis and Khnum, while some pictures of Hathor even show her with a human head and only the horns of a cow. (In this context, however, one should remember that the Ancient Egyptians had not recognized the central role played by the brain.)

All this merely serves to show that mankind has, from time to time, attributed various degrees of thought to animals. We must now turn to the question of how one is to determine whether animals really do think. And this, we will discover, is an issue fraught with difficulties. Even if an animal belongs to a species that is close to our own, judging the presence or absence of thought might still be a relatively tough task, and for our more distant relations the job could be nigh on impossible. For try as we might to be objective in our evaluation, our Achilles' heel will be our natural tendency to compare the behaviour of other animals with that displayed by *Homo sapiens*. How is one to judge, for example, whether a garden worm is conscious, consciousness presumably being a prerequisite for thought? When a chimpanzee shows almost human intelligence in its use of sign language, as we shall discuss later, there seems to be no doubt that it is thinking, but at what point on a descent down the evolutionary ladder does conscious awareness evaporate? Is it still there in the spider? One can place electrodes on the head of a cat, monitor its brain activity, and clearly distinguish between the sleeping and wakeful states. To this extent, at least, one can maintain that consciousness is present in that animal. But the exploitation of such techniques is not possible with lowly creatures like the ant, and it seems better to rely on observational criteria. If a creature can adapt to changing circumstances, for example, and display behavioural versatility, it seems safe to conclude that it is conscious in any useful interpretation of that term. Let us look at a few examples.

One aspect of animal behaviour that has been taken to indicate thought is the use of what could generally be referred to as tools. The woodpecker finch caused quite a stir when it was first observed to use a thin twig to coax insects out of holes that were too narrow to admit its beak. Later, the sea otter was found to use stones routinely recovered from the sea-bed to break open the shells of molluscs and sea-urchins. That forethought is involved in this feat is beyond question, because the creature finds a suitable stone and tucks it under its arm before starting on its aquatic forage. This behaviour is neither instinctive nor stereotyped, because these tools are used only in areas where suitable food cannot be obtained by other means. In some otter colonies, moreover, only the young and old members use stones, the otters that are in the prime of life being strong enough to pry the shells of their prey off the rocks with their claws and bared teeth.

Another tool user is the type of spider known as *Dinopis*. It makes a web, but not of the normal type that is strung permanently from convenient parts of the environment. The web of *Dinopis* is like a small net, which it casts over its prey to ensnare it, in much the same manner as that used by the gladiators in ancient Rome. The bolas spider, *Pasilobus*, goes one better. It fabricates a snare in the form of a thread (of the same material normally used for a web) that carries a sticky blob at one end. It then gives off a chemical substance that mimics the pheromones (i.e. sexual attractants) usually emitted by the females of some species of moth. When male moths respond to the promise of this odour, by flying to the vicinity of the spider, it swings its line until the moth is entrapped by the adhesive droplet, and then reels in its meal. Short of the fact that *Pasilobus* (probably) doesn't boast about 'the one that got away', this is about as close to the idea of fishing by our own species as one could wish to come.

Yet, even this feat is surpassed by the assassin bug, *Salyarata variegata*. Its favoured dish is the termite, and it too uses a pair of tricks to realize its dietary desires. Before embarking upon the hunt, it plasters itself with numerous little bits of twig and leaf stolen from an actual termite nest (rather than from the primary source of that material). This could serve as camouflage, but it seems that the main object is to make its outer surface feel and smell familiar to its intended victims, for the termite's sense of sight is quite limited. When the twig-bedecked hunter expectantly positions itself at the entrance to the termites' nest, its movements usually do attract the attention of the colony's well-armed soldier caste, but the camouflage apparently deceives them, for they soon lose interest and return to their posts. The way now clear, *S. variegata* carefully peers into the opening, grabs itself an *hors d'oeuvre* and sucks out all the victim's semi-fluid internal organs. Not satisfied with this act, impressive as it undoubtedly is, the bug now produces its *pièce de résistance*. The point is that termites apparently put a premium on good housekeeping, and they make virtue out of necessity by eating their own dead. Just how the disguised bug senses this is not clear, but it dangles the evacuated hulk of its first victim at the termites' front door. One of the termites latches on to this exoskeleton, prior to performing its duty of tidying up, only to find itself being hoisted out of the nest and into the jaws of the waiting predator. The bug repeats its fishing act until its appetite is satisfied.

We could find many other examples of the apparently thoughtful use of implements. There is an ant, for example, which builds a trap by digging out a funnel-shaped depression in loose sand, such that any prey trespassing on the slope will roll down into the centre, where it has positioned itself under a thin covering of the sand. Rather than merely wait for a victim to make its false step, the ant throws sand to put it off balance. A similar, but even more impressive, thing is done by some fish, which spit drops of water at insects perched on the limbs of plants just above the surface of the water. The amazing thing about this feat is that these fish actually compensate for the refraction caused by the water's surface (i.e. the effect which makes a half-submerged stick appear as if it is bent).

These and other examples of the use of implements are impressive, but perhaps we are inclined to attach too much importance to them, because we find them similar to our own brand of achievement. Is the fishing prowess of *Pasilobus* really more creditable than what is achieved by an ordinary spider, using its sticky and almost invisible web to catch its food? After all, the way in which the spider rushes out of its hiding place, to wind extra turns of web around a partially trapped insect, and thereby secure its meal, is also quite imposing. And what about that clever repair job that it carries out, after severing the strands that hold the sucked-out carcass so as to let the latter fall away?

Another criterion that we could apply in order to reveal the presence of thought in animals is evidence that acquired expertise is passed on from one member of a species to its fellows. This would effectively eliminate the possibility that the behaviour is dictated by instinct, which, as we saw earlier, can manifest itself in quite complex patterns. There is happily no shortage of examples where such learning is in evidence. Jane Goodall described the use of sticks by chimpanzees, to harvest termites. They select a suitably sized branch, remove the leaves, break off the ends until the size is optimal, and prod the resulting implement into the mound by using one of the holes employed by the insects. The interesting point, here, is that the young chimpanzees learn this art by watching the adults, and it invariably takes them many hours of practice before they have mastered the technique.

A similar thing is observed with Japanese macaque monkeys. In the early 1960s, Masao Kawai noticed that some members of this species had discovered a way of separating grain from sand. They simply threw the mixture into water, whereupon the sand sank, and the floating grain could be picked from the surface. This technique, no doubt stumbled on accidentally, was at first employed by just a few of the species, but it was gradually passed on to the others through observation and imitation.

A particularly well-documented example of learning by example was reported in 1951 by J. Fisher and R.A. Hinde. It had been noticed, as early as the 1930s, that two species of tits had learned how to penetrate the coverings of milk bottles so as to get at the liquid. When the milk is not homogenized, the cream floats on the top, and this apparently proves to be an added incentive to the birds. In those early days, the tops were made of cardboard, there being a centrally located circular region that had been scored so as to make for easy depression by the tip of a finger. Or, so the birds discovered, by the tip of a beak. When cardboard tops were later replaced by metal foil, the birds had to discover that these are even more readily pierced. (I have observed this at my sister's farm in Nottinghamshire, and she swears that the birds can even tell the difference between silver tops (standard milk) and gold tops (rich in cream).) The fascinating thing about this phenomenon was that it was quickly reported when first noticed, and that its subsequent spread amongst the tit population was carefully charted. That it was a case of learning by imitation could thus be established beyond doubt.

An especially endearing suggestion of forethought is seen in the behaviour of beavers. As is well known, the homes of these creatures are accessible only via a water-filled passage and this means that the young have to learn to swim for a considerable distance without attempting to inhale. Their first swimming lesson is thus a potentially lethal experience. But in fact it is not at all dangerous, because the entire family joins in. The older offspring take their usual deep breath and dive from the nest area into the opening of the tunnel. But instead of continuing on their way out, they turn around and wait just below the surface. The parents then push the infants into the water, the plunge carrying the tiny tots well below the surface.

Their senior siblings provide the necessary safety net by simply pushing them back to the brim of the nest. After numerous repetitions of this exercise, all the family's youngest members become sufficiently adept at holding their breaths, and they can traverse the entire length of the tunnel without undue risk. It is difficult to believe that this complex enterprise is merely the product of instinct.

There are two examples of differentiated behaviour which demand inclusion because of their strong suggestion of mentation on the part of the creature involved. The first is displayed by certain ground-nesting birds, such as the killdeer or piping plovers. They have developed remarkable strategies for leading predators away from their nests. When potential danger looms, in the form of an intruder, the bird will walk slowly to a point several metres from its nest, well before the alien could possibly have seen either the bird or its home. Then, when the intruder is within sighting distance, the bird flutters slowly and deliberately in a direction that would not take it back towards the nest's real location. The act is so conspicuous that it is clearly intended to give a false impression of the nest's actual whereabouts. This is indeed an impressive ruse, but the bird has an even more surprising encore up its sleeve. Quite often, when it is carrying out this decoy manoeuvre, it will hold its tail or one of its wings at an awkward angle, almost as if to suggest that one of these has suffered injury. This is precisely the intention, and the masquerade is sometimes extended to include a bogus semi-collapse, in which the creature stops and flops about on the ground. The bird is obviously feigning injury. But why this show of avian histrionics? It is related to the fact that predators instinctively know that an injured prey is easier to catch. Watch a cheetah attacking a herd of antelope, for example, and you will notice that it will always choose an animal with a limp, if one is available. During this predator-misleading operation, the bird keeps a close watch on the interloper, always contriving to stay within sight, but nevertheless just out of reach.

These birds indulge in a different mode of behaviour when the threat comes from an unknowing group of animals that might inadvertently trample on the eggs or fledglings. In this case the bird stays by the nest, and flaps its wings ostentatiously, where-upon the approaching herd usually veers so as to avoid trouble.

The use of these two alternatives, and the bird's unerring choice between them, is surely the acme of adaptive behaviour, and it is very difficult to believe that no thought is involved.

There is even better to come, however, because the vervet monkey has a numerical advantage over the plover: it can distinguish between no less than three different types of danger, and react with an appropriate response. Thomas Struhsaker reported, in 1967, that these apes tailor their alarm calls to the type of threat, and that they are apparently able to differentiate between three categories of predator: one that approaches from the ground, such as a leopard or hyena; one that attacks from the air, such as an eagle; and finally one that comes climbing towards them, namely a snake. The vervet has a distinctly different call for each of these types of threat. And the availability of three different warnings is potentially valuable because the situations to which they correspond require different evasion tactics. The appearance on the scene of an eagle, for instance, drives the monkeys into the cover of the trees, but this is a most unsuitable response when a leopard is around because leopards can climb. Avoidance of danger from that source requires the monkeys to move out to those tree limbs that are too thin to support the big cat's weight. When a snake is the threat, the monkey has merely to be careful to locate it and quickly move away. That these warning calls really are used to communicate information between members of a group of vervet monkeys was established by playing tape recordings of the calls through a concealed loudspeaker. Sure enough, a leopard-type call drove them up into the trees and out along the thinner branches. An eagle-type call sent them diving for the thickest available cover, and when the snake-type warning was played at them, they raised themselves high on their hind legs and frantically looked around for the snake. This confirmation was achieved by Peter Marler (who had used a similar field-trial approach in his studies of bird song, as described in an earlier chapter) together with his colleagues Robert Seyfarth and Dorothy Cheney.

Seyfarth and Cheney have shown that communication between these monkeys has a deeper dimension: they not only use nuances of voice to distinguish between individual companions, but also to identify relationships between them. The two colleagues recorded the screams of a juvenile member and played it back to the entire group, including the youngster's mother. The mother's reaction was, not surprisingly, stronger than those of the other adult females. The fascinating thing, however, was that all the latter responded not by looking in the direction of the loudspeaker but directly at the mother. They clearly knew which of their companions the young monkey belonged to. It was later established, in much the same way, that vervets can also identify the members of neighbouring groups and correctly associate them with particular stretches of territory.

There is no denying that animals are capable of numerous types of behaviour which, if they were being displayed by humans, would have to imply conscious thought. The big question is, however, whether they really are the result of conscious thought in the creatures involved or are merely the product, albeit impressively complex, of instinct. But how is one to resolve this issue? It would be a great advantage, of course, if one had a reliable means of unambiguously detecting consciousness in animals. This might be wishful thinking, however, in view of the fact that consciousness is a difficult enough concept to handle even in the context of our own species. And even if a means is ultimately found whereby consciousness can be monitored, and its presence established without disturbing the animal's behaviour, there will still be the problem of showing how what an animal thinks relates to what it does. This is certainly not a trivial question, as can be seen from contemplation of what we are able to achieve with very little help from consciousness. (I am sometimes quite alarmed to discover that I have driven to or from work with a problem on my mind, and that I have barely been aware of the act of controlling the car and responding correctly to the various traffic situations.) It is no wonder that there have been attempts to communicate directly with members of some species, for success in that quest might nicely bypass the problem. As we have just seen, there is ample evidence of communication between vervet monkeys, and the pioneering work of Karl von Frisch revealed the extensive language with which bees impart foraging knowledge to their comrades. And these are not isolated examples of what could be called intraspecies language. What is still lacking, however, is interspecies communication, and preferably with ourselves as one of the parties involved. Let us, therefore, take a look at what has been achieved on that front.

This might seem to inject us into a wide field of investigation, but in fact the issue can be narrowed down quite easily, for if we cannot communicate with those species to which we are most closely related it is not likely that we are going to have much verbal intercourse with an animal that is evolutionarily more remote. If we cannot talk to a lemur, what chance is there of intelligent conversation with an ostrich, even when the latter's head is not buried in the sand! Which species, then, lies closest to us? In earlier times, this was an issue of considerable debate, for although a stroll around any well-stocked zoo quickly shows us which candidates can be eliminated, the final choice depends upon which physical similarities are to be given the highest priority. Should one stress similarities in the arrangement of the teeth, for example, or permit relative arm length to have the deciding vote? Fortunately, modern genetic techniques allow us to give an unequivocal answer to the question. Comparison of genetic material from various species, the DNA that is, provides us with an unambiguous measure of the evolutionary distance between ourselves and our nearest cousins in the animal kingdom, and it naturally comes as no surprise to find that these are the apes. They all belong to the family known as Pongidae, while we are the only living members of the Hominidae family. One is even able to differentiate between these apes, in terms of their genetic proximity to us, and the result can be stated in terms of an arbitrarily defined distance scale, in which importance is to be attached to the relative values rather than to the absolute magnitudes. The outcome is as follows: chimpanzee 1.8, gorilla 2.4, orangutan 3.6, gibbon 5.2 and monkey 7.7. If we cannot talk to the chimpanzee, therefore, we are probably going to have to be satisfied with merely observing the animals with which we share this planet, without communicating with them. What, then, has been accomplished in our efforts to interact with chimpanzees?

Chimpanzees have been kept as household pets for much of human civilization. Their role as companions can be traced at least as far back as the Ancient Greeks and Egyptians. There have, however, never been reports of their acquiring language as a result of this proximity to our language-using race. But neither had there been any concerted effort to actually teach them to communicate to humans. Until the 1930s, that is, when several projects were initiated in the USA and the USSR. They were abject failures, because they aimed at teaching the animals to produce vocalized English and Russian. It was subsequently realized that these apes simply do not possess the appropriate anatomical machinery to enable them to produce the phonemes of which our words are composed. Even if the animals had understood English or Russian perfectly well, they would not have been able to speak it. As a result of these early disappointments, interest in man–chimpanzee communication languished for about a quarter of a century.

The early studies had at least established that chimpanzees do understand the spoken word, however. Winthrop Kellogg has written of his experiences during the nine-month training period of a chimpanzee named Gua. And the scientifically interesting thing about this investigation was that it also involved a human control subject, namely an infant child who shared Gua's learning environment. A marked difference between the two was obvious from the outset. The child babbled and prattled away of its own volition, seeming to experiment with sounds and probe the avenues of its vocal capabilities. As we noted earlier, these sounds later crystallize into spoken language. No ape, on the other hand, has ever been observed to go through such a stage, and Gua was certainly no exception. Gua's early performance in understanding language, nevertheless, actually outstripped that of its human nursery mate. Simple commands such as 'No no' and 'Come here', and longer phrases like 'Blow the [car's] horn', 'Close the door', 'Don't put that in your mouth' and 'Go to Daddy' were all quickly assimilated. Later, of course, the child's rate of development far exceeded that of the chimpanzee. Gua also developed a useful vocabulary of signs, such as throwing itself prone on the floor to indicate a desire for sleep. (This was no mere game; it would fall asleep immediately if it was put to bed promptly after making the gesture.) It would also remove its bib to indicate that it was finished eating, and it learned to hold on to its genitals to indicate a need to urinate.

It was these latter observations, as much as anything, which suggested the next step, for it emphasized the manual nature of the chimpanzee's natural flair for communication. The lead was followed up by R. Allen Gardner and Beatrice Gardner, who acquired, in June 1966, a female of the species aged somewhere between eight and fourteen months. They named her Washoe, after the county which provides a home for the University of Nevada, where they carried out their study, and chose the American Sign Language (ASL) as the sole means of interacting with her. This is the gestural system of communication used by the deaf and dumb in North America.

(The appearance of the word dumb, here, has an interesting dimension. It has recently acquired a second meaning, of course, namely lacking in intelligence or common sense. Even as late as the early part of this century, the deaf and dumb were indeed looked upon as imbeciles. To be either deaf or dumb is of course a great disadvantage in life, but the impairment can be overcome. To be both deaf and dumb is far worse, and to be deaf, dumb and blind must be absolutely devastating. Such a person has only the tactile sense with which to communicate, and if the deficiencies are congenital, how does one even acquire the concept of communication? As the moving case of Helen Keller showed, the concept is nevertheless simply waiting to be discovered, because the intact cortex will still be capable of recording correlations; it is always ready to pounce on causative connections previously denied it. This is what was exploited by Helen's gifted teacher, and when she held one of Helen's hands under running water and spelled out on the palm of the other W-A-T-E-R, the wonderful world of communication was suddenly opened up to her young companion.)

The chimpanzee also has a well-developed cortex, waiting to latch on to the stimulating correlation, and this is what provided the Gardners with ample scope for success in their fascinating venture. Their choice of ASL was well considered, and it was important to them that some of the signs are rather arbitrary in their form, and quite unrelated to any natural symbolism. Take, for example, the sign for 'always'. It consists of holding the hand in a fist, with the index finger extended, and rotating the arm at the elbow. There is not much symbolism in this action. The sign for flower is, on the other hand, quite symbolic; it is made by holding the fingers of one hand extended, all five fingertips touching, and putting these first to one nostril and then to the other, as if smelling. The Gardners felt that it was an advantage to use a sign language with varying degrees of symbolism.

The results of the study make for fascinating reading. Within 22 months, Washoe had acquired 30 signs, the criterion being that she spontaneously used these in an appropriate context on fifteen consecutive days. Her average use of signs was, by this time, about thirty per day. Amongst her early acquisitions were 'gimme' (made with a beckoning motion, with the wrist or knuckles as a pivot), 'more' (in which the fingertips are brought together, usually overhead) and 'sweet' (which is indicated by touching the wagging tongue with the index or index and second fingers). Later, Washoe learned to point an index finger at a person's chest to indicate 'you', and to point it at her own chest and thereby refer to herself: 'I – me'. Amongst the less obvious signs, learned after about two years had elapsed, were 'clothes', in which the fingertips are brushed down the chest, and 'clean', which is indicated by passing the open palm of one hand over the open palm of the other.

Washoe's use of the signs soon began to reveal considerable sophistication. She started to show what is known as transference. For example, she transferred the sign for 'dog' to the sound of barking by an unseen dog. But the thing that particularly thrilled the Gardners was her spontaneous use of combinations of signs. Her trainer–observers had carefully avoided using anything other than isolated signs, as a caution against accidentally giving her this ability. But here she was, happily stringing together couplets such as 'Gimme tickle' (before they had ever asked her to tickle them) and 'Open food drink' (for the refrigerator, which they had previously always referred to as the 'cold box'). Washoe even betrayed her innate lack of patience one day when she put together the signs for 'Please open hurry' and 'Listen eat', when the Gardners had not responded sufficiently quickly to an alarm clock which usually heralded mealtime.

Although some of the ASL signs are fairly arbitrary, as we have noted, they could not really be called abstract. An investigation carried out by David Premack, on a chimpanzee named Sarah, has gone much further towards demonstrating that these animals really are able to handle abstract concepts. He replaced ASL with coloured plastic shapes, and had soon trained Sarah to understand and react to such commands as 'Sarah give apple Mary' (Mary being the name of the human trainer). This was achieved after exposing Sarah to 'Mary give apple Sarah'. Later, Sarah was taught 'Insert' and learned to use it correctly, as in responding to 'Sarah apple dish insert'. The most elaborate tasks she succeeded with involved instructions such as 'Sarah apple cracker dish cracker pail insert', in which two different items were to be put in a dish, while only one was put in a pail.

Before we get too carried away by such triumphs, it would be well to inject a couple of cautionary notes. One, happily, proved easy to refute. It invoked what has come to be known as the Clever Hans phenomenon. Clever Hans was a German horse that stamped out with its hoof the answers to simple arithmetical problems written on a blackboard. The animal was 'unmasked' by Osker Pfungst in 1911, when it was demonstrated that its abilities evaporated when the trainer was prevented from seeing the answers. The creature had merely been sensing the slight alterations in the trainer's posture that had innocently been giving the game away; the trainer unwittingly relaxed when the correct answer was reached, and this did not escape the attention of Clever Hans. This difficulty would presumably also have been present in the investigations of sign language in chimpanzees, since these creatures are also sensitive to human mood. It can be circumvented by having them interact with a keyboard, as Duane Rumbaugh and Sue Savage-Rumbaugh have shown. The other point is more serious. The early success with the use of sign language must have tempted the researchers involved to entertain the idea of, one day, being able to read a chimpanzee's thoughts. That dream has fallen far short of realization, and David Premack has put this failure down to the fact that a chimpanzee is not able to think with its acquired language. It can make the associations necessary to permit use of the symbols, but these symbols do not become part of its internal software, as it were. This is not to say that the chimpanzee's achievement is unimpressive, and it emphatically doesn't prove that the animal lacks consciousness, as we will see shortly. It does tell us, however, that when Dr Doolittle dreamed of talking to the animals, he was probably wide of the mark. A better policy is to judge the issue of conscious thought in other species by simply observing their behaviour under the appropriate conditions.

Before bringing this fascinating story up to date, let us briefly look back at how attitudes to animal thought have changed over the most recent few centuries. René Descartes believed animals to be incapable of thought, while John Locke allowed them perception, memory and reason, but stopped short of crediting them with the power of abstraction. In his view 'Brutes compare but imperfectly' and 'Brutes abstract not'. David Hume took a more charitable view. He regarded animal inferiority *vis-à-vis Homo sapiens* to be a matter of degree rather than of kind. The mainspring of his argument was that animals can learn from experience, just as man does, and that they are thus able to draw the mental line from cause to effect. Animals, Hume reasoned, are able to draw inferences. Arthur Schopenhauer saw animals as enjoying the advantages of understanding and a free will, despite their incapability of learning a language. He believed them to be aware only of the present. 'The brute feels and perceives', he wrote, 'but man also thinks and knows.' It was left to Charles Darwin to bring the popular attitude back to that of Hume. 'The difference in mind between man and the higher animals', he wrote, in *Descent of Man*, 'great as it is, certainly is one of degree and not of kind'. In this, he received the staunch support of Herbert Spencer, Thomas Henry and George Romanes. The latter specialized in all manner of anecdotal supporting evidence, such as stories of cows opening gates, parrots talking in their sleep, and worker bees communicating information to their fellows (the latter subsequently being verified, of course). This is not to say that Romanes was a catch-all for the most outlandish claims. When Alexander Graham Bell wrote to Romanes, announcing that he had managed to train an English terrier to say 'How are you grandmamma?', Romanes flatly refused to believe him.

What would all these philosophers have made of the most recent observations on apes, one wonders? Hume, at least, might have revised his view of the animal mind even farther upwards, for chimpanzee behaviour has even been found to include what could be called sin. Chimpanzees, it seems, are masters of deceit. Emil Menzel was amongst the first to realize this. He revealed the location of a cache of food, within a large enclosure, to a chimpanzee that enjoyed only a modest position in the local pecking order. Then he admitted the rest of the

Until recently, it was believed that no animal other than the human being is capable of thought, but observations on a number of species have now refuted this oversimplification. In some cases, as with the one shown here, it has transpired that non-human animals are even capable of attributing thought to their fellow creatures. The picture shows a situation in which a female hamadryas baboon is grooming a young male that is hidden from her harem master's view by a rock. The female took twenty minutes to work her way casually over to the rock, in order not to arouse suspicion, and it is clear that she could calculate that the young male would be invisible to the senior baboon.

group. The animal with the knowledge of the food's whereabouts deliberately misled its senior companions in order not to lose out to them. David Premak extended these studies to include the chimpanzee—human relationship, and he demonstrated that a chimpanzee will attempt to misdirect an observer, especially if the latter has demonstrated that he too relishes the food that is at stake.

Baboons have been observed to get up to pranks that are even naughtier. Gelada baboons form harem groups in which a single male controls a number of females. In one study, Hans Kummer placed one of the females in a cage with an alien male, such that they were out of sight, but not out of earshot, from her normal harem male. When she subsequently began to groom the new male, he did not emit the loud sounds that males of his species usually vocalize when being thus groomed. Kummer also reported seeing a female hamadryas baboon manoeuvre herself and a young male beyond the gaze of her lord and master so that she could copulate with the willing upstart. In between these illicit goings on, she would periodically return to the 'old man', to give him a reassuring groom. Robin Dunbar observed similar adulterous behaviour in a female gelada baboon, and was fascinated to notice that the loud post-intercourse vocalizations that are standard for this species were suppressed by both the fallen female and her young paramour. They were wise enough to be able to anticipate the consequences of giving the game away.

An apparently higher order of anticipation and deception was observed in one of Kummer's hamadryas baboons. A female took twenty minutes to gradually work her way over to a rock just a couple of metres from where she had been sitting. She appeared to want to give the impression that her short journey was capricious and without ulterior motive. But in fact the rock was concealing a young male from her harem master's view. She then proceeded to groom the young fellow, adopting a stance in which all of her body, except her grooming hands, was visible to the older male. Her care in thus positioning herself indicates that she was able to calculate exactly how the scenario appeared from her master's point of view. Richard Byrne and Andrew Whiten have reported another intriguing case of baboon deceit. One of the youngsters was making quite a din because it had been bullied by an adolescent. This attracted the attention of a number of the adults, including the victim's mother, and they were soon in pursuit of the offender, bent on administering suitable retribution. But rather than flee or submit, the adolescent stood on its hind legs and scanned the horizon. This is the standard reaction of a baboon when it senses danger from a predator. His would-be punishers stopped in their tracks, and immediately joined in the reconnaissance, leaving the bully to slink away unpunished.

An important prerequisite for deceit is accurate anticipation, and any animal capable of anticipation might, in principle, be able to anticipate being anticipated; an animal which can deceive might be able to deceive a deceiver. Jane Goodall reported seeing a young chimpanzee suddenly notice a banana that observers had hidden in a tree, while the animal's companions remained oblivious of the tempting piece of fruit. A larger chimpanzee happened to be sitting closer to the tree than the observant youngster, and Goodall was fascinated to observe that the latter moved away so as to lead its potential competitor off the scent. When its senior colleague moved away, the youngster dashed back and quickly polished off the banana.

Franz Plooij has reported observing an even more complex piece of chimpanzee deception. A male who was on the point of eating some bananas that only he knew about was interrupted by the sudden appearance of one of his peers. He promptly acted just as Jane Goodall's young chimpanzee had done: he moved away and ostentatiously played the innocent. The intruder then also left the scene, but only to position himself behind a tree. When the first animal returned to claim his bananas, and of course reveal their location, the unseen observer rushed out and commandeered all the other's fruit.

As Richard Byrne and Andrew Whiten note, this complex of deceptions indicates that a chimpanzee is capable of saying to himself: The other fellow thinks that I think that he doesn't know where to find a banana . . . but I think he knows perfectly well where the banana is. If such behaviour is not a consequence of conscious thought, who then needs conscious thought?

● Summary

The mental ability of an animal is determined by the size of its brain relative to the size of its entire body. Measured in this manner, man is seen to be the best endowed of Nature's creatures, but other species, especially those close to us on the evolutionary tree, display impressive capacities for learning and adaption. Many show a pronounced social behaviour, and some can even acquire a rudimentary language. The lesser machines, capable as they appear to be of some degree of thought, are impressive, but their performance pales in comparison with that of Nature's senior machine. The current leader differs from its nearest competitors only in degree, however, not in type.

The final eclipse?
Consciousness and will

Every Christian Church has tried to impose a
code of morals of some kind for which it has
claimed divine sanction. As these codes have always
been opposed to those of the gospels a loophole has
been left for moral progress such as hardly exists
in other religions. This is no doubt an argument for
Christianity as against other religions, but not as
against none at all, or as against a religion which
will frankly admit that its mythology and morals
are provisional. That is the only sort of religion that
would satisfy the scientific mind, and it is very
doubtful whether it could properly be called a religion at all. No doubt many people hope that
such a religion may develop from Christianity. The
human intellect is feeble, and there are times when
it does not assert the infinity of its claims. But
even then:

> Though in black jest it bows and nods,
> I know it is roaring at the gods,
> Waiting for the final eclipse.

The scientific worker of the future will more and
more resemble the lonely figure of Daedalus as he
becomes conscious of his ghastly mission, and be
proud of it.

JOHN BURDON SANDERSON HALDANE
Daedalus, or Science and the Future

The icy little breeze sent a sudden shiver through us, and I
mutely remonstrated with myself for not having brought a
topcoat. But the directions, as given in the conference programme, had not made it clear that we were going to be

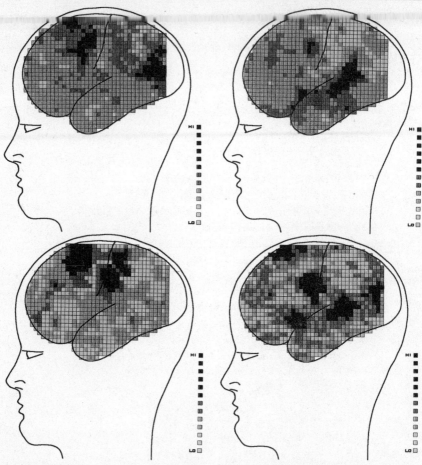

Positron emission tomography provides pictures of the brain in action. A mutant form of glucose, which cannot be fully metabolized, is preferentially absorbed by the most active regions and tends to accumulate in them. The glucose molecules are radioactively labelled, and they give rise to gamma rays, the detection of which yields a picture showing which parts of the brain are most active in a particular situation. In the four examples shown here, the subject was following a moving object with his eyes (upper left); listening to spoken words (upper right); moving his fingers on the side of the body opposite the hemisphere being monitored (lower left); and reading aloud (lower right). It is instructive to compare these pictures with the diagram shown below, which indicates the areas responsible for several of the faculties that have been localized through studies of patients with brain injuries.

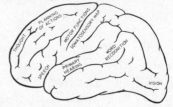

briefly out of doors. Despite the cold, it was difficult to ignore the deeply impressive structure that had held our attention for the past couple of minutes. Cologne Cathedral, after all, boasts some of the world's most spectacular architecture, and like some of the other great religious buildings in Germany, it was spared the devastation otherwise inflicted by the Allied bombing during the Second World War. Its Gothic buttresses were thrown into even sharper relief by the modernity of the surroundings.

That such edifices were not ravaged in the same manner as other civil (and of course military) targets attests to the fact that reverence for the houses of God readily transcends national boundaries. So does failure to heed the word of God, however, for that armed conflict, like so many others, pitted against each other peoples that supposedly belonged to the same faith.

This was just one of the thoughts that passed through my mind in rapid succession, that late September evening, as we gazed up at the soaring spire with its almost lace-like masonry. What, I wondered, were my colleagues thinking? And with that question, we have reached a very interesting issue, for thoughts are surely the most private of all things. They are inaccessible to all except their owner. This fact has indeed often caused so much political, religious and legal frustration that instruments such as the rack, the thumbscrew, and their even nastier modern counterparts, have been employed in attempts to prise them loose. And when a thought's possessor volunteers to make it public, a truth drug or lie detector is sometimes deemed desirable, to ensure that it emerges intact and unsullied from its owner's brain. Small wonder that the prospect of remote reading of thoughts has continued to fuel curiosity. The electroencephalograph (EEG) must, at one time, have seemed to hold promise of such revelations, but few experts in that area would now entertain such a possibility. Similarly, although the more recent technique of positron emission tomography (developed by Niels Lassen and David Ingvar, who built on earlier advances by Louis Sokoloff) permits one to detect which parts of the brain are active under a given set of circumstances, this is still a very far cry from exposing the actual thoughts that underlie that activity.

There is a related question which is no less intriguing. Can one even be sure that other people have conscious thoughts? If it seems obvious that they do, how would one go about proving it? By posing artfully designed questions, and by generally observing the responses to given stimuli? But what questions, and which stimuli? The more one ponders this issue, and it is a classic amongst philosophers, the greater looms the difficulty of establishing that one's fellow human beings are not in fact merely complex automatons. One's final resort must be to what seems most compatible with common sense: that since we all come from approximately the same mould, we either all have thoughts, or none of us has thoughts. The existence of my own thoughts, therefore, encourages me to believe that the pages of this book are not being scanned by an unthinking device, however sophisticated such a thing might admittedly be. And the existence of the reader's thoughts will (I hope) similarly convince her or him that this book is not the mere product of a thoughtless bit of hardware.

Authors seldom even require coaxing, let alone thumbscrews. They, at least, are prepared to divulge their innermost thoughts at the slightest excuse. So let me continue to expose what was running through my mind, that crisp evening in Cologne. I wrote earlier of armed conflict. Another of my thoughts was concerned with a different type of conflict: the conflict between what this cathedral, and all its lesser relations, stands for, namely the immortality of the soul, and the theme of the scientific meeting that had brought us to the Cologne area that week in the autumn of 1987. For our outing that evening was providing a brief respite from busy sessions in which we had been discussing the latest evidence supporting a decidedly mechanistic view of the mind. Sessions which, indeed, allowed precious little scope at all for the soul, immortal or otherwise.

Another of the feelings that I was experiencing was, if anything, even more sacrilegious. It was related to the fact that buildings like the one we were looking at seem to be generally taken as sufficient proof of the existence of everything they stand for. There are houses of God, therefore there is a God. This is their underlying message, and there must be many who would consider the truth of that proposition to be beyond question. That there are such buildings logically proves nothing of the kind, of course; it merely demonstrates that there were (and still are) people sufficiently motivated by a belief in God that they would erect temples, or pay for others to erect them.

We have already considered the emergence of the idea of the immortal soul, early in this book, and the concept hardly needs further clarification. There is a ramification which is worth considering at this point, however, because it will provide a springboard for the re-evaluation of the soul that I will be advocating later on. The point is that temples to deities, of whatever faith, seem to invoke respect irrespective of one's own particular conviction. The Westerner entering a Shinto shrine, for example, experiences a feeling of reverence even though he or she might know precious little about the Shinto canon. And what Christian would not feel humbled by the towering form of the giant Buddha in the temple at Nara? My own most intense experience of this type occurred during a visit to Le Corbusier's chapel of Notre-Dame du Haut at Ronchamps. Mention of it being *the* building of the twentieth century, in several architectural texts that I had read prior to the visit, had put me in a sceptical frame of mind, but such doubts evaporated the moment the structure came into view. And the feeling of communion with something almost cosmic increased tenfold upon entering the chapel. I would defy even the most hardened criminal to sit alone in Le Corbusier's masterpiece and not feel the presence of something larger than man.

But the question remains as to what this superhuman something actually is. Let me turn to another train of thought that I had that evening, as we mechanistically inclined neural conferees gazed up at the holy symbol of what our scientific sessions had been undermining. I was recalling a newspaper item, current at the time, which reported the inferred permanent demise of someone long since dead. This sounds so odd that it obviously ought to be spelled out in greater detail. The person in question had, in fact, passed away on 31 October 1926, but his soul was nevertheless the subject of a fascinating piece of litigation sixty-one years later. The point is that the departed individual had solemnly undertaken to contact his relations through messages transmitted from the hereafter and, because no such communications had been received, Judge George Choppelas of San Francisco's Court of Historical Review had reluctantly concluded that the man should be declared gone beyond recall. The case would have been of little interest had it not been for the identity of its central character. He was Harry Houdini, indisputably the greatest escape artist the world has ever known. His ability to emerge from the seemingly impregnable confines of all manner of claustrophobic containers, often submerged under water, his arms and legs usually having first been bound in ropes or chains, had made Houdini a living legend. Whence the interest in what the newspaper reported. If this master of the miraculous escape could not penetrate the barriers between life and death, who else was likely to bring off such a feat?

That Houdini has not been heard from is no proof that his spirit did not pass on to the hereafter, however. It merely shows that one cannot count on messages from the departed to bolster the case for immortality of the soul. It is thus interesting to note the recent appearance of several claims for what might seem to be a viable alternative, an acceptable second best, namely what has come to be known as the after-death experience. In these times of medical wizardry, it is not unusual for people to be resuscitated after their vital systems have stopped functioning. Hearts can now be restarted, and nervous systems can be re-galvanized. Some of the happy beneficiaries of this newly won expertise have reported on their mental experiences during the brief period in which they were essentially dead. There has, not surprisingly, been considerable interest in what these people have had to say about their fleeting sojourns on the far bank of death's Rubicon.

The obvious difficulty with this type of thing lies in its subjective dimension. Many of the people fortunate enough to be reprieved at the eleventh hour are going to let their impressions of the experience be coloured by their understandable gratitude. One might expect devout Christians to report being turned back by St Peter at the very threshold of the pearly gates, while adherents of other religions will probably have stories to tell which similarly reflect the figures and features of other dogmas. And the accounts can generally be expected to be all the more vivid if the person involved is convinced that there is a life after death.

There is nevertheless something impressive about many of the reports on the after-death experience: they tend to have a number of things in common that could not be said to be the product of cultural conditioning. One of these is the out-of-body experience. The person feels as if he has passed beyond his own physical confines, and is dispassionately observing his exterior. Another thing that crops up in many of the accounts is the sensation of a bright light, and descriptions of travelling through a tunnel are also quite common. Finally, and perhaps most commonly, there is the feeling that one's entire life is flashing through one's mind, while these other things are happening. It is almost as if there were a fundamental set of such experiences, one that even has a well-defined sequence. First there is a feeling of peace, then comes the separation from the body, closely followed by entry into the tunnel, at the end of which appears the bright light. Because reports of this train of events are essentially the same, irrespective of the religious conviction of the person in question, there is an obvious motivation for taking them seriously. What do the various happenings mean, however? There was a time when they were seriously taken to be related to the departure of what became known as the 'astral body', and there were several attempts to demonstrate the exodus by periodic weighing of a dying person. None of them was able to produce the desired evidence.

The apparent universality of the symptoms, as they could be called, admits of another type of explanation; they might simply be related to the way in which the nervous system breaks down as death approaches. This line of reasoning has latterly been championed, independently, by Susan Blackmore, Jack Cowan, and others. It takes as its starting point the fact that the brain's normal equilibrium is achieved not by quiescence on the part of its constituent cells but rather through the balance that exists between excitation and inhibition. We have encountered several examples of what can happen when this equilibrium is disturbed. Recall, for example, the peculiar optical illusion known as the motion after-effect, which was described in Chapter 4. There is another simple illusion which is even more relevant to what we are considering here. It, too, arises from a disturbance of the normal functioning of one of our senses. The reader can observe this for himself by closing both eyelids and gently applying pressure to the eyeballs with the fingertips. After a period that usually ranges from a few seconds to about half a minute, this pressure causes one to see flickering lights. They form a series of alternating light and dark patches, not unlike a vast warped chess board, but the pattern is perpetually in motion. In Chapter 4, I described the structure of the retina, and noted that the connections between its central region, the fovea, and the brain are particularly numerous. As the nervous system breaks down, therefore, it is quite probable that the spurious lights will appear most strongly in the centre of one's field of view, and give the illusion of travelling through a tunnel. Moreover, similar perturbations in the cortex could provoke the type of memory recall that was invoked in connection with the discussion of dreaming, in Chapter 6. This could be the reason why the dying person's life seems to flash before him.

The out-of-body sensation is more difficult to explain. Susan Blackmore and Harvey Irwin have stressed that what the brain interprets as being the real situation, under any given circumstances, is actually nothing more than the best rationalization of whatever information the senses are feeding to the cortex. They found that people who have had the out-of-body experience tend to be those whose dreams are recalled through bird's-eye views. Even in contexts that have nothing to do with death, these people appear to take a sort of abstracted view of themselves. But even in people who do not share this propensity, the disturbance to the mental system that occurs as death approaches will create a situation that has much in common with an hallucination. It has been found that the inhibitory systems are more vulnerable than those responsible for excitation, and the disinhibition of the cortex produces increasingly severe perturbations of the dying person's consciousness. In those rare cases where there is a return from the brink, the person often finds it difficult to shake off the feeling that the body is trivial and that the self is ephemeral. In the extreme form, the sense of identity is not fully recovered, and the unfortunate person never again feels that the world is tangible and solid. The same is true for some of those who have suffered prolonged exposure to hallucinogenic drugs, such as LSD. The term 'blown his mind' is often applied to such cases, and it may prove to be appropriate if it is demonstrated that there is a direct link between what goes on at the individual synapses and the brain's ability to form reliable representations of the

environment. The fragmented condition, whether brought about
by a close encounter with death or by the disturbing influence
of a narcotic, provides a glimpse into the way in which the
components of self are welded into the cogent whole. It may
reveal more about consciousness itself than about what might
or might not lie beyond the grave.

The dénouement of this story has crept up on us, for there
it is, in that one word: consciousness. Or rather, half of the
dénouement, because when consciousness is mentioned, it is
natural to think also of its travelling companion: free will. I have
deliberately placed my back against the wall, and forced myself
to declare what attitude to these concepts I feel is dictated by the
evidence reviewed in the preceding chapters. Consciousness, I
wish to suggest, is not what it seems, and free will might be
mankind's greatest self-delusion. My main argument against
what is normally meant by free will is going to be that there
is too much inherent and automatic control in the system to
permit it, and one of my more difficult tasks is going to be to
show how the phenomena of spontaneity and originality can be
salvaged from such a mechanistic picture.

Some of those who would refute my thesis, and their numbers
must be legion, would discount automatic control in the nervous
system, and maintain that it is an irrelevance. Their argument
would stress the difference between the unconscious and the
conscious processes in our brains, and maintain that I am
considering only the former. It is only with respect to conscious
processes, they would remind me, that free will is conjectured to
play a role. Such a division has long been recognized, after all; as
we have already seen, Freud was advocating it a hundred years
ago. But if we are to successfully distinguish between the parts
played by the unconscious and the conscious, we had better
be sure that we know what those terms mean. What, then, is
consciousness, and how do we acquire free will? Consciousness
could be defined as awareness of one's surroundings and one's
identity. Is my camera conscious, then? With its automatic
adjustments to varying light and varying distance, it not only
seems to be aware of its surroundings, it even reacts to changes
going on about it.

Some of today's psychologists are most comfortable with the
view that consciousness arises from the brain's ability to examine

its own thoughts. We will look at that idea a little later on. Another hypothesis is that consciousness is acquired simultaneously with language. This might seem to be an attractive idea in that both thoughts and language could be made possible only by the possession of some form of symbolism. There are two arguments against the language–consciousness link that readily come to mind, and I will present them in the context of our own species. One is that language appeared after our emergence. If the rationale for consciousness is that it permits the exercise of free will, therefore, this means that there was a period (probably occupying many thousands of years) when *Homo sapiens sapiens* enjoyed the genetic endowment of free will, but was not using it. (Without spelling out the intermediate steps of the reasoning, I believe that the delay would have led to massive overcrowding in purgatory!) The other argument against attaching decisive importance to the acquisition of language is that it would seem to deny consciousness to some of our fellow humans. What about the case of Helen Keller, for example, which was discussed in the preceding chapter. Her initial lack of even a symbolic language did not prevent her from observing the vital correlations which only subsequently allowed her to learn to read and write. Perhaps the ability to notice correlations between stimuli, indeed, gives us a better basis for ascribing consciousness. But, before settling on that, let us consider some of the phenomenon's other facets.

A useful clue might derive from the fact that we know of one well-defined state in which consciousness is lacking, namely sleep. As we noted earlier, sleep is a phenomenon encountered throughout the mammalian class. If we equate the waking state with the opposite of unconsciousness, it follows axiomatically that all our mammal relations share with us a capacity for consciousness. This would at least have the merit of being easier to square with the evidence for animal thought that we considered in the previous chapter. In the same vein, autistic people undoubtedly share the usual circadian sleep–wake cycle with their normal counterparts, even though they lack the usual powers of communication (some admittedly only partially). What is it, though, that occurs in the brain when we awake and regain the conscious state? Perhaps we can

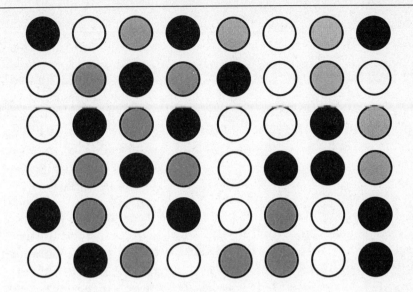

Studies of individuals who have sustained brain injury, and of others whose two cerebral lobes have been surgically separated, have established that the various faculties are governed by different sides of the brain. Logic appears to be associated with the left side, whereas appreciation of artistic qualities stems from the opposite lobe. The possibility of conflict between the brain's specialized areas can be demonstrated by comparing the times taken to read aloud the actual colours in the sequences above and below.

obtain insight by asking what useful abilities are conferred by consciousness. As I described in Chapter 6, we do at least know which centres of the brain are involved when sleep is replaced by wakefulness, but it is still not known precisely what they do at the neural level. On a grosser scale, however, one could say that these consciousness-generating regions enable us to react appropriately to the variety of situations we are confronted with in our daily lives. Consider a specific example, which is not as trivial as it might at first seem. Suppose one has consumed an excess of liquid before retiring. Because of the prolonged period of training which we underwent in infancy, this will not lead to bed-wetting. When the pressure on the bladder reaches a critical level, something in the brain induces consciousness, and we wake to make a brief visit to the bathroom. Compare this with another of the brain's sentinel functions which insures us against lying for such a long time on one of our arms, for example, that the blood's circulation is threatened. In the one case consciousness is induced, whereas in the other the evasive action is accomplished without the need for waking. But it is also clear that the trip to the toilet requires a higher degree of coordination; more of the senses are going to be involved if we are to avoid bumping into doors and furniture.

This argument can be taken a step further. One could say that the more difficult the task, the greater is the required degree of consciousness. And this carries us over to the related issue of attention, for it is easy to miss the point that there is often good cause to ignore most of the information that is constantly bombarding our senses, and concentrate on just a few stimuli. Psychologists sometimes refer to this as the cocktail party effect. One experiences it when, occupied in conversation with someone else at such a party, one suddenly notices that one's partner has attracted the attention of a person of the opposite sex. A husband, for example, discovers that his wife is chatting with a hairy-chested lothario ten years her junior, while a wife sees out of the corner of her ever-vigilant eye that her spouse is slipping into the clutches of some *femme fatale*. Under such circumstances, it is amazing how one can shut out virtually all the din of the other party-goers, not to mention the voice of the person with whom one is ostensibly conversing, in order to eavesdrop on one's partner and the threatening intruder, often over a distance of several metres. The cocktail party effect reveals that conscious awareness is the ability to narrow down one's focus of attention, to the exclusion of much of the other potential information that is simultaneously impinging on our eyes and ears. And the fascinating thing is that we can manage a host of other less important things without being distracted from the thing which is our main interest. A tray of drinks passes, for example, and we help ourselves to a martini and a handful of peanuts, without so much as shifting our gaze from our partner and the person who, if our worst fears are justified, is bent on seduction. (Samuel Johnson expressed the same ideas even more starkly when he wrote, in *Letter to Boswell*: 'Depend upon it, Sir, when a man knows he is to be hanged in a fortnight, it concentrates his mind wonderfully.')

If this example is reliable and representative, and I believe that it is both of those things, it reveals that conscious awareness is really only the tip of the mental iceberg. It also exposes the fact that the thing which lays greatest claim to our attention, at any instant, will be a reflection of our priorities. If the person carrying the drinks tray had tripped, and sent it, together with the entire consignment of glasses, canapés and serviettes, flying in our direction, we would have ducked! It seems doubtful that we are the only species which can simultaneously attend to one thing and be aware of others, but perhaps we have this faculty to a more marked degree. There is much more to be discussed, however. We have not yet even touched upon the important factor of timing.

If I accidentally place my hand on a hot stove, my reflexes cause me to withdraw it well before the sensation is registered by my brain. Yet, after the event, I am left with the impression that I pulled my hand away in response to the pain. It is as if the brain rationalizes in retrospect: a neurological equivalent of *post hoc, ergo propter hoc*. In 1979, Benjamin Libet reported the results of an experimental investigation which quantified these effects. The study is not widely known, and there must be many a philosopher presently oblivious of Libet's findings who will one day realize how devastating they are to the dogma of free will. Stating it simply, Libet showed that the conscious perception of an apparently voluntary act invariably lags about half a second behind the moment at which the decision to act is taken. The subconscious has much more of a say in things than we ever would have dreamed.

It is clear that I am approaching the climax of my case against the ghost in the machine, and it would be remiss not to slow down at this point and carefully weigh the pros and cons. Some of the heaviest ordnance is here being deployed on the battlefield and there is a premium on the return of accurate dispatches. The battlefield in question is the seemingly staid and dispassionate publication *Brain*, but let us not be deceived by the demure outer covers of that journal; Libet himself was well aware of the incendiary nature of the issue that brought him into the front line. The bombers might have spared the cathedral's spire but, in my opinion at least, Benjamin Libet is down in the basement, deputizing for Guy Fawkes. The gunpowder is in position, and the fuse is burning.

Let us begin by taking a look at the original results published by Libet and his colleagues, Bertram Feinstein, Dennis Pearl and Elwood Wright. Their human subjects were patients who were to have electrodes (i.e. electrical leads) surgically implanted into appropriate regions of their brains, as part of carefully planned therapy. Naturally, their consent was obtained before the experiments were carried out, and we should bear in mind that the brain itself has no pain sensors. The great advantage that derives from having access to the surface of the cortex lies in the possibility it offers of directly stimulating the somatosensory region (i.e. the area that serves the sense of touch) and thus of bypassing the normal route from the body's outer surface and inward through the afferent nerves. This is not to say that one is thereby going to avoid a long time delay, because knowledge of the speed of nerve impulses enables one to calculate that this delay would be a mere ten milliseconds or so. The availability of two alternative routes reveals something rather unexpected about the way in which the brain records sensations.

When the cortex is stimulated directly, the patient gets the impression that it is the corresponding part of the body that is being touched. There is nothing particularly surprising about this. It is a related mechanism which causes some amputees to feel pain or itching in an arm or leg that has long since been removed: the phantom limb effect, as it is usually called. In the experiments of Libet and his colleagues, the stimulation to the external surface of the body took the form of a half millisecond electrical pulse to the skin at the back of one of the hands. We will hereafter refer to this as an S stimulus, and sometimes simply use the letter S. For the main series of experiments, the cortical stimulus was applied to the region corresponding to the other hand, and it was composed of a train of electrical pulses, each again about half a millisecond in duration, the frequency of pulses being sixty per second (i.e. the inter-pulse interval was about 16 milliseconds). We will use the letter C for this mode of stimulation. The experiment's strategy was to give the subject both S and C stimuli at various times, and ask which was sensed first. The subject's answers were thus 'left first', 'right first', or 'together'.

The first surprise actually came during a preliminary experiment, when S and C were applied to the same hand (or hand area on the cortex). It was found that the subject could easily detect an isolated S pulse, in spite of its brevity. But consciousness of a C stimulus occurs only if the train of pulses is continued for at least 500 milliseconds (i.e. half a second). It might seem that this shows that direct cortical stimulation is too diffuse to be compared with the more normal S type. But Libet and his colleagues subsequently demonstrated that the delay is real enough, and that it also applies to S. It appears that even when a brief S pulse is given to the subject, the resulting avalanche of neural signals up in the brain takes about half a second in order to develop a conscious sensation. Libet and his colleagues coined the term neural adequacy to describe the point of development at which the subject becomes conscious of the sensation, and they underpinned the credibility of their important conclusion by a second type of experiment. If an S pulse is followed by a C train of pulses, applied to the same 'hand' but after a delay of about 200 milliseconds, the subject is never conscious of the S. It would be expected that the subject would report having felt two stimuli, but only one is reported. It is as if the C pulse is able to erase the S pulse which preceded it, and this demonstrates that the S pulse too needs considerably more time to make itself felt than the negligible time it takes just to reach the cortex. (The effect has been given the name backward masking.) The S pulse must therefore also touch off a neural avalanche that requires time to develop to the level where it gives a conscious sensation.

BACKWARD MASKING

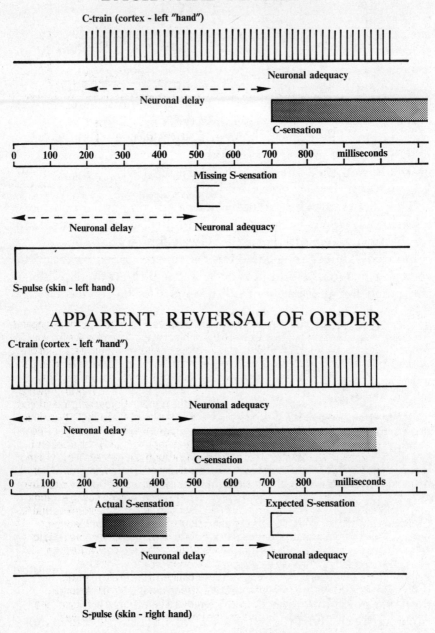

C-train (cortex - left "hand")

Neuronal adequacy

Neuronal delay

C-sensation

| 0 | 100 | 200 | 300 | 400 | 500 | 600 | 700 | 800 | milliseconds |

Missing S-sensation

Neuronal delay

Neuronal adequacy

S-pulse (skin - left hand)

APPARENT REVERSAL OF ORDER

C-train (cortex - left "hand")

Neuronal adequacy

Neuronal delay

C-sensation

| 0 | 100 | 200 | 300 | 400 | 500 | 600 | 700 | 800 | milliseconds |

Actual S-sensation

Expected S-sensation

Neuronal delay

Neuronal adequacy

S-pulse (skin - right hand)

RETROACTIVE REFERRAL OF SENSATION

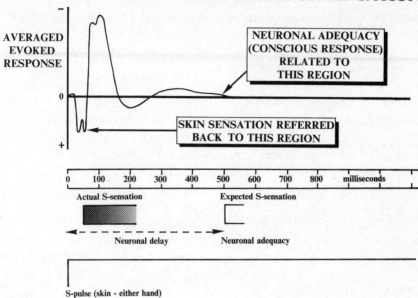

In the experiments of Benjamin Libet and his colleagues, stimulation (C) was applied directly to the somatosensory cortex while the subject was conscious. A stimulus (S) was also given to the skin of one hand, either before or after the cortical stimulation, and the subject was asked which one was given first. The results were surprising. If both stimuli are applied to the same 'hand' (above left), and S occurs less than about half a second prior to C, the subject does not experience S. This is known as backward masking. For stimuli applied to different 'hands' (below left), the subject will report having felt S before C even though S is actually applied after C, but within about half a second of the latter. There is thus an apparent reversal of order of the stimuli, in the subject's mind. The significance of the approximately half a second period was explained by Libet and his colleagues through reference to what is seen in the typical electroencephalogram, when this is averaged over many individual measurements. The average evoked response, as it is called, first shows a positive sweep around 50 milliseconds. It then develops both negative and positive trends, and finally decays away to zero at around half a second. The conclusion was that full conscious awareness does not develop until about half a second has elapsed, because this amount of time is required for the cortex's appropriate nerve cells to fully process the incoming information. Libet and his colleagues gave the term neuronal adequacy to the fully developed response (see above). The surprising experimental observations can be explained if the brain refers its conscious response back to the initial positive sweep around 50 milliseconds. Something like this occurs when we quickly remove a hand from a hot object; the pain is first felt somewhat later, but we get the impression that the hand was removed because of the burning sensation.

Turning to pairs of stimuli applied to different 'hands', Libet and his colleagues found that the subject would report that the hand receiving the S pulse was stimulated first even though it had in fact been stimulated 200 milliseconds, say, later than the hand corresponding to the C train of pulses. This remarkable observation showed that although, as explained above, the S pulse requires the half-second avalanche (or reverberation) period to develop into a conscious sensation, the subject nevertheless associates it with a time that is much closer to the actual event. The subjective sensation thus involves a backward referral in time, and Libet and his colleagues offered an explanation as to what the brain uses as a sort of internal marker of an event. In Chapter 6, we saw how the electroencephalogram (EEG) can be used to measure the brain's response to a stimulus. The technique is difficult, because reliable statistics can only be obtained if many sets of EEG traces are averaged. The resulting curve is called the average evoked response (or AER), and it has some distinctive characteristics. Around 50 milliseconds after the stimulus is applied, the AER shows a distinct swing in the positive direction. This is followed by a large negative swing, around 100 milliseconds, and there are also later mild swings in both the positive and negative directions, around 300 milliseconds. Libet and his colleagues made a good case for the positive signal around 50 milliseconds being the cue-giver. Once the neural adequacy has been established, there is a retroactive referral of time to the 50 millisecond point. Thus, although this enables the subject to make a remarkably good shot at an event's timing, he does get it wrong by about 50 milliseconds.

It would be easy to underestimate the profound nature of these experiments. And there is an obvious temptation to suggest what seem to be self-evident rebuttals. Normal reaction times, for example, are less than the half a second that Libet and his colleagues say is necessary for neural adequacy. My own students working in psychophysics routinely measure reaction times by exploiting the internal timing devices in personal computers. (The subject sits with a finger poised on one of the keys and depresses it as soon as a coloured disc appears on the screen.) They have now made so many measurements of this kind that their statistics are quite reliable. And the measured reaction times are typically 350 milliseconds, which is of course under half a second. But this does not refute the result of Libet *et al.*, for we have no proof that consciousness occurs during the 350 milliseconds. Our subjects are ultimately conscious of their reactions, naturally, but their consciousness need not intervene in them. When a decision is built into the test, such as asking the subject to depress the G key if a green circle is shown, and the R key if it is red, the reaction time jumps to 650 milliseconds.

One can imagine the excitement that Libet and his colleagues must have felt upon completion of their investigations. Here was evidence of a most unexpected separation in the timing of events and sensations, and Libet found it strongly suggestive of something that we have encountered at numerous junctures in this book: dualism. He concluded that he and his colleagues had finally stumbled on a way of experimentally establishing the failure of identity between brain states and mental states. Physiology, with its nerve impulses and its neurotransmitters, is one thing, but mind is something quite different. That is what they saw staring at them out of their painstaking experiments, and they did not have to wait long for support in that view. John Eccles and Karl Popper had strongly advocated the dualist standpoint in their monumental *The Self and its Brain*, and they leapt to endorse Libet and his colleagues. 'This antedating pro-cedure does not seem to be explicable by any neurophysiological process,' they wrote on their page 364, 'Presumably it is a strategy that has been learnt by the self-conscious mind.' And later they go on to suggest that 'the antedating of the sensory experience is attributable to the ability of the self-conscious mind to make slight temporal adjustments, i.e. to play tricks with time'. To Eccles and Popper, self-confessed 'interactionists' as they are, letting the self-conscious mind have a mind of its own, as it were, presents no special difficulty; it may play tricks with time, and with any other physical parameter for that matter, if it so desires. For they see the mind–body problem as one of convincing the rest of us that the mind alone, of all things in nature, need not feel itself shackled by physical laws. This is dualism in another guise, even though the parlance undeniably belongs to the twentieth century. Brain states, that is to say the myriad nerve impulses, synaptic transmissions, and what have you, which are demonstrably physical, give rise to mind states, which are non-physical. Conversely, non-physical mind states give rise to physical brain states. The normal state of affairs, in which physical effect dutifully follows physical cause, is thereby violated, and the physical world shows itself to be radically different from what we have always taken it to be. And it tolerates this aberration for the unique need of pandering to our spectral minds. This scenario, envisaged by Eccles and Popper, sounds like an incredible superstition, one which, as Geoffrey Warnock has remarked, is suspiciously flattering of human self-importance.

I believe that there is a more satisfactory explanation of these fascinating experiments of Libet and his colleagues. I feel they suggest that when we imagine consciousness to be both the dynamo that drives all our actions and the adjudicator that weighs all our decisions, we might be putting the cart before the horse. There are apparently events that lie deeper than consciousness, and they precede its development. We have to face the possibility, I believe, that our decisions could be programmed subconsciously, and initiated before our conscious minds are apprised of the fact. This might sound ominous, but it is quite compatible with Freud's ideas.

The idea that there is more going on in the brain, at any instant, than is directly orchestrated by consciousness might seem difficult to swallow, but there is evidence that parts of the brain can accomplish remarkable things in an apparently autonomous fashion. In the peculiar phenomenon of blind sight, for example, a person whose normal visual pathway is not functional, and for whom vision is thus not part of consciousness, is nevertheless able to react to a strong visual stimulus such as a suitably positioned lamp. (It is the superior colliculus which provides this remarkable faculty.) There is also the massive evidence for subliminal thought provided by the various experiments of Roger Sperry, and those who have followed his lead. In the 1950s and the 1960s, patients were treated for a number of ailments, notably epilepsy, by severance of the corpus callosum, which is the bundle of nerve fibres that joins the two halves of the cortex. Sperry observed some bizarre effects in such split brain individuals. Blindfolded, and allowed to identify an object with the left hand, such a person can subsequently retrieve it from a collection of different items, but only if the left hand is again used. Initial familiarization with the right hand produces the opposite bias. But asked to name the object, the patient reveals a clear one-sidedness, succeeding only if it is in the right hand. This is consistent with the location of Broca's area (on the left, but right-serving, side of the brain), as we have noted earlier, and it shows that information is unable to traverse the surgically imposed gap. As we have also noted, the right side of each retina feeds visual information to the right side of the brain, thus compensating for the inversion caused by the lens of the eye. This facilitates coordination of the visual and tactile senses, and Sperry demonstrated analogous left-hand discrimination between objects seen and selected without recourse to speech. The work of Roger Sperry, perhaps more than that of any other researcher in this field, has shown how competently local areas of the brain can go about their business. Conscious awareness, it seems, is not a prerequisite for mental function at the regional level.

But what use is consciousness? That is the question most often posed in connection with this mental property. What evolutionary advantage did it confer? Nicholas Humphrey has put forward an interesting argument for tying it to the complexity of mankind's social systems. The other animals close to us on the evolutionary ladder, he believes, have clever brains but blank minds. In Humphrey's view, our type of society, with its potential for disaster if individuals did not understand each other's feelings and motives, would be quite out of the question if we were not capable of the introspection that consciousness makes possible. Richard Gregory put it even more forcefully when he speculated that brains might be conscious because they can read themselves. And he suggests that because such a capacity for looking inward at its own workings could be built into a computer, we should be alert to the possible emergence of conscious versions of these devices.

The idea of the brain reading itself can be usefully considered in connection with a comparison that was made earlier. I contrasted the automatic and unconscious monitoring of body posture, which continues throughout a night's slumber, with the need for a brief regaining of consciousness in connection with a nocturnal visit to the bathroom. There is an essential difference between these two types of process. The monitoring of posture requires recognition of nothing that is external to the body. The foetus in the womb can derive just as much benefit from its own position monitors. The trip to the bathroom, on the other hand, puts small demands on our faculties of cognition. We see the bathroom door, and our consciousness enables us to check the door's appearance with our internal dossier on doors, the latter being of course couched in general concepts rather than specific images or pictures. And an entry in our door information file tells us that it is solid and that it must be opened if we are to progress further on our short journey. Regarded in this way, consciousness is seen as a sort of clearing house for information, and the need for such a mediating agency would be expected to be greater the larger the brain capacity. But although consciousness thus seems to occupy a position at the centre of the stage, the results of Benjamin Libet and his colleagues remind us that it is not the conductor's baton.

This reinterpretation of the results of Libet and his colleagues offers, I feel, all manner of advantages. Apart from the way in which it nicely dovetails into the ideas of Freud, which after all were based on a sizeable corpus of clinical observation, it suggests ways in which spontaneity and originality can be explained without the danger of getting bogged down in the morass of the free will paradox. With consciousness figuring as a station *en route* rather than the terminus, the subconscious is given free rein to attempt to put together novel responses to the challenges with which it is confronted. But the word attempt is important here, because the solutions the subconscious comes up with must nevertheless be tested against the prevailing mental constraints, and any responses judged and found wanting will be rejected before they can reach the surface level over which consciousness holds dominion. It is this division of labour that permits the sleeper to wake in the middle of night with the solution to the problem that was on the mind when he or she retired; released from the mental narrowing that is attention's hallmark, the brain can roam freely over the full range of its possible responses, and 'resonances' that went unheeded during consciousness now have the chance of 'ringing a bell'. This putting together of novel solutions could loosely be compared with two other biological mechanisms that produce almost an infinity of outcomes from an essentially limited number of components.

The one is the rearrangement of the various genes in the hybrid pairs of chromosomes present in the freshly fertilized egg cell. This is the mechanism that guarantees that no two individuals will have identical sets of genes; each fertilization constitutes a fresh throw of the genetic dice. The other piece of biological diversity that is reminiscent of the source of mental novelty is that seen in the immune system. A finite number of different molecular forms of the proteins that coat the membranous surfaces of the immune system's cells can combine in a virtually infinite number of ways, and thereby be sure of producing a form that can latch on to the antigen (i.e. the alien substance) that is currently threatening the body's defences.

We thus come to the thorniest issue of them all: the will. Is it free or is it not? I have already indicated that I believe free will to be an illusion, and of course I must explain how I arrive at that conclusion. But before we move on to that, let us consider what others have had to say about the question. My own favourite is a tale that Isaac Bashevis Singer tells. He was walking in New York with a friend who was holding forth on the obvious merits of determinism (and its lack of room for free will), which he held up to the great novelist as if it were a philosopher's panacea. The friend reached the climax of his argument just as the two of them were half way over a street crossing, and when the traffic lights suddenly changed from red to green the confirmed determinist broke into a trot in order to gain the safety of the sidewalk. When Singer reaches this point in his narrative he inserts a brief theatrical pause, and then, with a mischievous twinkle in his eye, he adds: 'So you see, we have to believe in free will . . . for we have no choice!'

The denial of free will is certainly nothing new. Baruch de Spinoza was quite set against it. 'What is often called will', he wrote in his *Ethics*, 'as the impulsive force which determines the duration of an idea in consciousness, should be called desire — which is the very essence of man.' 'Men think themselves free,' he continued, 'because they are conscious of their volitions and desires, but are ignorant of the causes by which they are led to wish and desire'. And Arthur Schopenhauer, in his book *The World as Will and Idea*, which appeared in 1844, tells us: 'Consciousness is the mere surface of our minds, of which, as of the earth, we do not know the inside but only the crust . . . The intellect may seem at times to lead the will,' he continues, 'but only as a guide leads his master; the will is the strong blind man who carries on his shoulders the lame man who can see.' There is scant room for freedom in these evaluations of the will. Immanuel Kant, on the other hand, felt that: 'only by placing duty above beauty, morality above happiness . . . can we cease to be beasts, and begin to be gods . . . but this absolute command to duty proves at last the freedom of our wills'. Later, in the same passage in *The Critique of Practical Reason*, however, he shows signs of hedging his bets, in the face of the issue's complexity. 'Our actions', he writes, 'once we initiate them, seem to follow fixed and invariable laws, but only because we perceive their results through sense, which clothes all that it transmits in the dress of that *causal* law which our minds themselves have made'.

More than a few people believe that twentieth-century physical science has thrust into our hands the means of finally settling the issue of will, and the coin has been taken to come down on the side of freedom. I do not share that opinion, but I feel that it would be well at this point to describe what are generally seen as the two chief candidates for liberating the will from the bondage of determinism. These are quantum indeterminacy and chaos. Let us take a look at them.

The twentieth century has seen the birth of many scientific revolutions, but none of these has been more profound than that produced by quantum theory. It was touched off by a bold hypothesis, in 1900, by Max Planck about the nature of electromagnetic radiation (namely that energy cannot be indefinitely subdivided; it is composed of standard indivisible – but very small – units), and it scored its greatest triumph when Niels Bohr showed that it led to an explanation of the structure of the atom. The quantum idea is counter-intuitive; it demands that we accept a radically different view of nature at the scale of distance relevant to atoms and molecules. We must give up the possibility of finding out just where an electron is, as it orbits around the nucleus in an atom, and even the concept of such an orbit must be radically modified. This is referred to as the uncertainty principle, and it does not merely arise from our inability to make sufficiently precise observations; even nature itself does not 'know' exactly where minute particles are at any instant. (The uncertainty principle of Werner Heisenberg actually refers to pairs of observable quantities, such as position and momentum, or energy and time, but we need not go into such detail here.)

Turning to chaos, we should note that remarkable discoveries have been made in the 1970s and 1980s. The biggest surprise has been the realization that chaos can be deterministic. Unless the laws which govern the temporal development of a physical system are sufficiently simple, it becomes impossible, even in principle, to predict the system's evolution further ahead than a rather small amount of time. And this is the case even though we might have a complete mathematical description of every interaction between the system's components. Such chaotic effects are the reason why one can confidently say, for example, that we will never be able to predict the weather more than about five days in advance.

Why should this be the case? The reason lies in what is known as non-linearity, which can be taken to mean lack of simple proportion. In nature, very few things do have simple proportions, and the chaotic effects are only now coming to light because science has until recently not had the means of coping with the complexities of the issues. The advent of fast electronic computers was the key breakthrough, and many of the fundamental truths about the chaotic state have emerged through computer simulations. Let us look at an example that is useful in the present context.

For the last hundred years or so, it has been known that the physical properties of gases derive from the motions of the molecules of which they are composed. A reasonable picture of the instantaneous situation in a gas can be obtained by contrasting it with what happens in an idealized game of snooker if the cue ball is struck so hard that it soon sets every other ball on the table in motion. But we need to imagine that instead of gradually slowing down, because of collisions with the cushion and with each other, and also because of the friction with the baize, the balls continue their motions and their mutual collisions indefinitely. Such a picture differs from the situation in a real gas in at least two respects. The less important difference lies in the fact that a snooker table is essentially two-dimensional whereas the molecules in a gas move about in three-dimensional space. The really significant difference lies in the nature of the interactions between the molecules. These interactions are quite different from those which govern the collisions between idealized snooker balls. The latter are operative only when the balls are in contact with one another (if we ignore the minute gravitational forces which admittedly are present), whereas two molecules start to exert non-negligible forces on each other well before they make contact. This makes the interactions in a gas highly non-linear, to use the term that was introduced earlier, and it gives the gas its chaotic behaviour; the minutest change in any one region is magnified by the interactions, making it impossible to predict the future development of the system.

Yet what might quantum uncertainty or chaos have to do with the functioning of the brain? The former, at least, could have no influence on the will, because it makes itself felt at much too small a scale. A single neuron is composed of millions of atoms, and the quantum phenomena of many individual atoms cooperate to give a macroscopic effect only under very special conditions, conditions which would not prevail in biological cells. It is similarly difficult to see how chaos could produce anything remotely reminiscent of the freedom conjectured to be characteristic of the will. For a start, neurons are essentially gelatinous solid membranes that enclose a liquid interior, not a gaseous one. And although molecular chaos is also a characteristic of the liquid state, it could hardly influence the firing properties of a neuron, since the latter are governed by the net effect of all the liquid-borne ions on the membrane's proteins. Chaos in the motions of the individual ions would not influence the situation. One could just as well attempt to credit a steam engine with free will because of the chaotic motions of the water vapour molecules in its boiler.

No, biology is not subject to such caprice. If it was, why has evolution gone to such extraordinary lengths to build in all the self-checks and correction mechanisms that have been described in the various chapters of this book? Even in the parallel arrangement of the cells in the neural network we see a system that, on the contrary, is robust against fluctuations in its components. Minds would be hopelessly unreliable servants of bodies if they reflected the whimsy of individual molecules.

One of the most remarkable scientific facts to emerge in recent times has been the existence of deterministic chaos. Systems that are completely described by well-formulated (and often surprisingly simple) interactions between their components are nevertheless capable of displaying dynamical developments that are chaotic. The example shown graphically in this picture is known as a fractal, and it was discovered by Benoit Mandelbrot. The study of such systems has done much to explain phenomena like turbulence and particle aggregation, and some have invoked chaos in explanations of the freedom of will. But the massive parallelism in neural networks, which seems ideally suited to counteract such chaotic effects, makes this explanation implausible. Deterministic chaos probably serves better as a metaphor for the intrinsic complexity of society.

But the chaos in a gas, at the microscopic level, nevertheless gives us a valuable analogy.

I am going to suggest that we turn the argument around, and take our cue from the typical molecule in a gas. We have seen that it is intrinsically impossible to precisely predict the future trajectory and speed of such a molecule, even if one has a complete description of its recent history and that of all the other molecules in the gas. This is true even though we have reliable knowledge of how an atom interacts (non-linearly, as we have seen) with its brethren. Another thing that is true of a gas is that no two of its molecules could possibly behave in exactly the same manner, because the probability of their finding themselves in precisely the same configuration of surrounding molecules is, to all intents and purposes, zero. When we bear in mind that the interactions between people are obviously more complex than the interactions between molecules, therefore, we see that the will would not have to be free to appear totally individual. Moreover, we have already seen that the inherent variations in nature and nurture conspire to give no two people the same subconscious baggage, for even identical twins will not have had exactly the same experiences. I believe that this, then, is the key to the paradox: we see individuality, and we are hoodwinked into interpreting it as freedom.

It takes but a small extension of these ideas to arrive at an analogous picture of the soul. For if there is one thing that the soul can be said to spring from, it is that one person can never have perfect knowledge of what is going on in the mind of any other individual. We might know what is *on* another person's mind, for this is often exposed through the interactions that were alluded to above, but we do not know what is *in* that mind.

There is an observation which strengthens this idea. A person deprived of all sensory input will, after a certain amount of time has elapsed, begin to hallucinate. The onset of this distressing state varies from one person to another, but it usually lies around three or four hours. (It might be significant that this is not radically different from the time interval between the periods of dreaming sleep.) In experimental investigations of this phenomenon, the subject is not only cut off from all visual or auditory stimuli; access is even denied to tactile inputs. This latter measure is achieved by placing the body in a closely fitting mould, and even the fingers are splayed out so that they cannot be used to stimulate each other. Such sensory deprivation has reportedly also been used as a method of torture, and it is every bit as cruel as physical maltreatment. In the context of our discussion in this chapter, the point to be made is that the personality is revealed as being precariously fragile; what one perceives as an individual's soul is perhaps better regarded as merely a share of society's collective soul. John Donne was closer to this point of view than he probably appreciated when he wrote, 'No man is an Island, entire of itself'.

Let me draw one last piece of inspiration from the properties of a gas. If it is so rarified that there are only a few molecules to contend with, the only physical phenomena that will be of interest will be the occasional collisions that were discussed earlier. But as the gas becomes more dense, the situation becomes dominated by such new phenomena as sound waves, convection, conduction, and so on. These are the collective properties, and they owe their existence to the sheer number of molecules that are present. Analogously, we have society's collective properties, though they obviously display a far richer variety, the interactions between people being that much more complex. And just as we cannot predict the course of the weather more than five days hence, so is it futile to try to anticipate society's future course. Institutes for the study of the future have tended to perform indifferently, at best, because they cannot handle the inherent complexity of human interactions. How, for example, is one to foresee the emergence of an Einstein or a Hitler?

This is the origin, surely, of the humility we feel when we are in the presence of those things that have been accomplished by the collective efforts of society. For not only our cathedrals, but also our libraries, our institutions of all kinds and our technological prowess, are, more than anything else, an expression of the fact that the whole of mankind is greater than the sum of its parts, even though the same need not be true of any one person. Some might feel that this picture leaves the individual unnecessarily impoverished, but it has to be ceded that the collective soul has given society dimensions which knowledge of Darwin's competitive principles would not have led one to anticipate.

Amongst these, altruism must surely take pride of place. It is
a quality which, quite understandably, has been credited as
deriving from the Creator.

Isn't there one enormous flaw in this entire line of reasoning,
however? The pages of this book are littered with evaluations of
all manner of evidence regarding the workings of the brain and
its associated mind. Who, pray, has been making these choices?
When I come down on the side of determinism, am I not putting
myself outside the jurisdiction of this gigantic piece of clockwork?
The answer is no. My words are no more the product of a free,
as opposed to an individual, will than are those of anyone else.
At every turn, what my senses have observed has been passed
through my consciousness, down to the subconscious levels of
my mind, there to be processed in a manner determined by all
that is already established in that inaccessible place, irrespective
of whether it got there by genetic endowment or by experience,
or indeed by a combination of both. I can of course guess at the
origins of the opinions that I hold, but I cannot be sure that
there are not other things lying in my unconsciousness that are
even more significant. And in any event, I had best keep these
murky memories to myself.

All but one of them, that is, because there is an experience
that I feel compelled to share. And I will have to recount it in
considerable detail. During the austere 1940s, when sporting
facilities were scarce, the mental hospital that lay a few kilometres from my home town generously opened its amenities to
the local youth. My friends and I thus found ourselves, several
times a month, enjoying the hospitality of what otherwise was
a closed world. I recall one event during a cricket match in
which I was an outfielder, right on the boundary. Throwing
occasional glances out through the wire fence that marked the
perimeter of the pitch, I observed a group of men who were
being supervised by a white-coated male nurse. These were not
the first patients that I had seen, but there was something sadly
special about them. They seemed totally bereft of all initiative.
The nurse's job that afternoon could not have been less onerous.
Irrespective of where they were shepherded, the men stayed put
once they had been positioned by their supervisor.

My subsequent enquiry revealed that these men were all
in the final throes of syphilis. They were in the state that I

touched upon in Chapter 9, namely that referred to as general paralysis of the insane, or GPI. Although this did not make grammatical sense, they were in fact called GPIs. When the opportunity later presented itself, I asked one of the nurses about the condition of these patients, and he illustrated his brief explanation by putting one of them 'through his paces'. It proved to be a quite unforgettable experience. The nurse mentioned a particular name, and I was shocked by the man's response: he sharply uttered the foulest of expletives. The nurse invited me to try saying the name. I did so, and the result was the same. (It is standard medical practice not to state any name that would expose the identity of a patient, so I cannot be more explicit regarding what words were actually used.) The nurse was called away to another patient at this juncture, and I was left alone with the GPI. My curiosity aroused, I could not resist trying the name again; it met with the same response. By this time, a normal person would have found such repetition tiresome, and he would have indicated a desire to move on to other verbal territory. But not so with the blank-eyed man who stood so immobile in front of me. I tried the name again, and again and again. Upwards of a dozen times, the impoverished little dialogue was repeated. I have no doubt whatsoever that the man would have been quite content responding all day, in the manner of an automaton. My request to observe the patients in the dining hall was granted, and the GPIs revealed themselves as being perfectly capable of handling the cutlery in the appropriate manner. But their style of eating was utterly mechanical; they displayed neither relish nor distaste. They had no conversation; their food was consumed in total silence. Indeed, there was not one aspect of their behaviour that involved anything other than stereotyped reactions.

Now let me come to my point in narrating this sad story. Did these poor creatures, docile to the point of immobility, possess free will? If they did, they were certainly not exercising it, and I frankly do not see how such unshackled volition could have been attributed to them. But if one assumes that they ever did enjoy freedom of will, before they contracted their dreadful disease, does this not throw us onto the horns of a philosophical dilemma? The point is that this final stage of the illness is not reached until the spirochaetes have been at their nasty work for a decade or more. When, during this prolonged process, would free will disappear? Is the transition gradual or sudden? It is difficult to believe that the latter could be the case, in view of the continuous loss of neural function over so protracted a period. Is there really a sharp corner to be negotiated as one goes round the bend? And yet, the other alternative seems no more attractive, for if the loss of free will is gradual, this must imply that wills are Orwellian: all are free, but some are more free than others! I would like to suggest that the facts of these depressing medical cases are easier to reconcile if one regards the will as being not so much free as individual. The gradual withdrawal into stereotyped behaviour, displayed by these GPIs, would then be seen as a natural consequence of their decreasing ability to react, with all the usual richness of nuance, to the complexities of the human environment.

There is another thing that ought to be stressed at this point. It is that the great majority of our interactions with our fellow human beings are based on predictability. We know the personalities of those around us, their peculiarities, their strengths and their weaknesses, and we adjust our own behaviour accordingly. In fact, we are put off balance when an acquaintance acts erratically. We speak of someone 'not being himself'. Inconsistency in a person's behaviour is, indeed, one of the symptoms that the psychiatrist takes as a sign of impending trouble. And even our interactions with strangers are governed by the assumption of certain behavioural norms. Society's rules, its customs and taboos, are the props that we rely on to ensure that our daily dealings with all manner of people are as trouble-free as possible. Freedom of will, I would argue, has very little to do with how we conduct ourselves, and I suspect that the concept's primary role is as a palliative for the ego. There are, however, two institutions to which the tenet of free will is usually seen as indispensable. One of these is our legal system, and the other is organized religion. Let us look at each of them in turn.

It might seem that the legal establishment would grind to a halt if it could be proved that the idea of free will is fallacious. This would be a risk, however, only in so far as one is to equate responsibility for one's actions with the possession of free will. And it is not clear that such a link necessarily follows. Litigation works perfectly well, after all, if deed is unambiguously identified with culprit, and it is only in the matter of sentencing that the moral side of the question really arises. But anyone who is tempted to look upon the issue as a mere piece of philosophical wrangling should try to put himself in the place of the solicitor who has the job of consoling the abandoned wife, the parent of the molested child, the owner of the property that has fallen prey to an arsonist, and the relations and friends of the victim of the terrorist's bomb. This, of course, is why we have to have a legal system. One could not let proof of culpability be sufficient justification for abandoning things to the emotions. That would be to open the door to the lynch mob. Since a perfectly sound case can be made for law simply serving the best interests of the majority, both deterrence and restraint are sufficient motivation for society's retribution; incarcerating an offender in prison, or making him pay a fine, does not have to imply that he was exercising free will when he committed his crime. According to this point of view, all legal sanctions, up to and including capital punishment, can be regarded as practical measures. But because that attitude also sees an individual's fate as being subject only to the combined factors of heredity, nurture and the current human environment, the moral desirability of clemency is clear. The association of violence with the triple-X chromosome syndrome, which I touched upon earlier in this book, provides a case in point. Restricting the movements of people with this genetic burden is ultimately beneficial for both society at large and for the individuals themselves. But it would surely be barbaric to apply the death penalty to a triple-X sufferer who had committed murder.

In the opening chapter of this book, I hinted at the possibility of similarly reconciling these ideas with organized religion, by invoking its steadying influence on society. I wrote of fear of the supernatural, and of the way in which this unites people by giving them something to look up to. If future developments in the science of the brain lead to further undermining of the concept of free will, and this must be entertained as a possibility, religion is going to find it hard to maintain its position. In this respect, the legal establishment enjoys an advantage in that its services cannot be dispensed with. It is now far more serious to be outside the law than to be outside the Church.

The latter admittedly presides over our hatches, matches and dispatches, but only if we do not merely prefer to put things in the hands of the registry office and the funeral parlour. And although the occasional scandal is capable of embarrassing the legal profession, it has at least avoided the wholesale moral disasters that the churches of various creeds have inflicted upon themselves. The reader will not have to pause for many seconds in order to recall examples of strife in which religion has actually been the driving force, including cases which pitted against each other peoples who ostensibly shared the same faith. While writing this book, my own memory acquired an indelible vignette from a television news report. The camera zoomed in on Mikhail Gorbachev standing amongst the ruins caused by the Armenian earthquake of late 1988. He was flanked by two men, one Christian and the other Moslem, and I will never forget his dazed look as he listened to them raise objections over having to dig each other's kinsmen out of the rubble. If that is religion, the atheist could be excused for congratulating himself over his status. Whereas the fact of organization has been a source of strength for the legal establishment, because of all the self-correcting principles that it has forced upon the system, the same has not always been true of its religious counterpart. On the contrary, it seems to have fostered schism. For when it comes to piety, as Alistair Cooke put it in one of his broadcasts, there is often an all too pronounced difference between the possession of it and the profession of it.

If such negative aspects were not counteracted by other factors, religion would already be a thing of the past. That it has survived is due in large measure to its laudable capacity for organizing the individual's power for doing good, and here at least it is the Church which deserves more credit than the law, for what lawyer gives his services free to the hapless inhabitants of society's lowest layers. But although this might sound niggardly, there is an important philosophical point regarding the goodness displayed by the religious good: are they good because they are religious, or are they religious because they are good? Discussion of that question could occupy an entire book.

It would be encouraging to think that the desire to do good was, in fact, the greatest motivation for attaching oneself to religion, but this factor pales in comparison to what I wrote about in the first chapter. For the fear of being extinguished by death will continue to be the major bulwark of the faith, even though it can hardly be regarded as a creditable asset. There is a scene in Evelyn Waugh's *Brideshead Revisited* in which a priest bends over the atheist patriarch, just as the latter expires, and then turns triumphantly towards the younger family members gathered around the deathbed. He announces that the dying man rescinded just as he was about to draw his last breath, and then he adds, smiling knowingly, that non-believers invariably undergo such a last-moment conversion. The point is well taken because, apart from the drive to reproduce, self-preservation has to be the strongest of the biological instincts. And it is this instinct which makes one grasp at any proffered straw, when the end is nigh. One does not even have to be on one's last legs to feel the chill of mortality creeping up. I usually experience such thoughts when sitting in dentist's or hairdresser's chairs. A glance up at the receding hair line is enough to set the mind working, and before long a small bead of perspiration breaks out on the forehead. It is at such moments that the thought of my own death scares the life out of me, and it is understandable why one could, as Doris Lessing has put it, find oneself catching religion. To Shakespeare's '*sans* teeth, *sans* eyes . . .', one would then be able to cheerfully add: Ah yes, but *avec* a ticket to the hereafter.

It is not with a view to salvaging a positive attitude towards religion, however, that I am going to change my tune, at the eleventh hour in this eleventh chapter. But change my tune I nevertheless must. The point is that this book has based its arguments on scientific evidence, and members of the scientific fraternity must conduct their discussions according to its rules. If I deliberately contravened these strictures, I should be drummed out of the regiment, and thoroughly deserve to be so. Had it been my intention to give the impression that the case against the soul is watertight, therefore, failure would have been inevitable, for it is an essential part of a scientist's creed that the mind is never quite made up. In such a misguided quest, I should have been undone by my calling. The proper thing to do at this point, and it is certainly not a chore, is to ask whether there is anything which could radically change the story. (I fear that it would be challenging fate to call this playing the

Devil's Advocate; too many readers will feel that this is precisely what I have been doing in the past ten chapters.) If the will is nevertheless to emerge as a free agent, however, something quite new is going to have to manifest itself to us, something which has not yet been encompassed by the natural sciences. Perhaps it will emerge out of the sheer complexity of a biological situation that does, after all, involve a staggeringly large number of cells. Maybe there are epiphenomena that we have never even dreamed of. (The nervous system has not exhausted its scope for surprising us. A recent publication by Masashi Kawasaki, Gary Rose and Walter Heiligenberg reported that certain neurons in the electric fish *Eigenmannia* are sensitive to temporal changes as small as a millionth of a second; that is quite astounding, when one recalls that a single nerve pulse lasts a thousand times longer than this.) Brian Pippard recently stressed the need to allow for such surprises when the system that one is considering is sufficiently complicated. A piece of ice, for example, appears to receive no warning of what radical change it is about to undergo as its temperature climbs towards zero degrees Celsius, and ice is a simple substance compared with the brain's grey and white matters. One cannot rule out the possibility that some even more spectacular change occurs in a many-neuron system when the degree of cellular activity exceeds a certain level. But by the same scientific token, one also has to allow for the possibility that things will be shown to be even less free than I have here been making them out to be.

There would, in any event, be ample compensation for seeing the thesis of this book proved wrong; if there is a hereafter, waiting to receive individual souls, this will at least provide an opportunity of satisfying one's curiosity about all sorts of things concerning that remote other world. But there is still that nagging question, raised in the first chapter, of how one is to explore it without a nervous system. And if, conversely, one is allowed to hold on to that asset, and thus continue to cogitate much as one does here on earth, will there not be another problem that is potentially even more worrying? I can only speak for myself, of course, but I fear that I would find it more of a burden than all the others combined. The issues that have been discussed in this book – consciousness, dualism, free will – and the rest, would pale in comparison: What am I actually going to do with myself for the next umpteen billion years?

● Summary

In spite of its relative complexity, the human brain exists solely for the processing of sensory information and the production of an appropriate response. The suitability of the latter is evaluated on the basis of past experience, and there are indications that the making of decisions actually precedes conscious awareness. Although the multiplicity of neural connections, together with the fact that consciousness does not control all the brain's processes, guarantees a certain degree of novelty, our reactions to a given stimulus are subject to comparatively severe restrictions. Our will is not so much free as individual. The brain, and its associated body, is an intriguingly sophisticated machine, but it is nevertheless just a machine; it conceals no spirit other than that which is a natural adjunct of its functioning and its interactions with its fellow machines. What is usually perceived as an individual's soul is probably better regarded as merely a share in society's collective soul.

Notes and bibliography

Chapter 1

Page 10 The Copernican view of the solar system won few adherents during the century after his death. The difficulties that new theories have in establishing themselves are discussed in Thomas Kuhn's *The Structure of Scientific Revolutions* (University of Chicago Press, Chicago, 1970).

Page 11 A highly readable modern defence of the traditional view of the soul is Richard Swinburne's *The Evolution of the Soul* (Clarendon Press, Oxford, 1986); it addresses such current issues as: are mental events identical with brain events?

Page 14 The various forms assumed by religious power were the subject of I M Lewis's *Religion in Context: Cults and Charisma* (Cambridge University Press, Cambridge, 1986).

Page 15 The first doctor to examine the hapless Phineas Gage was John Harlow, a few hours after the accident; his full report on the remarkable recovery was published after Gage's death, in *Massachusetts Medical Society Publications*, vol 2, pages 327–347, 1868.

Page 17 An extensive review of ancient ideas on the brain and its function, including a discussion of the *rete mirabile*, is given in D H M Woollam's contribution to F N L Poynter's *The History and Philosophy of the Brain and its Functions* (Blackwell Press, Oxford, 1958).

Page 18 Plato's ideas about the physical basis of sensation are described in section 31 of his *Timaeus*, a translation of which was made by F M Cornford (Routledge & Kegan Paul, London, 1937); Plato's section 49, on the difference between the sexes, provides some light relief.

Page 19 Galen's contributions to the study of the brain are described in C Singer's *Galen on Anatomical Procedures* (Oxford University Press, London, 1956).

Page 20 The relevant section (*libri septum*) of A Vesalius's *De humani corporis fabrica* (1543) can be found in C Singer's *Vesalius on the Human Brain* (Oxford University Press, London, 1952).

Page 21 Leonardo da Vinci's contributions to the study of the brain are reviewed in J P McMurrich's *Leonardo da Vinci the Anatomist (1452–1519)* (Williams & Wilkins, Baltimore, 1930).

Page 22 The mystic Robert Fludd (1574–1637) was possibly the first to use the concept of 'the mind's eye'; his work is discussed in A G Debus's *The English Paracelsians* (Oldbourne, London, 1965).

Page 22 Franciscus de le Boë (1614–1672) was also known as Sylvius, and the Sylvian fissure is named after him. He was responsible for shifting the focus from the ventricles to the cerebral cortex, as the habitat of the animal spirits. His work is discussed in F Baker's 'The two Sylviuses: An historical study', which appeared in *Bulletin of Johns Hopkins Hospital*, vol 20, pages 329–339, 1909.

Page 25 'Let us boldly conclude that man is a machine'. This strong statement by Julien Offray de la Mettrie, and others in the same vein, appears in the recent reprint of his *L'homme-machine* (Pauvert, Paris, 1966).

Page 26 Niels Steensen's *Lecture on the Anatomy of the Brain* (1669) opens with a remarkable disclaimer: 'Gentlemen, Instead of promising to satisfy your curiosity concerning the anatomy of the brain, I confess sincerely and publicly here that I know nothing about it.' The book, now available in a translation edited by Gustav Scherz (Arnold Busck, Copenhagen, 1965), nevertheless set a new high water mark in writings on the subject.

Chapter 2

Page 31 C Sherrington's early studies of the reflex arc extended the work of Jiri Prochaska, around 1780, and Ivan Sechenov (described by Pavlov as the father of Russian physiology), around 1865. Sherrington's first report 'On reciprocal innervation of antagonistic muscles' appeared in *Proceedings of the Royal Society*, vol 60, pages 414–417, 1897; it was placed in context in the book he wrote with four of his former students (R S Creed, D E Denny-Brown, J C Eccles and E G T Liddell): *Reflex activity of the spinal cord* (Oxford University Press, London, 1932).

Page 31 A recent version of J Locke's major publication is *An Essay Concerning Human Understanding* (Dover, New York, 1959).

Page 32 The work of T Willis originally appeared in his *Cerebri anatome* (Martyn & Allestry, London, 1664); an English translation is to be found in S Pordage's *Dr Willis's practice of physick* (Dring, London, 1684).

Page 34 Speculations such as whether a guillotined person's head can briefly retain consciousness can be found in a P J G Cabanis's *Rapports du physique et du moral de l'homme* (Bechet, Paris, 1824).

Page 35 F Gall's monumental six-volume work appeared during the period 1822–1825, under the running title *Sur les fonctions du cerveau et sur celles de chacune de ses parties* (Baillière, Paris); the entire bizarre enterprise was reviewed by Frances Hedderly, president of the British Phrenological Society at the time of its liquidation, in *Phrenology: A study of the mind* (Fowler, London, 1970).

Page 37 The work of M J P Flourens is described in his *Recherches expériment- ales sur les propriétés et les fonctions du système nerveux dans les animaux vertébrés* (Crevot, Paris, 1924); English translations of parts of this are to be found in J M D Olmsted's contribution to the second volume of E A Underwood's *Science, medicine and history* (Oxford University Press, London, 1953), and in G von Bonin's *Some papers on the cerebral cortex* (Thomas, Springfield Illinois, 1960).

Page 39 The famous debates at the anthropological society in Paris, in 1861, have been described by Henry Head in his *Aphasia and kindred disorders of speech* (Cambridge University Press, Cambridge, 1926).

Page 41 J Hughlings Jackson's own description his pivotal contributions appear in the monograph *A study of convulsions* (Odell & Ives, London, 1870); his work is also reviewed in J Taylor's *Selected writings of John Hughlings Jackson* (Hodder & Stoughton, London, 1931).

Page 42 English translations of the pioneering work of E Hitzig and G Fritsch appear in G von Bonin's *Some papers on the cerebral cortex* (Thomas, Springfield Illinois, 1960) and in H Wilkins's 'Neurosurgical classics XII' published in *Journal of Neurosurgery*, vol 20, pages 904–916, 1963. The related work of D Ferrier is covered in his *The localization of cerebral disease* (Smith, Elder, London, 1878).

Page 43 R Bartholow's own chilling account of his work on Mary Rafferty is the article 'Experimental investigations into the functions of the human brain' which appeared in *American Journal of Medical Science*, vol 67, pages 305–313, 1874.

Page 44 E Adrian's contributions to neuroscience are put in perspective in his *The physical background of perception* (Clarendon Press, Oxford, 1947).

Page 45 The most significant article by Gordon Holmes was his 'The symptoms of acute cerebral injuries due to gunshot injuries', which appeared in *Brain*, vol 40, pages 461–535, 1917.

Page 46 A good overview of C Wernicke's contributions is his *Grundriss der Psychiatrie in klinischen Vorlesungen* (Thiem, Leipzig, 1900).

Page 46 J H Macdonald has translated L Bianchi's work on the frontal lobes: *The mechanisms of the brain and the function of the frontal lobes* (Livingstone, Edinburgh, 1922).

Page 47 J Déjerine's account of his work on the corpus callosum appeared in *Semiologie des affections du système nerveux* (Masson, Paris, 1900).

Page 47 A good overview of Roger Sperry's ground-breaking studies is his 'Some effects of disconnecting the cerebral hemispheres', published in *Science*, vol 217, pages 1223–1226, 1982.

Page 48 The exacting work that did so much to establish the cortical map is described in K Brodmann's *Vergleichende Lokalisationslehre der Grosshirnrinde in ihren Prinzipien dargestellt auf Grund des Zellenbaues* (Barth, Leipzig, 1909); an English review of this, and the related work of W Campbell and the Vogts, is the book by W Haymaker and F Schiller *The founders of neurology* (Thomas, Springfield Illinois, 1970).

Page 49 P MacLean's views are presented in his *A Triune Concept of the Brain and Behaviour* (Toronto University Press, Toronto, 1973).

Page 50 Arthur Koestler's *The ghost in the machine* (Random House, New York, 1967) was, of course, the inspiration for the title of the present book; Koestler's title was borrowed from a remark in Gilbert Ryle's *The concept of mind* (Barnes & Noble, New York, 1949).

Page 52 C Bernard's pioneering efforts on the autonomic nervous system are described in his *Leçons sur les effets des substances toxiques et médicamenteuses* (Baillière et Fils, Paris, 1857).

Chapter 3

Page 55 An English description of G Aldini's independent work is given in his *An account of the late improvement in galvanism* (Cuthell, Martin & Murray, London, 1803).

Page 56 L Galvani's *De viribus electricitatis in motu musculari commentarius*, published by Ex typographia Instituti Scientiarum in 1791, appeared as an English translation, *Commentary on the effect of electricity on muscular motion*, by M G Foley (Burndy Library, Norwalk, Connecticut, 1953).

Page 57 J Walsh's account of his studies of aquatic electricity is 'Of torpedos found on the coast of England', which appeared in *Philosophical Transactions of the Royal Society*, vol 64, pages 464–473, 1774.

Page 57 C Matteucci's measurement of the electrical current generated by a muscle is described in his *Traité des phénomènes électro-physiologiques des animaux* (Fortin & Masson, Paris, 1844), and in the English translation by J Pereira, *Lectures on the physical phenomena of living beings* (Longman, Brown, Green & Longman, London, 1847).

Page 58 A van Leeuwenhoek communicated a number of his observations on nerve fibres to the Royal Society; a typical example appeared in *Philosophical Transactions of the Royal Society*, vol 17, pages 949–960, 1693.

Page 58 An English translation by H Smith of T Schwann's major publication, which appeared in German eight years earlier, is *Microscopical researches* (Sydenham Society, London, 1847).

Page 60 C Golgi and S Ramon y Cajal reviewed their major contributions to the study of the brain when they shared the Nobel Prize in 1906: the relevant articles are 'La doctrine du neurone' (Golgi) and 'Structure et connexions des neurones' (Ramon y Cajal) in *Les Prix Nobel en 1906* (Norstedt & sons, Stockholm, 1908).

Page 61 An overview of the achievements of A H Forel may be found in his *Out of my life and work* (Norton, New York, 1937).

Page 61 Waldeyer-Hartz's own evaluation of the significance of his contributions can be read in his *Lebenserinnerungen* (Cohn, Bonn, 1920).

Page 63 H von Helmholtz's epoch-making measurement of the velocity of a nerve impulse was reported in 'Messungen über Fortpflanzungsgeschwindigkeit der Reizung in der Nerven, zweite Reihe' which appeared in *Archives of Anatomy and Physiology*, pages 199–216, 1852.

Page 63 E Du Bois-Reymond surveyed his work in the two-volume work *Untersuchungen über thierische Elektrizität* (Reimer, Berlin, 1884).

Page 65 E Adrian's discovery of the action potential is described by him in 'The all-or-none principle in nerve', which appeared in *Journal of Physiology, London*, vol 47, pages 460–474, 1913–1914.

Page 66 The scope of J Z Young's writings on the brain, from the specific to the general, can be gauged by comparing his article 'Structure of the nerve fibres of Sepia' in *Journal of Physiology* (London), vol 83, pages 27–28, 1935, and his book *Programs of the brain* (Clarendon Press, Oxford, 1978).

Page 66 A L Hodgkin and A F Huxley's studies of nerve conduction culminated in their explanation of this in terms of conjectured channels: 'A quantitative description of membrane current and its application to conduction and excitation in nerve' in *Journal of Physiology* (London), vol 117, pages 500–544, 1952.

Page 69 C Sherrington's *Man on His Nature* (Cambridge University Press, London, 1951) puts his contributions into the overall picture, as it was perceived at the end of his long and highly productive life.

Page 70 O Loewi's Ferrier Lecture 'On problems connected with the principle of humoral transmission of nerve impulses', published in *Proceedings of the Royal Society*, vol 118B, pages 299–316, 1935, provides a concise summary of his neurotransmission breakthroughs.

Page 71 The quantal nature of neurotransmitter release was concluded by B Katz and R Miledi in 'A study of spontaneous miniature potentials in spinal motoneurones', published in *Journal of Physiology* (London), vol 168, pages 389–422, 1963; this built upon the paper by P Fatt and B Katz 'Spontaneous subthreshold activity at motor nerve endings', in the same journal, vol 117, pages 109–128, 1952; *Nerve, Muscle and Synapse* (McGraw-Hill, New York, 1966), by Katz, is a pocket-sized gem.

Page 72 H Dale's *Adventures in physiology* (Pergamon Press, Oxford, 1953) gives the background to his work on inhibition.

Page 73 D O Hebb's *The organization of behaviour* (Wiley, New York, 1949) has become one of the most cited of all books on the brain.

Page 75 I Pavlov's work appeared in English translation in *Lectures on conditioned reflexes* (Lawrence, London, 1941) by W H Gannt.

Page 76 E R Kandel's article 'Small systems of neurons' in *Scientific American*, vol 241, pages 66–76, 1970, is a good introduction to his seminal discoveries; his edited volume with J H Schwartz, *Principles of neural science* (Elsevier, New York, 1981), is a major reference work in brain science.

Page 79 The discovery of synapses that behave in a Hebbian fashion, in the rat hippocampus, was reported by S R Kelso, A H Ganong and T H Brown, in *Proceedings of the National Academy of Sciences USA*, vol 83, pages 5326–5330, 1986; the related effect known as long-term potentiation, in the rat visual cortex, was subsequently reported by A Artola and W Singer, in *Nature*, vol 330, pages 649–652, 1987.

Page 80 The experiment of R Held and A Hein was reported in *Journal of Comparative and Physiological Psychology*, vol 56, pages 872–876, 1963; that of C Blakemore and G F Cooper appeared in *Nature*, vol 228, pages 477–478, 1970.

Chapter 4

Page 87 F S Werblin and J E Dowling reported their observations of the visual system of the mudpuppy *Necturus maculosus* in *Journal of Neurophysiology*, vol 32, pages 339–355, 1969.

Page 87 S W Kuffler announced the discovery of centre-surround sensitivity in his article 'Discharge patterns and functional organization of the mammalian retina', published in *Journal of Neurophysiology*, vol 16, pages 37–68, 1953.

Page 89 The explanation of the Mach bands follows that given in T H Bullock, R Orkand and A Grinnell's *Introduction to nervous systems* (Freeman, San Francisco, 1977).

Page 90 The mysterious shadow phenomenon has been known since 1870, and it was announced by L Hermann in 'Eine Erscheinung simultanen Kontrastes' published in *Plügers Arch. geselschaft Physiologi*, vol 3, pages 13–45; it is still being investigated, a recent example being 'A comparison of perceptive and receptive fields in man and monkey' by L Spillman, A Ransom-Hogg and R Oehler in *Human Neurobiology*, vol 6, pages 51–62, 1987.

Page 92 A good source of quantitative information on the cellular arrangements in the visual system is W J H Nauta and M Feirtag's *Fundamental Neuroanatomy* (Freeman, New York, 1986).

Page 93 The blindsight that derives from the superior colliculus continues to attract scientific curiosity; a recent example is 'Blindsight and insight in visuo-spatial neglect', which J C Marshall and P W Halligan published in *Nature*, vol 336, pages 766–767, 1988.

Page 95 Information on the 'wiring diagram' of the cortex was obtained from O D Creutzfeldt's article 'The neocortical link: Thoughts on the generality of structure and function of the neocortex', in M A B Brazier and H Petsche's volume *Architectonics of the cerebral cortex* (Raven Press, New York, 1978).

Page 96 The discoveries of orientational selectivity and the cellular configurations that give rise to binocularity, by D H Hubel and T N Wiesel, were described in *Journal of Physiology*, vol 160, pages 106–154, 1962; this ground-breaking work was recently put in perspective in Hubel's *Eye, Brain and Vision* (Freeman, Oxford, 1988).

Page 97 The motion after-effect was first reported in 1894, by Sigmund (von Ewarten) Exner (1846–1926), in a communication to the scientific academy of Vienna.

Page 97 The article by H V B Hirsch and D N Spinelli, 'Visual experience modifies distribution of horizontally and vertically oriented receptive fields in cats' was published in *Science*, vol 168, pages 869–871, 1970; J P Rauschecker and W Singer reported their observations in the article 'The effects of early visual experience on the cat's visual cortex and their possible explanation by Hebb synapses' which appeared in *Journal of Physiology*, vol 310, pages 215–239, 1981; the Blakemore-Cooper article was cited in Chapter 3.

Page 98 C McCollough announced her discovery of the illusion in 'Color adaptation of edge-detectors in the human visual system', published in *Science*, vol 149, pages 1115–1118, 1965.

Page 103 The determination of the speed with which one can rotate mental objects was reported by R N Shepard and J Metzler, in *Science*, vol 171, pages 701–703, 1971.

Chapter 5

Page 107 V Braitenberg's data are conventionally collected in his *On the Texture of Brains* (Springer-Verlag, Berlin, 1977).

Page 108 The article 'The cerebellum as a computer: Patterns in space and time', by J C Eccles, appeared in *Journal of Physiology*, vol 229, pages 1–32, 1973.

Page 110 K S Lashley's article 'In search of the engram' was published in the *4th Symposium of the Society for Experimental Biology*, pages 454–482, 1950.

Page 112 A good introduction to W Penfield's pioneering work is the book he co-authored with T Rasmussen: *The cerebral cortex of man* (Macmillan, New York, 1950).

Page 114 The book by W James is *Psychology* (Holt, New York, 1890).

Page 114 The seminal paper 'A logical calculus of the ideas immanent in nervous activity', by W S McCulloch and W Pitts, appeared in *Bulletin of Mathematical Biophysics*, vol 5, pages 115–133, 1943.

Page 115 F Rosenblatt described his strategy in 'The perceptron: a probabilistic model for information storage and organisation in the brain', published in *Psychological Review*, vol 65, pages 386–408, 1958; M Minsky and S Papert's book is *Perceptrons* (MIT Press, Cambridge, Mass., 1969).

Page 117 Igor Aleksander's neural computer 'Wisard' was the subject of an article in *The Times*, October 19, page 10, 1984.

Page 117 A good introduction to the extensive work of T Kohonen is his book *Self-Organization and Associative·Memory* (Springer-Verlag, New York, 1984); two books by Stephen Grossberg have been referred to as the old and new testaments of neural networks: they are *Studies of Mind and Brain* (Reidel Press, Boston, 1982) and *The Adaptive Brain* (North-Holland, Amsterdam, 1987); together with Shun-ichi Amari, Grossberg and Kohonen established the International Neural Network Society in 1987, and its official journal, *Neural Networks*, was first published early in 1988.

Page 119 J J Hopfield's article 'Neutral networks and physical systems with emergent collective computational properties' is probably the most-cited paper in this branch of science; it appeared in *Proceedings of the National Academy of Sciences USA*, vol 79, pages 2554–2558, 1982.

Page 119 The book by W R Ashby is *Design for a Brain* (Wiley, New York, 1952).

Page 121 The fullest description of the back-propagation procedure is to be found in the article 'Learning internal representations by error propagation', by D E Rumelhart, G E Hinton and R J Williams, which appeared in the first volume of D E Rumelhart and J L McClelland's *Parallel Distributed Processing: Explorations in the Microstructure of Cognition* (MIT Press, Cambridge, Mass., 1986), pages 318–364; this two-volume work, and its companion exercise book (complete with a computer diskette), has rapidly established itself as the undisputed leader in its field.

Page 123 T J Sejnowski and C R Rosenberg's paper 'Parallel networks that learn to pronounce English text' appeared in *Complex Systems*, vol 1, pages 145–168, 1987.

Page 124 It is generally assumed that the antithesis of distributed processing by a parallel neural network would be a situation in which a single cell responds to an pattern 'observed' by an entire array of input cells, the often-cited case being the cell that becomes active if, and only if, the input is a picture of one's grandmother; the existence of such 'grandmother' cells has in fact been reported, examples being D I Perrett, A J Mistlin and A J Chitty's 'Visual neurones responsive to faces' in *Trends in neurosciences*, vol 10, Pages 358–364, 1987, Y Miyashita and H S Chang's 'Neuronal correlate of pictorial short-term memory in the primate temporal cortex' in *Nature*, vol 331, pages 68–70, 1988, and G Heit, M E Smith and E Halgren's 'Neural encoding of individual words and faces by the human hippocampus and amygdala' in *Nature*, vol 333, pages 773–775, 1988; these experimental observations are not in conflict with the distributed-network concept, however, because highly discriminative cells are present in such a network's output layer, once the system has been suitably trained.

Page 124 S R Lehky and T J Sejnowski's paper 'Network model of shape-from-shading: neural function arises from both receptive and projective fields' was published in *Nature*, vol 333, pages 452–454, 1988; the related work 'A back-propagation programmed network that simulates response properties of a subset of posterior parietal neurons', by D Zipser and R A Andersen, also appeared in *Nature*, vol 331, pages 679–684, 1988.

Page 127 The brain's pleasure centres were discussed by J Olds and P Milner in the article 'Positive reinforcement produced by electrical stimulation of the septal area and other regions of rat brain', in *Journal of Comparative Physiology and Psychology*, vol 47, 419–427, 1954; the self-starvation phenomenon was reported in A Routtenberg and A W Kuznesof's paper 'Self-starvation of rats living in activity wheels on a restricted feeding schedule' in *Journal of Comparative Physiology*, vol 64, pages 414–421, 1967, while related effects were described in A Routtenberg, E L Gardner and Y H Huang's paper 'Self-stimulation pathways in monkey *Macaca mulatta*', published in *Experimental Neurology*, vol 33, pages 213–224, 1971.

Page 127 The reward system of the brain is described in A Wauquier and E T Rolls' book *Brain Stimulation Reward* (North-Holland, Amsterdam, 1976).

Page 128 S M Kosslyn's work on mental images was described in his article 'Information representation in visual images', in *Cognitive Psychology*, vol 7, pages 341–370, 1975, and later in his book *Image and Mind* (Harvard University Press, Cambridge, Mass., 1980).

Page 130 A good example of the type of complexity that is quite beyond the scope of present theoretical neural networks is discussed in R A Nicoll's article 'Neurotransmitters can say more than just "yes" and "no"', which appeared in *Trends in neurosciences*, vol 5, pages 369–374, 1982.

Page 131 The general aspects of autism are surveyed in L Wing's book *Autistic children: a guide for parents* (Constable, London, 1971); the special sub-group of autistics known as *idiots savants* were the subjects of D Treffert's *Extraordinary People* (Bantam, London, 1989).

Chapter 6

Page 134 Hans Berger's pioneering discoveries were reported in his article 'Über das Elektrenkephalogramm des Menschen', which appeared in *Arkiv fur Psychiatrie und Nervenkrankeiten*, vol 87, pages 527–570, 1929.

Page 135 A good general description of the EEG is given in E Basar's *EEG-Brain Dynamics* (Elsevier/North-Holland, Amsterdam, 1980); this book also deals with evoked potentials, as does E J Moore's *Bases of Auditory Brain-Stem Evoked Responses* (Grune & Stratton, New York, 1983).

Page 136 Many different aspects of sleep, including the role of the PGO waves, were covered in the conference proceedings *Sleep 1976* (Karger, Basel, 1977), edited by W P Koella and P Levin; other general sources of information on the subject are E L Hartmann's *The functions of sleep* (Yale University Press, New Haven, 1973), and J Horne's *Why we sleep* (Oxford University Press, London, 1988); the idea that sleep's primary function is to immobilize an animal, and thereby increase its chances of survival, was discussed in 'On the function of sleep' by R Meddis, in *Animal Behaviour*, vol 23, pages 676–691, 1975.

Page 137 Representative papers on REM are E Aserinsky and N Kleitman's 'Regularly occurring periods of eye motility and concomitant phenomena during sleep' in *Science*, vol 118, pages 273–274, 1953, and W C Dement and N Kleitman's 'Cyclic variations in EEG during sleep and their relations to eye movements, body motility, and dreaming' in *EEG Clinical Neurophysiology*, vol 9, pages 673–690, 1957; the issue of REM loss was addressed in W C Dement's paper 'The Effect of Dream Deprivation', published in *Science*, vol 131, pages 1705–1707, 1960.

Page 139 A modern imprint of S Freud's classic *The Interpretation of Dreams* was published by Basic Books (New York, 1955); that same publisher produced J A Hobson's *The Dreaming Brain* in 1988.

Page 140 R W McCarley and J A Hobson's discussion of the dreaming state appeared in the articles 'The neurobiological origins of psychoanalytic dream theory' and 'The brain as a dream state generator: An activation-synthesis hypothesis of the dream process', which appeared in *American Journal of Psychiatry*, pages 1211–1221 and 1335–1348, vol 134, 1977.

Page 140 M Jouvet's paper 'Neurophysiology of the states of sleep' appeared in *Physiological Review*, vol 47, pages 117–177, 1967.

Page 140 Pathologies of sleep are covered in C Guilleminault's *Sleeping and waking disorders: Indications and techniques* (Addison-Wesley, Menlo Park, 1982).

Page 142 W Robert's book is *Der Traum als Naturnothwendigkeit Erklärt* (Hermann Seippel, Hamburg, 1886).

Page 142 The papers that appeared in *Nature* 1983, vol 304, were F Crick and G Mitchison's 'The function of dream sleep' (pages 111–114) and J J Hopfield, D I Feinstein and R G Palmer's ' "Unlearning" has a stabilizing effect in collective memories' (pages 158–159); a follow-up paper 'REM Sleep and Neural Nets' was published by Crick and Mitchison in *The Journal of Mind and Behaviour*, vol 7, pages 229–249, 1986; the concept of 'brainwashing', which is comparable to the above 'unlearning', was introduced in J W Clark, J Rafelski and J V Winston's 'Brain without mind: Computer simulation of neural networks with modifiable neuronal interactions', which appeared in *Physics Reports*, vol 123, pages 216–273, 1985.

Page 143 The apparent lack of dreaming in the spiny anteater was discussed in T Allison, H Van Twyver and W R Goff's article 'Electrophysiological studies of the echidna, *Tachyglossus aculeatus*', published (in English) in *Archives Italiennes de Biologie*, vol 110, pages 145–184, 1972.

Page 146 H Piéron's contributions were covered in his *Problèmes physiologiques du sommeil* (Masson, Paris, 1913).

Page 149 E Hartmann's article 'The 90-Minute Sleep-Dream Cycle' appeared in *Archives of General Psychiatry*, vol 18, pages 280–286, 1968.

Page 150 F Goltz's work on decerebrated dogs was reported in his paper 'Der Hund ohne Grosshirn. Siebente Abhandlung über die Verrichtungen des Grosshirns', which was published in *Pflügers Archives*, vol 51, pages 570–614, 1892; an English translation of a summary of the work is given in the chapter 'On the functions of the hemispheres' in editor G von Bonin's *The cerebral cortex* (Thomas Springfield Illinois, 1960).

Page 152 An alternative view of the origin of dreaming was given in B D Davis's article 'Sleep and the maintenance of memory', published in *Perspectives in Biology and Medicine*, vol 28, pages 457–464, 1985, and also in R M J Cotterill's article 'The brain: An intriquing piece of condensed matter', which appeared in *Physica Scripta*, vol T13, pages 161–168, 1986.

Page 153 J-P Changeux and A Danchin's paper 'Selective stabilisation of developing synapses as a mechanism for the specification of neuronal networks' was published in *Nature*, vol 264, pages 705–712, 1976.

Page 154 Recent evidence for external controllability of the circadian rhythm is given in F W Turek and O Van Reeth's review 'Altering the mammalian circadian clock with the short-acting benzodiazepine, triazolam', published in *Trends in Neurosciences*, vol 11, pages 535–541, 1988; evidence that the rhythm can be altered by mutation of a single gene was given in M R Ralph and M Menaker's article 'A mutation of the circadian system in golden hamsters', published in *Science*, vol 241, pages 1225–1227, 1988; reviews of the general issues are A T Winfree's article 'Human body clocks and the timing of sleep', in *Nature*, vol 297, pages 23–27, 1982, and his book *The Timing of Biological Clocks* (Freeman, New York, 1987).

Chapter 7

Page 160 A concise illustrated summary of the biology of genes and proteins is provided by R M J Cotterill's book *The Cambridge Guide to the Material World* (Cambridge University Press, London, 1985).

Page 165 The genetic evidence of the hereditary proximity of humans and apes is presented in J J Yunis and O Prakash's article 'The origin of man: A chromosomal pictorial legacy', which appeared in *Science,* vol 215, pages 1525–1530, 1982; a genealogical tree, based on this evidence, was compiled by B Dutrillaux and summarized in his contribution 'Chromosomal evolution of the great apes and man' to R V Short and B Weir's edited volume *The great apes of Africa* (Journals of Reproduction and Fertility, Colchester, 1980).

Page 167 R W Sperry's discoveries were reported in his paper 'Chemoaffinity in the orderly growth of nerve fiber patterns and connections', published in *Proceedings of the National Academy of Sciences USA*, vol 50, pages 703–710. 1963.

Page 168 R Levi-Montalcini described her pioneering work on nerve growth factor in the article 'NGF: An uncharted route' in F G Worden's edited volume *The Neurosciences: Paths of Discovery* (MIT Press, Cambridge, Mass, 1975).

Page 169 The discovery of long-sought morphogens was reported by C Thaller and G Eichele in their article 'Identification and spatial distribution of retinoids in the developing chick limb bud', published in *Nature*, vol 327, pages 625–628, 1987; the general issues involved in brain development are discussed in A Gierer's article 'Spatial organization and genetic information in brain development', which appeared in *Biological Cybernetics*, vol 59, pages 13–21, 1988, while the specific question of genetically-dictated effects on individual neurons was dealt with in J Palka and M Schubiger's paper 'Genes for neural differentation', in *Trends in Neurosciences*, vol 11, pages 515–517, 1988.

Page 171 A general survey of behavioural traits that have been linked to chromosomal aberrations is given in the W Schmid and J Nielsen's edited volume *Human Behavior and Genetics* (Elsevier/North-Holland, Amsterdam, 1981).

Page 172 D C Turner, J Feaver, M Mendl and P Bateson reported their observations on feline 'friendliness' in the article 'Variation in domestic cat behavior towards humans: a paternal effect', which appeared in *Animal Behaviour*, vol 34, pages 1890–1892, 1986.

Page 173 G E Robinson and R E Page Jr's observations on bees were reported in their article 'Genetic determination of guarding and undertaking in honey-bee colonies', published in *Nature*, vol 333, pages 356–358, 1988; P C Frumhoff and J Baker's complementary study was reported in their article 'A genetic component to division of labour within honey bee colonies', also published in *Nature*, vol 333, pages 358–361, 1988.

Page 174 Hereditary effects in human mental performance were dealt with in D W Fulker, J C DeFries and R Plomin's article 'Genetic influence on general mental ability increases between infancy and middle childhood', published in *Nature*, vol 336, pages 767–769, 1988.

Page 175 During the 1987 Himalaya climbing season, upwards of three dozen people tried to reach the summit of the difficult mountain known as K2. As the surviving members of some of the earlier expeditions returned to the base camp, it became clear that the chance of any individual actually dying in the attempt was about fifty per cent. This did not deter the later climbers, however, and many of them spoke of the challenge as if it were a narcotic.

Page 175 M Zuckerman's findings are placed in a wider context in his book *Sensation-seeking: Beyond the Optimum Level of Arousal* (Lawrence Erlbaum, Hillsdale New Jersey, 1979).

Page 179 J Dum and A Herz produced a critical review on 'Opioids and Motivation', which was published in *Interdisciplinary Science Reviews*, vol 12, pages 180–190, 1987; important biochemical aspects of the issue were covered in A Mansour, H Khachaturian, M E Lewis, H Akil and S J Watson's paper 'Anatomy of CNS opioid receptors', which appeared in *Trends in Neurosciences*, vol 11, pages 308–314, 1988.

Page 179 C Claiborne Park's book *The Siege* is available as a Pelican paperback (Penguin, London, 1972); the subject of autism is also dealt with in the volume *Infantile Autism: concepts, characteristics and treatment* (Churchill & Sons, London, 1971), edited by M Rutter.

Page 179 C Benbow's findings were reported in the paper 'Physiological correlates of extreme intellectual precocity', published in *Neuropsychology*, vol 24, pages 719–725, 1986.

Chapter 8

Page 181 The two different extremes of the issue have both been the subject of books published in the Pelican series: V H Mottram's *The physical basis of personality* (Penguin, London, 1946), and S Rose, R C Lewontin and L J Kamin's *Not in our genes* (Penguin, London, 1984).

Page 182 A good introduction to the work of K Z Lorenz is his book (translated by R Martin) *Studies in Animal and Human Behavior* (Harvard University Press, Cambridge Mass., 1971).

Page 183 The observations of M H Johnson and his colleagues were briefly reported in the article 'Brain maturation and the development of face recognition in infancy', which appeared in *Behavioural Brain Research*, vol 23, page 224, 1987; and in the article 'The role of a restricted region of the chick forebrain in the recognition of individual conspecifics', published in the same journal, vol 23, pages 269–275, 1987.

Page 183 The classical observations on babies were reported by C C Goren, M Sarty and P Y K Wu in the article 'Visual following and pattern-discrimination of face-like stimuli by newborn infants', which appeared in *Pediatrics*, vol 56, pages 544–549, 1975.

Page 186 O J Bradick and J Atkinson's measurement of a baby's capacity to focus was reported in the article 'Some recent findings on the development of human binocularity', published in *Behavioural Brain Research*, vol 10, pages 141–150, 1983.

Page 188 I P Pavlov's work is described in his book *Conditioned Reflexes* (Oxford University Press, London, 1927).

Page 189 The 'brainwashing' episode that dashed candidate George

Romney's hopes is described in T H White's *The Making of the President 1968* (Athenium, New York, 1969), pages 69–73.

Page 191 F Bogdany's discovery was reported in the article 'Linking of learning signals in honeybee orientation', published in *Behavioral Ecology and Sociobiology*, vol 3, pages 323–336, 1978; K von Frisch looked back on his pioneering work on bees in his article 'Decoding the Language of the Bee', which appeared in *Science*, vol 185, pages 663–668, 1974.

Page 192 W H Thorpe's pioneering work on bird song is covered in his book *Bird-song* (Cambridge University Press, London, 1961); it has recently transpired that new neurons appear during the learning of song by birds, as reported in K W Nordeen and E J Nordeen's article 'Projection neurons within a vocal motor pathway are born during song learning in zebra finches', published in *Nature*, vol 334, pages 149–151, 1988.

Page 192 The classic study in which P Marler established the existence of dialects in bird-song is described in his article 'Species distinctiveness in the communication signals of birds', published in *Behaviour*, vol 11, pages 13–29, 1957.

Page 192 An example of recent analysis of bird-song appears in D Margoliash and M Konishi's paper 'Auditory representation of autogenous song in the song system of white-crowned sparrows, published in *Proceedings of the National Academy of Sciences USA*, vol 82, pages 5997–6000, 1985.

Page 194 Representative of N Chomsky's many writings on the subject of language are his books *Aspects of the theory of syntax* (MIT Press, Cambridge, Mass., 1965) and *Reflections on language* (Fontana, London, 1976).

Page 196 N Geschwind's ideas were put forward in his 'Disconnexion syndromes in animals and man', which appeared in *Brain*, vol 88, pages 237–294, 1965; recent supporting evidence is presented in the article 'Is the left hemisphere specialized for language at birth?' by B T Woods, published in *Trends in Neurosciences*, vol 6, pages 115–117, 1983.

Page 198 N Juel-Nielsen's book is *Individual and environment: A psychiatric-psychological investigation of monozygotic twins reared apart* (Munksgaard, Copenhagen, 1965).

Page 198 A typical example of the many papers that have been produced in connection with the Minnesota study is A Tellegen, D T Lykken, T J Bouchard Jr, K J Wilcox, N L Segal and S Rich's 'Personality similarity in twins reared apart and together', which appeared in *Journal of Personality and Social Psychology*, vol 54, pages 1031–1039, 1988.

Page 199 D Goodwin's somewhat depressing findings were reported in his articles 'Genetic and experiential antecedents of alcoholism – prospective study', published in *Alcoholism – Clinical and Experimental Research*, vol 1, pages 259–265, 1977, and 'Alcoholism and heredity – Review and hypothesis', published in *Archives of General Psychiatry*, vol 36, pages 57–61, 1979.

Page 199 The equally disconcerting results of the Swedish study were reported in C R Cloninger, M Bohman and S Sigvardson's article 'Inheritance of alcohol-abuse: cross-fostering analysis of adopted men', published in *Archives of General Psychiatry*, vol 38, pages 861–868, 1981.

Chapter 9

Page 204 The still-sparse evidence for temporary remission of schizophrenia by such physical factors as raised body temperature was reviewed in S Lipper and D S Werman's article 'Schizophrenia and Intercurrent Physical Illness: A Critical Review of the Literature', which appeared in *Comprehensive Psychiatry*, vol 18, pages 11–22, 1977.

Page 206 The ancient Egyptian writings were described in J H Breasted's *The Edwin Smith surgical papyrus* (Chicago University Press, Chicago, 1930).

Page 207 A modern source of fungus lore is R Gordon Wasson's *The Wondrous Mushroom: Mycolatry in Mesoamerica* (McGraw-Hill, New York, 1988).

Page 209 Myasthenia gravis has been the subject of reviews by D B Drachman: 'Biology of myasthenia gravis', in *Annual Reviews of Neuroscience*, vol 4, pages 195–225, 1981, and 'Myasthenia gravis: immunobiology of a receptor disorder', in *Trends in Neurosciences*, vol 6, pages 446–450, 1983.

Page 209 The affliction was the subject of M D Yahr and K J Bergmann's edited volume 'Parkinson's disease', which appeared as *Advances in Neurology*, vol 45, 1986; the specific issue of external factors was reviewed in C M Tanner's paper 'The role of environmental toxins in the etiology of Parkinson's disease', in *Trends in Neurosciences*, vol 12, pages 49–54, 1989.

Page 210 A general survey of Huntington's disease is given in M R Hayden's book *Huntington's Chorea* (Springer, New York, 1981); recent genetic findings are described in the article by J J Wasmuth, J Hewitt, B Smith, D Allard, J L Haines, D Skarecky, E Partlow and M R Hayden: 'A highly polymorphic locus very tightly linked to the Huntington's disease gene', in *Nature*, vol 332, pages 734–736, 1988.

Page 211 A good introduction to the disease is given J T Coyle, D L Price and M R DeLong's paper 'Alzheimer's disease: A disorder of cortical cholinergic innervation', which appeared in *Science*, vol 219, pages 1184–1190, 1983; the recently-established genetic links were announced in three articles in *Nature*, vol 331, 1988: P Ponte, P Gonzalez-DeWhitt, J Schilling, J Miller, D Hsu, B Greenberg, K Davis, W Wallace, I Lieberburg, F Fuller and B Cordell's 'A new A4 amyloid mRNA contains a domain homologous to serine proteinase inhibitors' (pages 525–527), R E Tanzi, A I McClatchey, E D Lamperti, L Villa-Komaroff, J F Gusella and R L Neve's 'Protease inhibitor domain encoded by an amyloid protein precursor mRNA associated with Alzheimer's disease' (pages 528–530), and N Kitaguchi, Y Takahashi, Y Tokushima, S Shiojiri and H Ito's 'Novel precursor of Alzheimer's disease amyloid protein shows protease inhibitory activity' (pages 530–532).

Page 212 The Down syndrome (mongolism) is included in O J Epstein's book *The Consequences of Chromosomal Imbalance: Principles, Mechanisms, and Models* (Cambridge University Press, New York, 1986); recent findings at the genetic level are described in D Patterson's article 'The causes of Down Syndrome', in *Scientific American*, vol 257, pages 42–48, 1987.

Page 213 The continuing plight of the mental patient is the subject of D Cohen's sensitively-written book *Forgotten Millions* (Paladin, London, 1988).

Page 214 The affliction is the subject of A J Friedhoff and T N Chase's edited volume *Gilles de la Tourette Syndrome* (Raven Press, New York, 1982); it is also featured in O Sacks's *The man who mistook his wife for a hat* (Gerald Duckworth, London, 1985).

Page 215 Various aspects of syphilis are covered in M M Singh's *Mental Disorder: A problem with many facets* (Pan Books, London, 1967).

Page 217 A good general survey of schizophrenia is provided by J M Neale and T F Oltmanns's book *Schizophrenia* (Wiley, New York, 1980); a concise account of recent developments is given in D R Weinberger's article 'Schizophrenia and the frontal lobe', which appeared in *Trends in Neurosciences*, vol 11, pages 367–370, 1988.

Page 219 S Freud's 1895 article 'An outline for a scientific psychology' was reproduced in M Bonaparte's edited volume *The origins of psychoanalysis* (Basic Books, New York, 1954).

Page 222 The two papers that recently caused so much excitement, both published in *Nature*, vol 336, 1988, were R Sherrington, J Brynjolfsson, H Petursson, M Potter, K Dudleston, B Barraclough, J Wasmuth, M Dobbs and H Gurling's 'Localization of a susceptibility locus for schizophrenia on chromosome 5' (pages 164–167), and J L Kennedy, L A Giuffra, H W Moises, L L Cavalli-Sforza, A J Pakstis, J R Kidd, C M Castiglione, B Sjogren, L Wetterberg and K K Kidd's 'Evidence against linkage of schizophrenia to markers on chromosome 5 in a northern Swedish pedigree' (pages 167–170).

Page 226 A selection of the brilliant autistic artist Stephen Wiltshire's works were reproduced in his *Drawings* (Dent, London, 1987).

Page 227 Apart from the books on autism listed in Chapters 5 and 7, there is a book that includes this in its discussion of a number of different pathologies, namely *Children in need of special care* (Souvenir Press, London, 1971), by T J Weihs; *Autism Research Review*, the quarterly whose first edition appeared in 1987, gives the latest news in this area.

Page 227 R M J Cotterill's article 'Fever in autistics' was published in *Nature*, vol 313, page 426, 1985.

Chapter 10

Page 229 Three excellent general books in this area are S Walker's *Animal Thought* (Routledge & Kegan Paul, London, 1983); D R Griffin's *Animal*

Thinking (Harvard University Press, Cambridge Mass., 1984); and P Evans's *Ourselves and Other Animals* (Century, London, 1987).

Page 230 The question of whether fish can experience pain was also discussed by Peter Spinks, in his article 'Fear of fishing', which appeared in *New Scientist*, vol 114, page 25, 1987.

Page 230 The rights of animals are championed by Andrew Linzey in his *Christianity and the Rights of Animals* (SPCK, London, 1987).

Page 231 Weird tales of animal executions are related in E P Evans's *The Criminal Prosecution and Capital Punishment of Animals* (Faber & Faber, London, 1986).

Page 232 A review of animal deities appears in G Parrinder's edited volume *Man and his Gods* (Hamlyn, London, 1971).

Page 234 The exploits of the assassin bug were related in E A McMahan's article 'Bait-and-capture strategy of a termite-eating assassin bug', which appeared in *Insectes Sociaux*, vol 29, pages 346–351, 1982.

Page 235 Some of Jane (van Lawick) Goodall's observations are recorded in her article 'Behaviour of free-living chimpanzees of the Gombe Stream area', published in *Animal Behaviour Monographs*, vol 1, pages 165–311, 1968, and in her book *The Chimpanzees of Gombe* (Harvard University Press, Cambridge Mass., 1986).

Page 236 Masao Kawai's remarkable discovery was announced in his paper 'Newly-acquired Pre-cultural Behavior of the Natural Troop of Japanese Monkeys on Koshima Island', published in *Primates*, vol 6, pages 1–30, 1965.

Page 236 The ability of various birds (primarily blue tits and great tits, but also magpies, blackbirds and woodpeckers) to open milk bottles was discussed in J Fisher and R A Hinde's articles 'The opening of milk bottles by birds' and 'Further observations of the opening of milk bottles by birds', which appeared in *British Birds*, vol 42, pages 347–357, 1949, and vol 44, pages 393–396, 1951.

Page 238 The differentiated behaviour of vervet monkeys was described in R M Seyfarth, D L Cheney and P Marler's article 'Vervet monkey alarm calls: semantic communication in a free-ranging primate', which appeared in *Animal Behaviour*, vol 28, pages 1070–1094, 1980.

Page 241 W N Kellogg's article 'Communication and Language in the Home-Raised Chimpanzee' appeared in *Science*, vol 162, pages 423–427, 1968; prior work was described in Keith J Hayes and Catherine Hayes's article 'Imitation in a home-raised chimpanzee', published in *Journal of Comparative Physiological Psychology*, vol 46, pages 470–474, 1952, and in Alison Jolly's article 'Lemur Social Behavior and Primate Intelligence', in *Science*, vol 153, pages 501–506, 1966.

Page 242 R A Gardner and B T Gardner's observations were recorded in 'Teaching Sign Language to a Chimpanzee', published in *Science*, vol 165, pages 664–672, 1969.

Page 243 D Premack's observations were published in his 'Language in chimpanzee?', in *Science*, vol 172, pages 808–822, 1971, and also in his book *Intelligence in Ape and Man* (Lawrence Erlbaum, Hillsdale, 1976).

Page 244 The phenomenon is described in T A Sebeok and R Rosenthal's edited volume *The Clever Hans Phenomenon: Communication with Horses, Whales, Apes and People* (The New York Academy of Sciences, New York, 1981); the unmasking episode is described in O Pfungst's *Clever Hans, The Horse of Mr von Osten* (Holt, Rinehart & Winston, New York, 1965).

Page 244 A representative publication is E S Savage-Rumbaugh, R A Sevcik, D M Rumbaugh and E Rubert's 'The capacity of animals to acquire language – Do species-differences have anything to say to us?', which appeared in *Philosophical Transactions of the Royal Society of London*, vol B308, pages 177–185, 1985.

Page 245 L A Selby-Bigge edited a version of D Hume's *A Treatise on Human Nature* (Clarendon Press, Oxford, 1888); a modern two-volume version of J Locke's crowning work is *An Essay Concerning Human Understanding* (Dover, New York, 1959); W Durant edited the *Works of Arthur Schopenhauer* (Simon & Schuster, New York, 1951); H Spencer's relevant work was *The Principles of Psychology* (Longman, Brown, Green & Longman, London, 1855); the ideas of G J Romanes are to be found in his *Animal Intelligence* (Kegan Paul, London, 1886); the culminating work in this context is of course C Darwin's *The Origin of Species* (John Murray, London, 1901).

Page 246 See the article 'Conditions of innovative behaviour in primates', by H Kummer and J Goodall, in *Philosophical Transactions of the Royal Society of London*, vol B308, pages 203–214, 1985; and also H Kummer, A A Banaja, A N Abokhatwa and A M Ghandour's article 'Differences in social-behavior between Ethiopian and Arabian hamadryas baboons', which appeared in *Folia Primatologica*, vol 45, pages 1–8, 1985.

Page 246 See H H C Vanderijtplooij and F X Plooij's paper 'Growing independence, conflict and learning in mother–infant relations in free-ranging chimpanzees', published in *Behaviour*, vol 101, pages 1–86, 1987.

Page 247 The behaviour that strongly supports the concept of animal thought was reported in R W Byrne and A Whiten's article 'Tactical deception of familiar individuals in baboons', which appeared in *Animal Behaviour*, vol 33, pages 669–673, 1985.

Chapter 11

Page 249 Useful background reading for this chapter is provided by Steven Rose's *The Conscious Brain* (Penguin, Harmondsworth, 1976), and also by Viggo Mortensen and Robert C Sorensen's edited volume *Free Will and Determinism* (Aarhus University Press, Aarhus, 1987).

Page 250 The proceedings of the meeting in question appeared in R Eckmiller and C von der Malsburg's edited volume *Neural Computers* (Springer-Verlag, Berlin, 1988).

Page 251 Positron emission tomography is described in N A Lassen, D H Ingvar and E Skinhøj's article 'Brain function and blood flow', published in *Scientific American*, vol 239, pages 50–59, 1978; a good idea of the way in which the technique has been honed to a fine observational edge can be gained from S E Petersen, P T Fox, M I Posner, M Mintun and M E Raichle's article 'Positron emission tomographic studies of the cortical anatomy of single-word processing', which appeared in *Nature*, vol 331, pages 585–589, 1988.

Page 254 Amongst the several books that have recently been written on the subject are: Susan Blackmore's *Beyond the body* (Heinemann, London, 1982); Raymond Moody's *Life after life* (Mockingbird, Covington Georgia, 1975); Kenneth Ring's *Life at Death: A Scientific Investigation of the Near-Death Experience* (Coward, McCann & Geoghegan, New York, 1980); and Michael Sabom's *Recollections of Death: A Medical Investigation* (Harper & Row, New York, 1982).

Page 258 Helen Keller's experiences were related in her *The Story of My Life* (Hodder & Stoughton, London, 1951).

Page 260 C von der Malsburg and W Schneider have actually tried to model this effect, as described in their article 'A Neural Cocktail-Party Processor', which appeared in *Biological Cybernetics*, vol 54, pages 29–40, 1986.

Page 261 The experiments were described in B Libet, E W Wright Jr, B Feinstein and D K Pearl's article 'Subjective referral of the timing for a conscious sensory experience: A functional role for the somatosensory specific projection system in man', which appeared in *Brain*, vol 102, pages 193–224, 1979.

Page 267 K R Popper and J C Eccles present their case in their book *The Self and Its Brain: An Argument for Interactionism* (Springer International, Berlin, 1977).

Page 268 R W Sperry's pioneering experiments were reported in his article 'Hemisphere deconnection and unity of consciousness', published in *American Psychologist*, vol 23, pages 723–733, 1968, and they were put in context in his brief review that followed the award of the 1981 Nobel Prize for Physiology or Medicine, namely 'Some effects of disconnecting the cerebral hemispheres', which appeared in *Science*, vol 217, pages 1223–1226, 1982.

Page 268 Those who feel inclined to accept the view that we acquired consciousness when we developed language ought to contemplate Frank Trippett's essay 'Why so much is beyond words', in the July 13, 1981, edition of *Time Magazine*, pages 55–56.

Page 269 N Humphrey's ideas about consciousness were the subject of his essay 'Consciousness: a just-so story', which appeared in *New Scientist*, vol 95, pages 474–477, 1982, somewhat related ideas emerge in J H Crook's *The evolution of human consciousness* (Oxford University Press, London, 1980); a broad range of attitudes toward the issue appear in B D Josephson and V S Ramachandran's edited volume *Consciousness and the physical world* (Pergamon Press, London, 1980).

Page 269 R L Gregory's ideas were reviewed in his contribution 'Consciousness' to R Duncan and M Weston-Smith's edited volume *The Encyclopedia of Ignorance* (Pergamon Press, London, 1977).

Page 270 Those who share my weakness for name coincidences might be intrigued by the excellent article 'Some reflections on brain and mind' written by Lord Brain, which appeared in *Brain*, vol 86, pages 381–402, 1963 (I think of this paper as 'Brain on brain in Brain'); in his section on the physical basis of consciousness, Lord Brain cites the work of Henry Head!

Page 272 A good review of the modern concept of chaos is provided by J Gleick's book *Chaos* (Heinemann, London, 1988).

Page 283 The remarkable capabilities of certain nerve cells in electric fish were reported in M Kawasaki, G Rose and W Heiligenberg's article 'Temporal hyperacuity in single neurons of electric fish', which appeared in *Nature*, vol 336, pages 173–176, 1988.

Page 283 A B Pippard's cautionary advice was offered during his Eddington memorial lecture 'The invincible ignorance of science', which was published in *Contemporary Physics*, vol 29, pages 393–405, 1988.

Glossary

Acetylcholine: the first neurotransmitter identified; its excitatory action is blocked by curare.

Action potential: the all-or-nothing electrochemical signal (having a standard amplitude) emitted out along the axon by a neuron's soma, if the threshold has been exceeded. Also known as a nerve impulse.

AER: see *average evoked response.*

Afferent: conducting information inward; said of nerve fibres in the nervous system that bring messages to the brain, and of dendrites in a nerve cell.

Alzheimer's disease: a condition characterized by deterioration of primarily short-term memory, but ultimately all forms of memory; a sort of premature senility, it affects about four per cent of all people over the age of 65.

Amacrine cell: a type of retinal neuron in which the processes extend in the plane of the retina.

Amino acids: organic compounds which come in twenty different types and which, when joined together chain-fashion, form proteins; some, like aspartic acid, glutamic acid and GABA, also serve as neurotransmitters.

Amygdala: an almond-shaped structure in the limbic system; it participates in the integration and control of emotional and autonomic behaviours.

Aphasia: an impairment of the ability to produce or comprehend spoken or written language.

Aplysia: a marine mollusc, also known as the sea hare; studies of its simple nervous system have elucidated molecular mechanisms at the synaptic level.

Association: the ability to relate different sensory information; it is mediated by neural networks.

Auditory cortex: a region of the neocortex which processes auditory frequencies in the range 20–20,000 Hertz; its 'tonotopic' arrangement links specific neurons to specific regions of the inner ear's cochlea.

Autism: a severe developmental disorder, affecting 4 in every 10,000
children (80 per cent of whom are also retarded); characterized by partial
or total inability to communicate and relate to the social environment,
the syndrome is thought to have genetic origins.

Autonomic nervous system: an involuntary part of the nervous system
which controls such life-sustaining functions as circulation, digestion,
excretion and reproduction; divided into the sympathetic and
parasympathetic subsystems.

Average evoked response: the average of a number (usually several
dozen) of electroencephalograms or magnetoencephalograms which have
been recorded following a repeated stimulus.

Axon: a single fibre (or process) extending from a neuron's somatic
region, out along which the latter emits nerve impulses (i.e. action
potentials). The axon divides into numerous branches at its extremity,
and each of these makes synaptic contacts with other neurons.

Backward masking: the suppression of the perception of one stimulus
by a second subsequent stimulus.

Basal ganglia: a group of closely connected structures in the forebrain
which help to control movement and posture, and which also influence
cognitive aspects of behaviour; the group includes the striatum, the globus
pallidus and the substantia nigra.

Binary logic: a system in which variables can adopt one of only two
different values, usually zero or unity (equivalent to no and yes).

Bipolar cell: a type of neuron in the retina, located between receptors
and ganglions.

Bit: short for 'binary digit'; the unit of binary information, the bit is
the coded answer to a yes-no question.

Blindsight: a mechanism whereby visual information produces a physical
response despite the lack of conscious visual sensation.

Brainstem: the structures around the upper part of the spinal cord,
below the midbrain, including the medulla oblongata and the pons;
also known as the rhombencephalon or hindbrain.

Broca's area: the part of the cerebral cortex that controls speech.

Catecholamines: a group of chemicals that serve as neurotransmitters;
including dopamine and noradrenaline.

Causality: the doctrine that everything has a cause; that every event
is completely determined by preceding events.

Cell assembly: a group of interconnected neurons that collectively
functions as a unit, under given circumstances.

Central nervous system: the brain and the spinal cord.

Central sulcus: the groove separating the motor cortex from the
somatosensory cortex.

Cerebellum: a structure surrounding the rear of the hindbrain that governs motor coordination; its neuronal structure is remarkably regular, with few cell types (e.g. Purkinje, Golgi and granule cells).

Cerebral cortex: the outer (grey-matter) layer of the cerebral hemispheres, comprising regions which receive sensory inputs and others responsible for forming associations; evolution's most recent addition to the nervous system, it is particularly well developed in mammals. Also known as the neocortex.

Cerebrum: the brain proper, in front of and above the cerebellum.

Chiasm: a point at which nerve fibres cross.

Chromosome: a strand of genetic material in a cell's nucleus, comprising a large number of genes; visible under a microscope during cell division, a chromosome consists of DNA and histone.

Commissure: a major sheaf of nerve fibres connecting different regions of the brain.

Consciousness: the totality of one's thoughts and feelings; awareness of one's existence, sensations and circumstances.

Convolution: see *gyrus*.

Corpus callosum: the Latin name for the great commissure, the approximately 200 million fibres of which link the left and right hemispheres of the cerebral cortex.

Cortical areas: specific regions of the cerebral cortex dedicated to sensor, motor or association functions.

Corticofugal: said of efferent nerve fibres that carry feedback signals from the brain to sensor structures.

Curare: a common chemical blocker of acetylcholine's action at the neuromuscular junction.

Cyclic AMP: a cyclic form of adenosine monophosphate that is derived from the energy-storing molecules of ATP (adenosine triphosphate); it serves as a signalling substance in cells.

Dendrites: highly branched afferent structures (processes) of a neuron; they receive chemical signals from the axon brances of other neurons, via synaptic contacts, and convey the resultant electrochemical signals towards the soma.

Depolarization: reduction of the voltage (which, in the quiescent state, is negative inside, to the extent of about 0.1 volts) across a neuron's bounding membrane.

Determinism: in general, the theory that a given set of circumstances inevitably produces the same consequences; in particular, the doctrine that human action is not free but determined by external forces acting on the will.

Deterministic chaos: the situation in certain systems in which the dynamical development cannot be precisely predicted even though the system itself is deterministic.

DNA: see *nucleic acid.*

Dopamine: a neurotransmitter of the catecholamine class; schizophrenia is possibly caused by an excess of dopamine in the limbic system.

Dualism: the doctrine that mind and body have independent identities.

EEG: see *electroencephalogram.*

Effectors: neurons at terminal regions of the nervous system, which act on glands or muscles.

Efferent: conducting information outward; said of nerve fibres in the nervous system that carry messages from the brain, and of the axon of a nerve cell.

Ego: the conscious thinking subject.

Electroencephalogram (EEG): a record of the net electrical activity measurable (with attached electrodes) at the scalp, due to the brain's internal workings; the characteristic EEG rhythms reflect general states of arousal, consciousness and the sleep-waking cycle.

Electrode: in the present context, a needle-like conductor with which the electrical activity of a neuron can be monitored.

Endocranial: within the skull.

Endorphins: a group of small internally-produced peptides which function as neurotransmitters, and influence emotional state.

Engram: the conjectured physical change in the association cortex's neural network caused by the storage of a memory.

Enkephalins: a group of small internally-produced peptide neurotransmitters possessing a morphine-like analgesic capacity.

Epilepsy: a disorder of brain function characterized by sporadic recurrence of seizure caused by avalanche discharges of large groups of neurons; known already to the ancient Greeks, it affects about one per cent of humans.

ERP: see event-related potential.

Event-related potential: a discrete pattern of EEG activity reflecting specific perceptual or cognitive processes.

Evoked potential: the EEG response measured for a specific stimulus.

Feature detector: a neuron or small group of neurons which become active only if a particular feature is present in the sensory input.

Feedback: the return of nerve signals to a sensory region such that the original signal sent from there is reinforced (positive feedback) or dampened down (negative feedback).

Forebrain: the evolutionary most recently developed part of the vertebrate brain; it comprises the reticular formation, the limbic system and the cerebral cortex.

Frontal lobe: the part of the cerebral cortex that lies within the forehead; it is responsible for various aspects of thought and the planning of actions.

GABA: see *Gamma-aminobutyric acid*.

Gamma-aminobutyric acid: an amino acid that serves as an inhibitory neurotransmitter.

Ganglion cells: the neurons that transmit the partially processed signals from the retina to the lateral geniculate nucleus; the ganglion axons form the optic nerve.

Gene: a section of chromosomal DNA that either codes for a given protein (structural gene) or controls such a structural gene (regulatory gene).

Genetic code: the relationships between the sequences of nucleotide bases in DNA and the amino acids that they specify.

Genome: the totality of expressible DNA in a cell's nucleus.

Genotype: the genetic make-up of a specific member of a species.

Gilles de la Tourette syndrome: a mental disorder characterized by a number of bizarre behavioural patterns, it has been linked to overactivity in certain dopamine-active systems; no definite genetic origin has been identified, and about half the (mostly male) patients improve towards middle age.

Glial cell: a non-signalling type of brain cell that performs nourishment and scavenging duties for the neurons; the most common type of brain cell.

GPI: short for general paralysis of the insane, the terminal stage of syphilis; patients with this affliction appear to be devoid of initiative.

Grey matter: the outer part of the cerebral cortex; it contains the somas of the cortex's neurons.

Gyrus: one of the curved elevations (convex towards the outside) on the surface of the cerebral cortex.

Hebbian learning: a mechanism whereby the transmission efficiency of a synapse is strengthened if the neurons it connects are both active at roughly the same time, and weakened otherwise.

Hemisphere: one side, left or right, of the cerebral cortex.

Hindbrain: see *brainstem*.

Hippocampal commissure: a small sheaf of nerve fibres connecting the cerebral hemisphere near the hippocampus.

Hippocampus: a centrally-located structure, lying under the cortex, implicated in the formation of memories; an evolutionary development of a more primitive structure found in the reptilian brain.

Hologram: literally the 'whole picture'; the distributed record of an image, which can be recovered by illuminating the hologram with one of the two stimuli used during the recording.

Homeostasis: the automatic control of such vital properties as heart beat, blood temperature and blood pressure, by part of the nervous system.

Homunculus: literally the 'little inner man', conjectured by the ancients to reside in the head, observe the environment via the senses, and respond appropriately; his abstract form still survives as the dualist 'ghost in the machine' – this book's adversary.

Horizontal cell: a type of retinal neuron in which the processes extend in the plane of the retina.

Hormones: internally-secreted organic compounds that control various vital body functions.

Huntington's disease: a mental disorder characterized by progressive involuntary dancelike movements (whence the alternative name Huntington's chorea), psychological deterioration and dementia; the victim usual dies of cardiac or pulmonary failure after about two decades.

Hyperpolarization: an increase of the voltage across a neuron's bounding membrane, thus decreasing the likelihood of pulse emission.

Hypothalamus: a small but very important structure in the limbic system that controls body temperature, eating, emotional tone, drinking, hormonal balance, various metabolic processes, and sexual drive.

Id: the instinctive impulses of an individual.

Ion: an (otherwise neutral) atom which has either gained or lost one or more electrons, thereby acquiring an electrical charge.

Ion channel: a protein present in neural membranes whose structure possesses an adjustable pore that regulates the passage of ions; channels selective for sodium and potassium provide the basis for the action potential.

Interneuron: a neuron which exerts an influence only on other neurons in its immediate vicinity.

Lateral geniculate nucleus: a group of neurons in the thalamus which receive connections from the retina, and also both send connections to and receive connections from the primary visual cortex.

Lateralization: the separation of mental faculties between the two hemispheres of the cerebral cortex.

Lesion: a localized injury; to a part of the brain, in the context of this book.

LGN: see *lateral geniculate nucleus*.

Libido: the emotional craving that underlies any human action.

Limbic system: a group of structures intermediate, in both position and evolutionary development, between the brainstem and the cerebral cortex; comprising the amygdala, hippocampus, hypothalamus, thalamus and septum, this region controls emotional behaviour.

Lobotomy: surgical disconnection of a cerebral lobe; often the frontal lobe.

Locus coeruleus: a structure in the brainstem which exerts its influence through the neurotransmitter noradrenaline; implicated in the sleep-wake cycle.

Long-term memory: memory retained beyond the period of immediate recall.

Macroscopic: said of things visible to the unaided eye.

Masking: see *backward masking*.

Mechanistic: explainable in terms of known physical laws.

Medulla oblongata: a part of the hindbrain near the upper part of the spinal cord.

Membrane: in this book's context, the lipid (i.e. fatty) 'skin' of all cells, including neurons; its embedded channels, pumps and receptors, all of which are proteins, give the neuron its special signalling capacity.

Memory: the mental faculty provided by the superimposed changes at the synaptic level.

Microscopic: literally visible only under a microscope; also applied to such smaller scales as the molecular and the atomic.

Midbrain: the region of the brain located between the forebrain and the hindbrain.

Motor cortex: the elongated and centrally located regions on each cerebral hemisphere which control muscle movement via nerve fibres which they send to the spinal cord.

Muscle spindle: a receptor structure present in all muscles; it senses muscular tension, thereby providing a means of controlling it.

Mutation: a chance or deliberate modification of the base sequence in chromosomal DNA; inheritable by subsequent generations if it occurs in the reproductive system.

Myasthenia gravis: an auto-immune disorder caused by depletion of the acetylcholine receptors at neuromuscular junctions; formerly often fatal, the condition can now be counteracted by various therapies.

Myelin: an electrically insulating lipid (fatty) layer that coats some nerve fibres.

Natural selection: the reproductive advantage of organisms better adapted to their environment; it provides the driving force for evolution.

Neocortex: see *cerebral cortex*.

Nerve cell: see *neuron*.

Nerve fibre: a single neural axon or a bundle of these.

Nerve growth factor: a chemical substance that promotes the growth of neural processes, in the direction of the substance's gradient.

Nerve impulses: see *action potential*.

Neural network: the brain's actual interconnected mesh of neurons (biological wetware); a theoretical model that attempts to simulate its electrophysical properties (computer software); a brain-inspired computational strategy (computer software); or a brain-inspired computational device (computer hardware).

Neuron: (sometimes spelled 'neurone'), the nerve cell, whose

electrochemically excitable membrane qualifies it as the fundamental
signalling unit of the nervous system.

Neuropeptides: a group of small molecules whose amino acid chains
serve as neurotransmitters.

Neurotoxins: a large group of chemical substances that are able to
disrupt nerve signal transmission; examples are alcohol, curare, nitrous
oxide and tetrodotoxin.

Neurotransmitter: a chemical substance whose molecules can physically
dock with (protein) receptor molecules, and thereby pass on nerve signals;
several dozen such substances are known, and the list is probably not
complete.

Noradrenaline: (also known as norepinephrine), a neurotransmitter of
the catecholamine class; widely used in the nervous system.

Nucleic acids: polymeric chains of nucleotide bases which store and
mediate translation of the genetic message; a gene is a stretch of DNA
(deoxyribonucleic acid), that molecule being located in a cell's nucleus,
while RNA (ribonucleic acid) transports the messages of the genes
out of the nucleus, into the cytoplasm, where they are expressed through
formation of proteins.

Nucleotide: one of the building blocks of the nucleic acids; there are
four types, adenine (A), thymine (T), guanine (G) and cytosine (C), and
the fact that the only pairings compatible with double helical DNA are A
with T and G with C guarantees perpetuation of the genetic message
stored in the chromosomes.

Occipital lobe: the region of the cerebral cortex at the back of the head.

Olfactory bulb: elongated extensions of the forebrain which receive and
perform the initial processing of the signals from the odour receptors.

Opiate: chemical substances with molecular structures similar to
morphine, which have analgesic properties; several are present in opium.

Optic chiasm: the point where a fraction of the optic nerves cross.

Optic nerve: the bundle of (approximately a million) neural axons that
connect each retina with the corresponding lateral geniculate nucleus.

Parasympathetic: pertaining to that part of the autonomic nervous
system that tends to decrease activity; its afferent fibres come from
the brainstem.

Parietal lobe: the region just rear of centre, high up on each cerebral
hemisphere.

Parkinson's disease: a syndrome characterized by tremor and loss
of motor control, due to a deficiency in the dopamine system, which
normally counterbalances excitatory acetylcholine activity; it usually
strikes between the ages of 50 and 65, and it affects almost one per cent
of humans.

Peptide: more correctly 'polypeptide', a chain of amino acids.

Perceptron: a system of two or more layers of idealized neurons, with interconnecting synapses between the layers, that functions as an input-output device; the synaptic strengths are automatically adjusted during a training period in which known input-output matchings are presented to the network, which thereafter is able to recognize, associate and generalize.

Phantom limb: the paradoxical tactile and pain sensations that seem to emanate from an amputated limb; their occurrence demonstrates the overriding role played by the somatosensory cortex.

Phenotype: the collective physical characteristics and properties that an organism develops through the expression of its genes.

Photoreceptors: two light-sensitive types of neuron present in the retina, which convert incident radiant energy into electrochemical signals; the rods primarily sense intensity, while the cones mediate detection of colour, contrast, motion and size.

Phrenology: the (now discredited) science which purported to relate the skull's bumps and depressions to mental capacities.

Pituitary gland: the supreme endocrine gland, located in the limbic system, which controls the secretions of the other endocrine glands.

Plastic: in the present context, modifiable by experience.

Pons: part of the brainstem that links the medulla oblongata and midbrain.

Positron emission tomography (PET): a technique which provides brain images that reveal the currently active areas.

Postsynaptic: pertaining to the receiving side of a synapse; the receptor laden membrane of a dendrite, gland or muscle.

Presynaptic: pertaining to the transmitting side of a synapse; the neurotransmitter laden axon terminal.

Primates: a group (taxonomically, an order) of mammals comprising apes, humans, lemurs and monkeys.

Process: in this book's context, a filamentous outgrowth from a cell's central (somatic) region; a dendrite or an axon.

Proprioceptive: sensitive to body posture or limb position.

Protein: a molecule composed of chain-linked amino acids, its structural or enzymatic properties deriving from its three-dimensional (often folded) structure, this being determined by its actual amino-acid sequence; together with nucleic acids, proteins are the major macromolecules of life, and they provide the nervous system with its channels, pumps and receptors.

Psychophysics: the science that seeks to quantify sensation, and mathematically model the relationship between brain and mind.

Psychosomatic: related to the mind's influence on bodily processes.

Pump: a protein molecule that transports a specific type of ion through a

neural membrane, thereby helping to maintain the ionic imbalance across
the latter; the various pumps collectively use about a quarter of all the
energy a person consumes in the form of food.

Purkinje cell: the main type of neuron in the cerebellum; identified by
the dense branching of its dendrites.

Pyramidal cell: the principal class of neurons in the cerebral cortex;
pyramidal cell axons form the white matter.

Receptor: see *receptor cell* and *receptor molecule*.

Receptor cell: a sensory neuron that converts a specific stimulation
(light, pressure, odour, etc) to nerve impulses.

Receptor molecule: a membrane-bound molecule capable of recognizing
the molecules of a specific substance (neurotransmitter or hormone) and
responding by generating a chemical or electrochemical signal.

Receptive field: the distribution of light that produces the maximum
response of a neuron in the visual system.

Reflex arc: a neural route from receptor neuron to motor neuron.

REM-Sleep: short for 'rapid eye movement' sleep; the portion of sleep
devoted to dreaming.

Reptilian complex: the evolutionary earliest part of the brain; it governs
the faculties related to survival.

Resting potential: the voltage difference (about 0.1 volts) across a
neuron's membrane, when that cell is in the quiescent state; caused by
the (pump mediated) concentration imbalance of sodium and potassium
ions between the inside and outside of the cell.

Reticular formation: a group of structures stretching from the medulla
oblongata to the thalamus; they collectively govern consciousness, and
even partial damage can produce coma.

Retina: a mesh of receptor and intermediary neurons at the back
of the eye which partially processes incident visual information before
transmitting it to the lateral geniclate nucleus.

RFLP: short for 'restriction-fragment length polymorphism', a genetic
engineering technique that facilitates gene identification.

RNA: see *nucleic acids*.

Sensor: a structure composed of a number of receptor cells, which
converts a stimulus to nerve impulses.

Septum: a group of neurons in the limbic system, adjacent to the
amygdala; together with the other limbic structures, it is implicated in the
emotions.

Serotonin: a neurotransmitter derived from the amino acid tryptophan;
its resemblance to lysergic acid diethylamide (LSD) explains the
hallucinogenic properties of the latter.

Schizophrenia: a mental syndrome popularly attributed to a 'splitting
of the mind', it manifests different clinical symptoms: withdrawal and

emotional dampening (hebephrenia), delusions (paranoia), disturbances in attitudes and movement (catatonia), and impairment of mental faculties (dementia); it is now thought to have a partially genetic origin.

Short-term memory: memory that cannot be recalled beyond a few hours.

Soma: the body; in an individual neuron, the cell body that contains the nucleus and related organelles.

Somatosensory cortex: the cortical region that receives sensory information from the body's mechanical (tactile) receptors in the muscles and skin.

Stellate cell: a type of cortical neuron that influences only its local environment; its axons do not enter the white matter.

Stretch reflex: the automatic tendency for a muscle to contract when it is stretched by an external agency (e.g. the knee jerk).

Striate cortex: the primary visual cortex, which receives input from the lateral geniculate nucleus; its name derives from the striped appearance after staining (with, for example, cresyl violet).

Substance P: one of a group of peptide neurotransmitters (called tachykinins) that are implicated in pain transmission; high concentrations are found in the substantia nigra.

Substantia nigra: a structure adjacent to the pons that is involved in the control of awareness.

Sulcus: a groove on the cortical surface.

Superior colliculus: a structure that helps control eye movement; it produces blindsight when the primary visual system is non-functional.

Sympathetic: pertaining to that part of the autonomic nervous system that tends to increase activity; its afferent fibres come from the spinal cord.

Synapse: the junction of a neuron with another neuron, gland or muscle; message transmission across a synapse is usually chemical (and neurotransmitter-mediated), but electrical examples are known.

Synaptic vesicle: see *vesicle*.

Sylvian fissure: a major cortical groove (gyrus) running from a point just above the ear, in a forward and downward direction, roughly towards the eye.

Temporal lobe: the region of the cerebral cortex below and behind the sylvian fissure; it comprises the auditory cortex, the limbic cortex and the temporal association cortex.

Tetrodotoxin: a neurotoxin that inhibits the action potential by mechanically blocking the sodium channels.

Thalamus: a composite structure in the limbic system that serves as a relay station for nerve fibres from the senses to the neocortex, and the corresponding feedback fibres; the visual system's lateral geniculate nucleus is a prominent component.

Threshold: the minimum membrane depolarization that causes a neuron to emit action potentials.

Tourette syndrome: see *Gilles de la Tourette syndrome*.

Triune brain: the model, propounded by Paul MacLean, that the brain comprises three evolutionary (and to some extent functionally) independent cognitive systems.

Uncertainty principle: a quantum mechanical rule that limits the precision with which pairs of physical attributes (position and momentum, for example) can simultaneously be measured.

Ventricles: a series of four interconnected cavities in the brain; filled with cerebrospinal fluid, they were believed by the ancients to harbour animal spirits.

Vesicle: a small membrane-bounded container of neurotransmitters present near an axon terminal's presynaptic membrane; spherical for excitatory substances, elongated for inhibitors.

Vestibular system: structures in the inner ear which collectively govern balance.

Visual cortex: the region of the neocortex that receives (primary) and processes (higher) visual information.

White matter: the layer lying inside the (grey matter) cerebral cortex; it consists of the pyramidal cell axons that connect various cortical regions.

Will: the faculty by which one decides, or conceives oneself of deciding, upon and initiating action.

Wernicke's area: the cortical region that handles the understanding of language.

Zygote: a fertilized egg cell.

Index